RETHINKING COMMUNITY IN MYANMAR

Practices of We-Formation among Muslims and Hindus in Urban Yangon

JUDITH BEYER

University of Hawai'i Press
HONOLULU

Printed in the United States of America

Published in 2024 in the Americas by
University of Hawaiʻi Press
2840 Kolowalu Street
Honolulu, HI 96822
www.uhpress.hawaii.edu

This edition of *Rethinking Community in Myanmar* is published
by arrangement with NIAS Press.

First published in 2023 by
NIAS Press
NIAS – Nordic Institute of Asian Studies
Øster Farimagsgade 5, 1353 Copenhagen K, Denmark
www.niaspress.dk

Library of Congress Cataloging-in-Publication Data

Names: Beyer, Judith, author.
Title: Rethinking community in Myanmar : practices of we-formation among
Muslims and Hindus in urban Yangon / Judith Beyer.
Description: Honolulu : University of Hawaiʻi Press, [2024] | Includes
bibliographical references and index.
Identifiers: LCCN 2024005297 (print) | LCCN 2024005298 (ebook) | ISBN
9780824898069 (paperback) | ISBN 9780824898083 (epub) | ISBN
9780824898076 (pdf) | ISBN 9780824898090 (kindle edition)
Subjects: LCSH: Communities—Religious aspects—Islam. |
Communities—Religious aspects—Hinduism. | Burma—Religious life and
customs. | Rangoon (Burma)—Religious life and customs.
Classification: LCC BL2053 .B47 2024 (print) | LCC BL2053 (ebook) | DDC
306.609591—dc23/eng/20240224
LC record available at https://lccn.loc.gov/2024005297
LC ebook record available at https://lccn.loc.gov/2024005298

University of Hawaiʻi Press books are printed on acid-free paper
and meet the guidelines for permanence and durability of the
Council on Library Resources.

Cover image: Scene from Arbaʻeen ceremony, 2015 (photo by author).

To Felix and Constantin –
I am through you so I.

Contents

List of Figures

(colour illustrations marked in **bold***)*

Acknowledgments

Many people and institutions have helped bring this book to fruition and accompanied me along the way and I would like to thank them here:

မြန်မာနိုင်ငံမှာရှိ သူငယ်ချင်းမိတ်ဆွေတွေ၊ ဆွေးနွေးဖက်ဆွေးနွေးဖက်တွဲနဲ့ သတင်းပေးသူတွေကို ကျွန်မ ကျေးဇူးတင်ပါတယ်။။ သူတို့ရဲ့ကိုယ်ပိုင်လုံခြုံရေး အတွက်နဲ့ သူတို့ဆီကို အနာဂတ်ကာလမှာလည်း ကျွန်မ သွားရောက်လည်ပတ်ချင် လို့ သူတို့အမည်တွေကို မဖော်ပြလိုဘူး။။ ကျွန်မ ဒီမှာ ဘယ်သူတွေကို ဆိုလိုတယ် ဆိုတာကို အသင်တို့ သိမှာပါ။။ ကျွန်မ အသင်တို့ကို မဖော်ပနိုင်လဲကတ်အဆင် ကျေးဇူးတင်ပါတယ်။။ အသင်တို့ ကျွန်မအပေါ်မှာ ယုံကြည်စိတ်ချမှု ပါ့ခြိတာကို လည်း ကျေးဇူးတင်လို့ မဆုံးပါ။။ အသင်တို့ရဲ့အဖွဲ့အပျက်ဇာတ်လမ်းတွေ၊ ပျက် ရွှင်မှုတွေနဲ့ စိုးရိမ်ကြောင့်ကြမှုအကြောင်းတွေကို ယုံကြည်စိတ်ချစွာ ပြောပြ့တဲ့ အပြင့် အသင်တို့ရဲ့ အိမ်ရာတွေ၊ ဗလီတွေနဲ့ ဘုရားကျောင်းတွေမှာ ကျွန်မနဲ့ ကျွန်မ မိသားစုကို ဖိတ်ခေါ်လက်ခံခဲ့တဲ့အတွက်လည်း ကျွန်မ အသင်တို့အားလုံးကို ရင်ထဲ အသည်းထဲက လိုက်လိုက်လွဲလွဲ ကျေးဇူးတင်ရှိပါတယ်။။ [1]

To my research assistants – or, as Felix Girke has called you, my Kachin Research Army (KRA) – Esther Htu San, Seng Mai Lanau, Seng Myaw, and Ja Mai Lone Hkum: I learned so much from you and enjoyed watching you blossom into successful women along the way. I will forever be grateful!

I have received financial support from the Centre for Cultural Inquiry at the University of Konstanz. The French Ministry for Higher Education and Research selected me to participate in the Fernand Braudel Associate Directorship Programme, which came along with a research stay at the Fondation Maison des Sciences de l'Homme (FMSH) in 2018 and a

---

1. 'I would like to thank my interlocutors and my friends and informants in Myanmar, who need to remain anonymous for reasons of their own security and because I would like to continue visiting them in the future. You know who you are and I owe more to you than I can say. I thank you from the bottom of my heart for the faith you bestowed in me, for trusting me to tell your stories, for sharing your joys and your worries, and for accepting my family and me into your homes, mosques, and temples.'

Visiting Professorship at the École des Hautes Études en Sciences Sociales (EHESS) in 2019. A research grant from the German Research Foundation (DFG) allowed me to carry out follow-up fieldwork in Myanmar.

In Paris, I would like to thank Yazid Ben Hounet, Bénedicte Brac de la Perrière, Baudouin Dupret and Stéphane Dudoignon for hosting me at FMSH and EHESS. I am grateful to the *Maison Suger* for providing excellent writing conditions in the middle of Saint-Germain; to Lucie Buffavand for exploring the city with me, to the ghosts of Jean-Paul and Simone, and to Soprano for his music.

In Konstanz, I thank Laura Rischbieter, Christina Zuber and Anne Kraume for joining me on the track to tenure, for providing consultation, consolation, and coffee! Thank you to Kirsten Mahlke, Thomas G. Kirsch, Christian Meyer, and Stefan Leins for their support. To my doctoral students, Carolin Hirsch, Benedict Mette-Starke, Sarah Riebel, Nickey Diamond, and Jessica Schmieder: thank you for enabling me to learn how to be a supervisor and to everyone in the various colloquia for valuable feedback on my texts. To Conny Heuer, Hedvig Johansson, Leila Dedial and Silva Schilling: Thank you for being such a great team! To Peter Krause for always reminding me to slow down. To all my students for enabling me to rethink the value of anthropology with each new semester.

I thank Uta Gärtner for introducing me to Myanma and for helping me with translations and transliterations, Bénedicte Brac de la Perrière, Patrice Ladwig, Mateusz Laszczkowski, Laura Rischbieter, Alicia Turner and especially Felix Girke for reading chapter drafts, and Jutta Turner for providing the maps to this book. To the anonymous reviewers for their detailed, thoughtful and constructive comments and suggestions. I am grateful to Brian Donahoe for his editorial guidance and his sharp eye and to Gerald Jackson for taking my book on board and seeing it through to publication.

To Winnie Öhrlich: Thank you for being you!

I thank Tobias Nitsch for listening unconditionally, for challenging me, for quietly reading in the background, for tea, and for *da sein*.

℘

This book is dedicated to my family, Felix and Constantin: It is through you that I get to experience all that is truly important in life.

Author's Notes

On naming

The names of my interlocutors are anonymized with the exception of those who have passed away. Some Yangon street names have been altered so as to not disclose my interlocutors' private residences. What remains identifiable, however, are the religious buildings around which much of my ethnography is centred. These are understood as public spaces to a large extent and the very location of where what I will call *we-formation* and *the work of community* can be experienced and become observable. In 1989, the country has been renamed from Burma to Myanmar, which is a more formal or literary version of the same word. In this book I use Burma to refer to the time before 1989 and Myanmar for the time thereafter. I use Rangoon when referring to the pre-1989 period and Yangon when referring to precolonial and post-1989 events.

On language and notation

I carried out fieldwork in English and Myanma. Having worked with Sunni Muslims for a long time in a very different Muslim context (Beyer 2016), I am familiar with Arabic-, Urdu-, and Farsi-based vocabulary and could therefore follow conversations, particularly about matters concerning religion. But I only realized the symphony of languages my interlocutors communicated in once I had already started my research: they often spoke Gujarati, Urdu, Memon, Tamil, or Hindi at home or in the temples and mosques. Very often they would switch from Myanma to Urdu or other languages in the same context. While I do understand Myanma and am able to communicate in it, I speak none of the other languages and thus often had to rely on my interlocutors to help me understand. What helped make the research possible was that many of my interlocutors, particularly of the older generation but also the very young and the well-educated, spoke English well. All of the older interlocutors had gone to 'missionary school', regardless of their religious beliefs, and profited from the education system before it was nationalized in the 1960s, when English ceased to be taught. As my interest was devoted to understanding the *work of community*, I did not want to restrict my research to one particular ethno-religious group and thus had to muddle through.

For better readability, I will refrain from putting the word 'community' as well as other collectivizing (and often essentializing) terms such as Hindus, Muslims, Buddhists, race, caste, etc. in quotation marks. When I occasionally do so, it is to remind the reader that these are not unproblematic terms, but value-laden conceptual and categorical abstractions. All words in italics denote terms in languages other than English. If an entire paragraph is set in italics, then it is a direct quote from transcribed audio files or a verbatim account from my fieldwork journals.

On currency

In Myanmar the local currency is the *kyat*. Before the attempted military coup of 1 February 2021, 1 Euro was approximately 1,600 kyat. It is also common in Myanmar to calculate with the unit *lakh*, which is part of the Indian numbering system. One *lakh* is the equivalent of 100,000 of whatever unit is being discussed.

On historical and legal sources

Historians working on Burma regularly rely on colonial-era documents compiled by state officials and housed in the India Office Records, that is, the archives of the East India Company (1600–1858), the Board of Control (1784–1858), the India Office (1858–1947) and the Burma Office (1937–1948), nowadays all located in the British Library in London. I also consulted these archives in 2010 and 2012. In writing this book, I have also profited from Mandy Sadan's meticulously researched *A Guide to Colonial Sources on Burma* (2008), in which she has compiled extensive lists of references from all four archives, with a specific focus on what she calls 'minority histories'. These documents provide important insights into how the colonial apparatus engaged with and presented the 'minority question' in India and Burma, but they generally offer little information about the perspectives of the individuals who were themselves subjected to these policies. While we get plenty of accounts of 'communities', we are lacking accounts of real people. Individuals' life stories through eyewitness accounts, biographies, genealogies, auto-ethnographies, or oral histories are still seldom pursued today (but see Dalrymple 2019), and were no concern then, especially as regards the colonized: the history of the British empire is to a large degree the history of imputed collectivity. It is also a gendered body of literature, the product of predominantly male colonial writers writing about male colonial state practices (see Ikeya 2013; Saha 2013; Stoler and Cooper 2002). Moreover, present-day literature based on colonial-era documentation regularly dissects and deconstructs terms such as race and nationality, whereas authors tend to leave the category of community (i.e., 'the village community', 'the Muslim community', 'the Hindu community') intact without scrutinizing the work of this first-order 'groupness' (see Mazumder 2013, Sadan 2008). This also goes for ethnohistorical works on colonial India and Burma.

Materials from court cases and legal files are an exception to this rule, as it is through these cases, which include testimonies and complaints, that the voices of individuals can be heard. But what has been published by the British colonial administration is highly selective and often portrays only the lives of wealthy urbanites. Interpreted through the language of the law, these documents often give us more insight into the reasoning of judges than that of the disputing parties. While historians such as Alicia Turner, Chie Ikeya, and the late Andrew Huxley, as well as legal and political scholars such as Melissa Crouch and Nick Cheesman, have investigated a large variety of legal sources on colonial Burma, anthropologists have thus far generally not engaged with this rich material. The important exception is Edmund Leach, who began his famous *The Political Systems of Highland Burma* ([1954] 1964) with a verbatim account of a witness at a confidential court of inquiry in the Northern Shan states from 1930. He thereby demonstrated how the judiciary construed 'the Shans' and 'the Kachins' as a single ethno-religious group, which stood in sharp contrast to their own accounts of living largely separate lives. This material allowed him to argue that individual accounts – such as the one given by an old headman whose 'race' and 'religion' were recorded as 'Lahtawng Kachin (Pawyam, Pseudo-Shan)' and 'Zawti Buddhist', respectively – 'cannot readily be fitted into any ethnographic scheme, which, on linguistic grounds, places Kachins and Shans in different "racial" categories. The problem, however, is not simply one of sorting out Kachins from Shans; there is also the difficulty of sorting out Kachins from one another' (Leach [1954] 1964: 2–3).[1]

In a way, this problem has remained unsolved. In my book I therefore focus on how individuals themselves categorize distinctions and diagnose relations between people. I argue that one of the most dominant categorizations that prevails to this day – community – is not indigenous but was, rather, introduced by the very colonial officers and anthropologists who then found it difficult to place their colonial subjects and informants within their own schemes.

On working with research assistants

Throughout the different stages of my fieldwork I worked with research assistants. Unintentionally, all of them turned out to be Christian Kachin, and three out of the four knew each other from their hometowns in Myitkina and Lashio. When one would move on to her very successful career in another field (journalism, music, business, and law), she would suggest another to serve as her successor. As a result, I was almost always accompanied by at least one of them in most of my fieldwork situations. Looking back, the most fruitful element of working with Esther, Ja Mai Lone, Seng Mai, and Seng Myaw was that for them, too, engaging with Hindu and Muslim fellow Yangonites was something entirely new. Some of them had never entered a mosque or a Hindu temple before; some had never spoken to a Muslim fellow citizen; for all of them the religious practices of my interlocutors were quite novel. I profited enormously from their interpretations as they learned along with me about what it means for Hindus and Muslims to grow up, live, work, and pray in a predominantly Buddhist society. They frequently noticed things that had escaped my attention – not because of the language barrier, but because *all* of our socializations had been different. However, there was much that united them with my interlocutors besides the fact that they were all citizens of Myanmar (with a few exceptions among my interlocutors). They, too, positioned themselves as belonging to an

---

1. It might have been Leach's willingness to allow for individuality outside of structure in the heyday of structural-functionalism that led Sherry Ortner to describe Leach as 'an unclassifiable (if admired) freak' (Ortner 1984: 142). For a restudy of Leach's famous ethnography, see Robinne and Sadan (2007).

ethno-religious community. They could thus share what that meant from their individual experiences as well as from the perspective of the communities they considered themselves to be members of.

Although I had not planned any of this in advance, this constellation allowed all five of us to move with ease in what became my fieldsite over the course of several extended periods of research. While Christians, Muslims, and Hindus do not interact much beyond the usual networks of business and in public space, there is – quite in contrast to their Buddhist fellow citizens – very little negative stereotypification in place. There is, in other words, no established narrative about the *other* that one could fall back on when entering into a dialogue or other type of interaction. I learned a great deal from listening to the conversations that developed among my research assistants and between them and my interlocutors.

On addressing

I address my interlocutors in three different ways: in Burmese, the polite standard is to address an older woman as *Daw*, an older male as *U*, a younger woman as *Ma*, and a younger man as *Ko*, in each case followed by their full name. I addressed my older Shia Muslim interlocutors by their Muslim first name and the suffix *Baji* (for women) and *Bhai* (for men), both indicating my junior position to them. If I was not familiar with them, I would use their full Muslim name and the prefixes *Daw* or *U*. This is also how I would address my Hindu interlocutors. If I knew them well, I would call them by their first name with the English Auntie or Uncle (e.g. Kathleen Auntie), either as a prefix or a suffix, depending what was expected in the given situation. All of my Muslim and Hindu interlocutors had two names: one reflecting their origins, the other a Burmese name. In all cases, only their Burmese names would be mentioned in their official documents, but within their families and networks they would very often only be addressed by their Hindu or Muslim name. I sometimes did not even know their Burmese names, as they never used them when interacting with me or with familiar others.

On learning from 'marginal men' and women

Over the course of fieldwork, I realized that it was mostly marginal women and men with whom I interacted. Anthropology, in general, has always been a discipline of 'marginal men', as the sociologist and founder of the Chicago School, Robert Park (1928), had labelled those who were most likely to offer support to the foreign ethnographer. My topic, in particular, was one where each and every individual was marginal in comparison to the Buddhist majority population or in the eyes of the nation-state. As members of officially classified ethno-religious minorities, they were structurally disadvantaged no matter how influential or individually important they had been. However, the people with whom I have interacted on a regular basis over the past several years were fringe walkers even more so than others. This could mean that they did not possess Burmese citizenship, that their ethnic backgrounds (i.e., the origins of their forefathers) were regarded as 'lower' within their own community than those of others, or that they shared a religious identity with a particular temple community, but their ethnic identity prevented them from being counted among its members at all. Moreover, many of the women with whom I developed friendships were either widows with children whom they had to raise by themselves or women who were childless, thus, in both cases, diverging from the ideal type of a married woman with children.

On fieldwork

This book is based on anthropological fieldwork in urban Yangon that began in December 2012, with a longer research trip (six months) in 2013. However, most of the data I use in this book stem from another six months of research I conducted in 2015–2016, as well as from follow-up research in 2018. While in 2013 I had focused on Christians, establishing only initial contacts with Hindus and Muslims apart from a few cases that I had begun to study in detail even then, I switched to researching 'Burmese Indians' full-time only during the later stages of my fieldwork. For this book, I decided to omit all data on Christians in Myanmar, as their migratory history is different; while a comparison to Burmese Indians would have been possible, I reserve this for a later publication. I carried out a month of follow-up research in 2018 and returned in early 2020 with the book manuscript to discuss my findings with my interlocutors.

For the most part I conducted participant observation in the course of various aspects of people's everyday lives as lived in and around their religious buildings. While relations of property and ownership of these buildings have been long disputed, this does not hinder access to them. I also focus on the ritual objects inside these buildings and those that are brought out into the streets during processions (such as statues), as well as on the material traces these buildings and objects leave in legal and administrative documentation. Rather than passing over these sites and objects as the *loci classici* of studying community and, therefore, the tired tropes of earlier ethnographies, I re-evaluate their importance from the emic perspectives of my interlocutors. I attended daily or weekly religious services and participated in activities revolving around official religious holidays, processions, meetings, internal elections, protest events, and political campaigns. In people's homes I collected the life histories and genealogies of my main interlocutors. In the local bookstores, through personal contacts, and online, I collected legal documentation, statistical information, and newspaper articles, and I followed all my interlocutors on Facebook – the main social media in Myanmar. Moreover, I took photographs and made video recordings and kept a fieldwork journal. Being in the field with my family, i.e., a husband, who carried out his own research project, and our young son, who attended a local school in Chinatown that catered mostly to ethnic Chinese families, brought many advantages to all of us. It allowed us to establish relations of trust, lent legitimacy to my initially unusual requests to 'hang out' with people I did not know, and allowed us to gain additional insights into the everyday lives of ethnic Chinese Yangonites with whom I did not directly work. My husband has reflected in detail on what 'sharing the field' has meant for all three us (Girke 2020).

Introduction

'We are Shia', the woman in black tells me. I can barely make out her face in the dark street as we move steadily forward, part of a crowd of a few hundred people all marching towards a brightly lit building down the road a bit on the right side. Being much taller, I have to look down to communicate with her. Her face is half-covered with a black scarf, just like mine. Her body is veiled in black clothes, just like mine. I stand out to her, while to me, she stands for everyone else present. She immediately recognizes me as other, but even if we had met before, it would have been difficult for me to pick her out of the crowd. She approaches me, briefly touching my arm with her right hand, then swings her arm back towards her body in a brisk movement and slaps her right hand onto her chest, just above the heart. I have been performing the same movement for the last two hours at least. We follow the sound of the men's chanting through the dimly lit streets of night-time Yangon. My chest hurts, my heart hurts, and I feel very much alert. We march onward, slapping our hands against our bodies, a few hundred men and women, all clad in black. The women stick together, with some walking side by side for a while to exchange a few words, or sometimes in silence, then regrouping with others, taking pictures on their cell phones or receiving calls from relatives, friends, or acquaintances asking after their whereabouts in the mass of people. Up ahead, some of the men are marching in a segregated block that is illuminated by glowing rods suspended from an electric wire that is in turn held aloft on long poles by some of the marchers. Electricity comes from a car that follows them at a walking pace. As a section of the procession, they are literally highlighted, as is the replica of a coffin that four of them carry on their shoulders. The technical arrangements and the distinction between those in the light and those in the darkness also serve to draw a boundary between those who have a special duty to

1

Fig. 0.1: In front of the Mogul Shia Mosque, the replica of the decorated sepulchre (*zaree*) of the third Shia imam, Hussain ibn Ali (a.s.[1]), comes to a halt at 2:50 a.m. after having been carried around downtown Yangon for more than four hours on the occasion of Arba'een, celebrated every year on the fortieth day after the Day of Ashura, which commemorates the tenth day after the third imam was martyred. Yangon, 2 December 2015. Colour version on page 287.

perform or a special skill to display, such as reciting prayers, and those who follow, who witness, who walk as an undifferentiated mass, like me and my temporary companion, none of us crossing the demarcated lines that separate the women from the men.

At one point, all participants stop to listen to the imam reciting a prayer, their hands resting on their hearts for the entire time, becoming still, only to then resume the beating rhythm once more. Some men and women strike themselves with such force that you can hear a hollow thud every time the hand comes down. Others only touch their chests lightly, especially when engaged in conversation with someone. While many men, particularly those inside the illuminated space, use both hands to hit themselves on either side of their chests in an alternating rhythm, the women only use their right hand, and so do I. Every time

---

1. The abbreviation 'a.s.' is Arabic and stands for Alayhi al-Salām, meaning 'Peace be upon him'. This is a reverential form of greeting and my Shia interlocutors asked me to use it throughout my book whenever I mention one of The Fourteen Infallibles: the Prophet (a.s.), his daughter Fatima (a.s.), and the twelve imams.

my hand touches my chest, I exclaim, 'Ya Hussain!'[2] – the 'Ya' (Oh!) coinciding with the muffled sound of my hand hitting my chest, the 'Hussain!' when I move my hand away from my body again. I chant along, not as loud and pronounced as the others around me, for I am still a bit shy, but loud enough so that I can feel the words resonating in my chest, feel them in my throat and how saying them impacts my breathing, how the movement of my hand and the recitation of these words and the force with which my hand comes down shake my body. I learn how to coordinate the movement of my feet with the movement of my right hand and to modulate the force of my hand with the calibration of my words; I learn to coordinate with those around me, moving steadily forward, without touching bodies, while still synchronizing the rhythm of beating my heart with that of the others. I feel like I belong to the crowd. That 'we' have, in fact, become one huddled mass of mourners. A collective body. At times I curiously turn inward, trying to sense how all of this makes me feel, thinking about the entwined meaning of heartbeat and beating one's heart. At other times I concentrate on observing everyone around me with the heightened attention typical of anthropologists engaging in participant observation.

I smile and nod to the friendly woman who had separated herself from the crowd to approach me. How should I answer her? There was already so much to do that listening and thinking of a reply to her statement was more than I could handle in that moment. I had encountered these same words ['We are Shia!'] in other situations over the course of fieldwork before, and they had always struck me as curious. If I answered, 'I know', I might have put her down. If I said, 'Oh, really?', I would only have made myself look foolish. What did she think I was doing in the middle of hundreds of others, mourning the loss of Imam Hussain (a.s.), dressed exactly as she was dressed (I thought), doing exactly what she was doing (I thought)?

2. The exclamation expresses the pain one is in, remembering – and embodying – how Imam Hussain ibn Ali (a.s.), who was the grandson of Prophet Muhammad (a.s.), was martyred in the Battle of Kerbala (10 October 680). Every year during Moharram, the mourning period, particularly on the tenth day after the imam was martyred (Ashura; Arab. ten), and on the fortieth day (Arba'een; Arab. forty), Shiites commemorate his passing, which led to the twelve-year Second Islamic Civil War which, in turn, predicated the eventual split into Shia and Sunni sects.

> *By approaching me, she began to stand out as an individual, and I began to stand in for everyone else absent. Despite my attempt to blend in and feel along with everyone else, I had remained an other the entire time. But my companion's utterance did not really require a response, and I remained quiet as we moved along until we reached the commemoration hall (imambargah). Everyone stopped for a prayer led by one of the mosque's leaders (mawlanas), for a cup of hot, sweet milk tea, only to then return to the street once more, continuing with the procession that would go on for another two hours throughout downtown Yangon.[3]*

The utterance 'We are Shia!' declares who someone 'is'; it contextualizes what it is that one is doing, and it also draws a boundary around a *we*. At the time, I was not sure what my companion intended to say. It is possible that she meant to actively include me in a *we*, as opposed to an imagined *they*, a third party not taking part in the procession but perhaps gazing at *us*. But it seems more likely that the *we* served to exclude me, as she sought to fill an assumed gap in my knowledge, thereby forcing me to see *them* as an *other* to which I did not belong. Even more: I myself might have been perceived as the *tertius* (Fr. *tiers*) who helped constitute in her eyes what Jean-Paul Sartre ([1943] 1992) has called a 'we-object': under someone else's gaze, two humans begin to become the same, begin to stand for something else and form, as a result of being observed by a third, a common situation against a common enemy by means of mutual alienation or mutual reification. Sartre clarified that '*every* human situation, since it is an engagement in the midst of others, is experienced as "Us" as soon as the Third appears' (1992: 543; emphasis in original). That there was no way to hide in a crowd became apparent to me during another nightly procession when some of my female interlocutors suddenly started speaking in hushed tones, asking each other who 'that face' was. They had, despite the darkness and the hundreds of women in black, immediately identified one other person they could not 'sort in'. They only stopped wondering when one of them found out that the stranger was, in fact, the cousin of a member who had come from London for a visit.

My companion's utterance likely addressed a lack – of me not belonging, and therefore of me not understanding – even if it seemed an odd

---

3. The preceding description has been excerpted from my field notes, 2 Dec. 2015.

assumption in the face of my walking and chanting with them, being dressed like them, and behaving like them, or at least appropriately. My walking alongside the other mourners for two hours had not provoked any reactions up until that moment; one reason might have been that some of the women and men already knew me well and allowed for my 'passing', nodding to me in a friendly manner when they saw me. Another reason for my being able to go unmarked is, I believe, that the practices that were part and parcel of the procession were neither exclusively 'performed' for an observing audience nor 'enacted' to produce a somewhat functionalist effervescent solidarity to forge a stronger cohesion among all members of the Shia community. While much of what goes on during processions is orchestrated and planned well in advance, a lot simply occurs when individuals happen to be in the same place at the same time, bringing with them a certain momentary disposition, and exposing themselves to sensory and intercorporeal experiences for which their membership in a community is not necessarily of any relevance. This book explores and theorizes such practices of *we-formation*, which were in evidence whenever I encountered or participated in activities that should be understood, as I will argue later, as largely pre-reflective. But the woman's utterance indicates a tipping point where pre-reflexivity changes into claims-making. This is where what I call *the work of community* starts: when my companion declared, 'We are Shia!', she was invoking an ethno-religious *we*, a collective *we* that activates a particular register of associations, historical trajectories and meanings. 'Community', I argue in this book, was actively turned into a category for administrative purposes during the time of British imperial rule. It has been put to work to divide people into ethno-religious selves and others ever since.[4] This understanding of 'community' does not equate to a *we* of individuals rhythmically beating their chests as they march together in a night-time procession, but a *we* that has become reflexive of itself by means of an observing *other* (whether imagined or in fact present); a *we* for which the act of slapping one's chest and heart has turned from a collectively shared

---

4.   The English term 'community', possibly because of its colonial origins, has no single equivalent in Myanma, the dominant language spoken in the country. Rather, there are a number of related concepts in Myanma with a range of translations that depend on who is speaking, who is listening, and what the context is. I explore the semantics of the term in Chapter 2.

sensory experience into a (stereo-)typical performance of symbolized action linked to the social category *Shia*.

During another procession, one week later, a woman in black asks me, 'Are you Shia?' I noticed her the second she came into my view – she must have picked me out at the same time. We both stand out. While wearing black just like everyone around us, we are taller. It seems to me that we must really be noticeable to the others around us, to whom we probably look alike. She has addressed me in English, so I reply, 'I am Judith … from Germany', giving her my country of origin instead of a possible religious affiliation. What I had interpreted as suspense in her face while she waited for my answer diminished: 'Oh. I thought you were Shia.' Her answer ruling out the possibility that I might share her religion despite my nationality. She introduced herself as being from Qom; an Iranian, married to one of the local *mawlanas* in Yangon whom she met while he was studying at the Islamic school in her home town. She was now giving Farsi lessons to local students in Yangon while study-ing Myanma herself. I was surprised, for it is rare for women from Iran to move to Myanmar to marry a local Shia. We continued walking side

Fig. 0.2: Once the procession came to an end in the early morning hours, men and women started intermingling, chatting, calling each other up, preparing to leave 30th Street where the mosque is located. I felt simultaneously exhausted and energized. In that moment I took a 'selfie'.

by side for a while, continuing to beat our chests with our right hands, but not chanting along with the others, rather exchanging information about ourselves. I was eager to get to know her better. I felt close to her, as if we had known each other before, as if we had something in common. Later I wondered whether it had been only the fact that neither of us belonged that made us belong together. We exchanged numbers and I remember thinking that perhaps she could become my friend, someone to go out and have coffee with? We arrived at an intersection where her husband was waiting for her, and she had to leave. I called her up a few times, but she never had time. Perhaps our shared foreignness was not a strong enough bond to overcome our lack of common ethno-religious belonging after all?

Starting out from an existential dilemma

How do I write about my interlocutors as individuals when they present their understanding of the world to me in terms of categorical belonging? What if my interlocutors predominantly viewed our encounter through a socio-cultural lens that focused on differences rather than commonalities? In an idealistic statement, Joao Pina-Cabral has posited that

> the ethnographer and the informant are not only exchanging information, they are jointly attentive to the world. Being jointly attentive, however, is a gesture that goes beyond communication, as it is formative of the worldview of those involved. The desire to help mutual understanding is part and parcel of the ethnographic process. (Pina-Cabral 2013: 261; see also Salmond 1986)

My encounters drove home to me that my attempt to engage with others on an individual-to-individual basis was also idealistic. Our anthropological ways of making sense of other people's lifeworlds are often different from those of our interlocutors; this is to be expected, and for some people, it is the entire point of anthropology. We should nevertheless seek access to our interlocutors' views of the world and aim for mutual understanding. But through encounters such as those described above, the difficulties of equitably focusing on individual beings became apparent: I wanted to enter into situations with my interlocutors from the perspective of two humans meeting each other, to try to establish rapport by leaning in to their very existence at a specific moment in time and space. My interlocutors, on the other hand, often took my existence as an occasion to demonstrate their awareness of themselves as members of a 'community' to which I did not belong, or perhaps it would be more accurate to say that my presence reminded them of such membership. Akber Hussain, one of my key interlocutors, never tired of teasing me about this. 'Hey, when will you become Shia?' he often asked, which indicated to me that it would have been easier for him to conceive of me as a converted 'member' than as someone who was simply very interested (and increasingly knowledgeable) in what it means to be a Shia in Yangon. My interest and knowledge in the Shia religion were fine, but they were not what mattered in the end: membership in the community did.

In this monograph, I explore the dialectics of *we-formation* and *the work of community* in urban Myanmar. This interplay is marked by my interlocutors' own interpretations and expectations regarding individuality and membership aligning at one time and clashing at another. While any practice of *we-formation* springs from an individual's pre-reflexive self-consciousness, which I understand as a minimal form of self-consciousness whereby the self is not (yet) taken as an intentional object, *the work of community* describes reflexive acts of claims-making in the name of community. This often occurs in the form of self-othering, for example, when individuals perform and present themselves as members of a community. In the context of Myanmar, this usually means a collectivity with clearly flagged-out ethno-religious markers that set it apart from the majority population and the cultural and social default. I establish *we-formation* and *the work of community* as concepts in order to cast doubt on the categorizations that are often taken for granted not only by people in Myanmar (including our collaborators in the field), but by scholars as well. While the analytical default is to conjure up a *we* in opposition to a *they*, a *we* without a *they* becomes apparent if one engages with individuals in their unique existence in the world and with their various ways of co-existing beyond their roles as members of corporate groups.[5] This insight goes well beyond the case at hand; it is just as relevant for the analysis of integration, belonging, and social categories more generally understood.

---

5. In anthropology, at least since Fredrik Barth's seminal *Ethnic Groups and Boundaries* (1969), the assumption has been that ethnic groups only become aware of themselves *as a group* when confronted with the need to define and defend the boundaries between themselves and others.

This book fills a research gap in that it is among the first to complicate the exclusively 'communal' portrayal of 'Muslims' and 'Hindus' in the literature on Myanmar and the wider region. In approaching the so-called 'Burmese Indians' as *a priori* ethno-religious communities, scholars have often simply reproduced the emic perspectives that their interlocutors have presented to them. We find few explorations of the tensions between individuality and membership, of the possibility of togetherness apart from collectivity, or of the strategic essentializing that people have learned to display for various reasons. While there is literature *about* these minorities in Myanmar, almost no qualitative data have been obtained from engagement *with* the individuals who are said to constitute these collectivities.

To reinforce this point, my encounters always start with individuals, and throughout the book the focus is on them. This monograph is not another book about 'community'. I do not take it for granted that community, as an object, exists to begin with. To set out to study community ethnographically would endow it with a reality it does not readily possess. Paying attention to my interlocutors' own accounts and drawing on historical sources demonstrates how the category of community has been able to acquire and retain its dominance to the present day, and illuminates how 'the ethno-religious community' in particular has become such a naturalized object not only in contemporary Myanmar, but in other places as well, including (and perhaps especially) in academia.

My interlocutors primarily shape their selves in relation to and as part of a community, often anchored in religious buildings and around religious practice. But people engage with their material world and with one another not only to enact 'community', but also to navigate and negotiate their individual being in the world. We should pay as much attention to such an existential *habitus* as we have become accustomed to paying to 'communal' interaction. Grasping such practices of we-formation requires an ethnomethodological perspective that recognizes interactions at a micro level, as well as an existential anthropological perspective that understands the human being not only as a member of a larger collective. In other words, community significantly shapes an individual's experience and sense of self, but never entirely.

I thus ask the anthropologists who are not familiar with Southeast Asia and Myanmar to follow me into the weeds of colonial personal law and the ethnographic details of contemporary ethno-religious life in Yangon. I also ask the regional specialists to become curious about ethnomethodology and existential anthropology. It is my hope that both groups of readers will thereby not only acquire new familiarity with an unfamiliar field, but also come look at individual subjectivity and human intersubjectivity from an unconventional perspective – one that might transcend their own regional or disciplinary boundaries.

Fig. 0.3: Country map of Myanmar showing the author's principal field site, Yangon.

The setting

My study is situated in Yangon, a rapidly expanding metropolis that doubled in population between 1995 and 2020, from 3.5 million to about 7 million inhabitants. Migrants now make up roughly 20 per cent of the city's population, living predominantly in the outskirts of the city. They come from rural areas, mostly in search of jobs, though some have fled violence in the northern regions, where clashes between the national army and armed ethnic organizations have never really ceased, affecting especially the Kachin, Chin and Shan ethnic groups. Many others have been displaced following natural disasters such as cyclone Nargis in 2008, which rendered hundreds of thousands of people homeless in the Ayeyarwaddy Delta, adjacent to the regional state of which Yangon is the administrative centre.

Yangon is nestled in the wedge of land created by the confluence of the Yangon (Hlaing) River and the Bago River, and as it grows it is increasingly spilling over the Yangon River to the west and sprawling up to the north. The river empties into the Andaman Sea south-east of the Bay of Bengal. In the eighteenth century, the small and swampy settlement Dagon – long dominated by ethnic Mon – became the trading hub Yangon when the Burmese king established connections with European trading companies that had begun to export teak in large quantities. Ever since then, housing has remained one of the most challenging problems. The steady population increase has led to the expansion of squatter settlements on the city's outskirts, where people live in makeshift huts, often without electricity and almost always without running water. Those with family members or relatives already residing in Yangon receive temporary shelter and organizational support until they have learned to navigate the dense streets, the ever-increasing traffic, and the logistics of a city whose colonial chess-board layout downtown is barely visible nowadays, as new skyscrapers made of material imported from China block the sunlight and the view of the two major landmarks of the urban topography: the Shwedagon Pagoda in the uptown area which, according to legend, was erected during the lifetime of the Buddha, and the Sule Pagoda in the downtown area of the city (see Stadtner 2011).

The downtown area is markedly different from the expanding northern part of the city and the ever-growing outskirts stretching eastward and westward from the centre: built directly on the banks of the Yangon

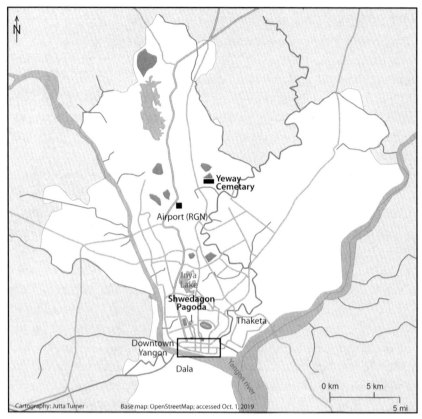

Fig. 0.4: Yangon city.

River, its rectangular grid cannot extend any further. This was the colonial centre of Rangoon, as the city came to be called during colonial times. The name of the city was changed in 1988 back to its precolonial name Yangon, along with those of other towns. The issue of the city's name remains a sensitive one to this day. For example, a new café opened in 2015 under the name Rangoon Tea House. When it became clear after a couple of months that it was going to be a huge success among tourists as well as locals, city authorities pressured the owners to change the name in order to avoid any positive connotations with the country's colonial past, encapsulated in the nostalgia-tinted 'Rangoon' in the name of the café. However, many streets are still remembered and referred to by their colonial names by long-term inhabitants such as my interlocutors. Another distinctive feature of the downtown Central Business District is the number of religious buildings in the area: in addition to the ubiquitous

Buddhist temples and pagodas, there are numerous impressive churches, mosques and Hindu temples on street corners or sometimes hidden in side streets. Despite the rapid change and the continuous expansion at its outskirts, downtown Yangon has remained and continues to be a religious place both inside and out. Downtown Yangon is, in fact, a densely populated village within an ever-growing city.

This material diversity speaks of the early days of the cosmopolitan qualities of modern Rangoon: the city was literally created by the muscle, sweat, and skill of Muslims and Hindus who were brought

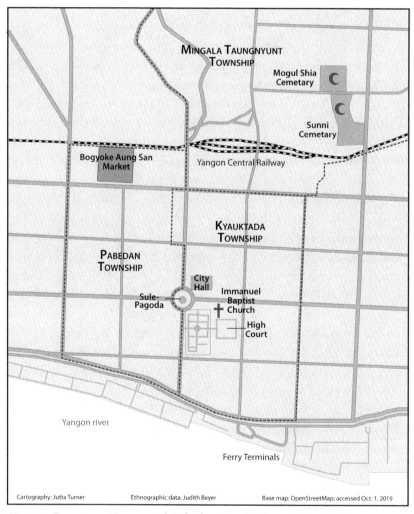

Cartography: Jutta Turner   Ethnographic data: Judith Beyer   Base map: OpenStreetMap; accessed Oct. 1, 2019

Fig. 0.5: Downtown Yangon with Pabedan, Kyauktada, and Mingala Taungnyunt townships.

here from other parts of British India. Some of them received land grants downtown as incentives to build their houses of worship – the mosques and temples around which they then began to settle, as well as the churches that catered to members of the Catholic, Baptist, and Methodist denominations and, more recently, Evangelical groups. At the same time, colonial architects were developing the downtown area in a grid-like fashion similar to other cities such as Singapore and Hong Kong (see Chapter 2). Religious buildings defined the character of downtown Yangon, and they continue to do so in present-day Yangon.

Urbanism, religion, and community

There is a widely held assumption that cities are secular places where cosmopolitan identities overshadow religion and ethnicity, which, despite decades of attempts to overcome such binary thinking, are regularly still regarded as being more 'traditional' forms of identification. At the beginning of the last century, thus at a time of rapid industrialization worldwide, the city was imagined as a place where 'the old clan and kinship groups are broken up and replaced by social organization based on rational interests and temperamental predilections' (Park 1928: 890). This has proved to be untrue – 'religion' and 'community' have retained their influence in the urban context (Cox 1965; McLeod 1978). However, only recently has the nexus between urbanism and religiosity become a topic of interest.[6] Anthropologists have shown that '[t]he dissolution of community ties' – an expectation that had been 'at the core of the urbanization paradigm and key to theories of secularization in which cities were depicted as epicentres of religious decline and became spatialized expressions of secularization' (Burchardt and Becci 2013: 5) – had in fact not taken place. Today, it is acknowledged that urbanism, religion, and community do not stand at opposite ends of a chronological (past–present) or geographical (rural–urban) continuum, but rather go hand in hand. Vered Amit has even argued that '[c]ommunity appears to have obtained greater analytical prominence when anthropologists began to shift their research to cities ... when they converged on to the terrain of complex societies they had hitherto consigned to sociologists'

---

6.   See, among others, Becci, Burchardt, and Casanova (2013), Hegner and Margry (2017), Kong (2005, 2010), Narayanan (2016), Orsi (1985, 1999), and van der Veer (2013, 2014, 2015).

(Amit 2002: 2). In India, the phenomenon of communalism, particularly in its form of communal conflict, has been viewed by some as being more pertinent in cities than in the countryside. It is in the metropolis, argued the Indian scholar Ashis Nandy (1990, 1991, 1993), that religion has come to be wielded as an ideology by the political elite in order to pursue their own interests.[7]

I was struck by the public pervasiveness of ethno-religious communities in urban Yangon when I first visited the city in 2009, and it has fascinated me ever since. There is something about big cities that makes the role of religion in this part of Asia particularly prominent – much more so than in my other field site in northern Kyrgyzstan, for example. In those Central Asian villages, being Muslim is part of people's everyday lives as well, but has never come to dominate public space to the extent I experienced in Yangon. Despite the fact that there are ever more mosques being built, Islam is not so much what happens in and around the mosque, but what takes place inside people's houses. This corresponds to the role religion had come to play during the Soviet period, when practising Islam was relegated to the private sphere. But 'being Muslim' was equally ascribed to people as part of their ethnic identity, and as such was detached from what a person believed in or practised – if, indeed, they practised at all. Roughly around the same time, in the British empire, it was precisely by anchoring religion in public space that governance was realized. The boundaries that were drawn and materialized via this procedure proved to be long-lasting and were much more consequential than people could have imagined. It is this particular way of positioning religion 'in the open' during colonial times that accounts for how cities such as Yangon come to be experienced by outsiders like me. This, however, is by no means the perception of my local interlocutors, for whom it is not their religious identification as such, but their membership in a community that is relevant, always in dialectical and dynamic relation to individuality. This tension has been almost completely neglected in the literature on so-called ethno-religious minorities in general and 'the Burmese Indians' of Myanmar in particular.

---

7. See also Dumont (1980), for whom 'communalism' was an indication that Indian society had undergone a process of modernization.

I argue that in contrast to other parts of Asia, where we observe 'power struggles over hegemonic religious definitions of urban spaces' (Burchardt and Becci 2013: 9), in Myanmar the state privileges Buddhist expression in practice and is thoroughly intertwined with it (Smith 1965; Schober 2011; Turner 2014; Brac de la Perrière 2015, 2017a; Walton 2017). In their overview of religion in the city, Burchardt and Becci emphasize that '[s]ecular discourses and practices are the context of the social location of religion and vice versa, meaning that secularism must be approached jointly with religion' (2013: 11–12), but end up positioning 'the state' against religion, even though they recognize that the state's 'parameters of neutrality strongly resonate with the features of religious majority traditions' (2013: 9). Technically, the Myanmar Constitution of 2008 and state formations that precede it back to 1962 are and have been officially neutral regarding religion. Nevertheless, there are no serious challenges to Buddhism's clear dominance and 'hegemonic religious definitions of urban spaces', as ethno-religious minorities need to tread very carefully in the public sphere, and have little chance of successfully contesting Buddhism's primacy. The country has a long history of discrimination against members of so-called non-indigenous ethnic groups – those that are not counted among the official 135 'national races' (*tain-yin-tha:*). If one is not a recognized member of one of these 'races', access to state services will be severely limited. Many of my interlocutors do not own a Citizenship Scrutiny Card (CSC), but only a Foreigner Registration Certificate (FRC). This renders them ineligible to buy property, for example, or to vote in elections. The possibilities of expression for members of ethno-religious minorities, I argue, have to stay in the realm of essentialized ethno-religious practice in order to be accepted and tolerated by others at all.

What needs greater scrutiny, then, is not the cross-fertilizing impacts of religion on the city or of the city on religion, but on what the archaeologist David Wengrow (2019) calls 'unbounded groups'. He recently argued that 'living in cities may not have been difficult or counter-intuitive at all, because cities are a certain type of unbounded group, and – from the standpoint of human cognition – living in unbounded groups is effectively what we had been doing all along'. Wengrow's argument relates to the question of secular spaces, too: it is quite difficult to 'opt out of' religion if religion is what has come to identify community in the first place.

In Myanmar, it is not feasible to free an 'individual who is persecuted on essentialist communal or fundamentalist religious grounds ... from involuntary forms of association and subordination', as Amit and Rapport (2002: 123–127) had in mind when they positioned cosmopolitanism as a way out of what Rogers Brubaker (2002) has called 'groupism' – that is, 'the tendency to take discrete, sharply differentiated, internally homogeneous and externally bounded groups as basic constituents of social life, chief protagonists of social conflicts, and fundamental units of social analysis' (Brubaker 2002: 164).[8] In Myanmar, community is historically and politically tied to 'identity by religion' in such a way that a crossing of religious borders always also means a significant alteration in an individual's possibilities to self-identify as a member of a community – and of being identified as such by others.[9]

I have come to understand that when my interlocutors, often in one of our first encounters, announced that 'We are Hindus' or 'We are Shia' or 'We are Memon', they were declaring not their religious faith, but their belonging to a community. To generically say 'We are...' instead of 'I am...', as I heard so often during fieldwork when I met someone new, is to present oneself first not as an individual, but as a member of a group. 'Being Hindu', for example, thus first of all denotes a collective category. Only rarely did I encounter an individual who would emphasize their individual faith over their membership to an ethno-religious community. And when this occurred (as I will specifically demonstrate in Chapter 3), it was to establish a difference to the 'other Hindus', thus retaining the collective label, but counting oneself out of the equation. My interlocutors, in other words, did not relate to me by means of their religiosity, but via their roles as members of a community, and some – in addition – on the basis of being fellow human beings with whom I shared other ways of identifying: as a parent, as a wife, or as a scholar. It is for these reasons that I do not consider this to be a book about religion. Rather, my ethnographic case studies centre on human activities marked as religious as they take place in mosques, temples and shrines in the densely populated downtown area of Yangon. In the words of Carol Breckenridge, who studied a Hindu temple in Madras in 1974: '[T]he

---

8. See also Moerman (1965, 1968, 1993) for an earlier analysis.

9. See Robinne (2019) for a recent attempt to apply the concept of cosmopolitanism to multi-ethnic Myanmar.

Temple was not so much the object of my study, as the place in which I wanted to pose my questions' (Breckenridge 1976: 36) – or, in my case, the place where I spent my time observing, participating and listening.

We-formation and the work of community

Community is a Late Middle English term that is derived from the Latin *communitas*, the Old French *comunete*, and the English *common*. Its proto-Indo-European roots are *kom-*, which means 'with', and *mei-*, which can mean 'to move', 'to (ex-)change', but also 'to bind' and 'small'. A derived term is the Latin *moenia* or *munia*, cognate with *murus* (wall), meaning 'city walls' or 'fortifications'. The meaning of the term thus oscillates between confinement and expansion, between keeping things inside, confined and safe, and engaging in interactional and transformative activities. In short, its etymology does not help clarify it as a category, let alone define it, but rather shows its semantic ambiguity. Hillery (1955) collected more than ninety definitions of the term in the mid-1950s. The *Oxford English Dictionary* lists eleven different meanings, each substantiated with historical sources illustrating its use in such contexts. This will surely remind anthropologists of the history of attempts to nail down 'culture' in our discipline. According to the OED, then, community is mostly about having something in common, whether an attribute or character, a property or interests, or rights and ranks; it evokes people being together through fellowship, interaction, religion, or nativity, and separated from those (often a demographic majority) who do not share in these respective identifiers. As such, community can acquire a spatial or organizational characteristic. This vast terrain of possible applications of the term calls to mind the words of the French philosopher Georges Bataille, who once said that 'a dictionary begins when it no longer gives the meaning of words, but their tasks' (Bataille 1985: 31).

'Community as "normative prescription" has all too frequently interfered with "empirical description" to the extent that a systematic sociology of community has proved to be impossible to construct', wrote Peter Hamilton in the foreword to Anthony Cohen's pathbreaking study *The Symbolic Construction of Community* (1985: 8). To push this argument further, I suggest that in anthropology's long-term efforts to concretize the inherent vagueness of community, authors have tended to focus on either prescription or description or, increasingly, deconstruction; convincing attempts at a synthesis are quite rare, especially when compared to encompassing – and ultimately sterile – critiques of the entire field. In this book I do not recapitulate the vast literature in anthropology and sociology on community per se. Many others before me have done so.[10]

For me to focus on community in this book in full awareness of its inherent ambiguities requires an initial commitment to Hamilton's systematic sociology of community. I only reproduce prescriptive statements as they were uttered by my interlocutors from Myanmar who generally use the English word, as there is no direct equivalent in the Myanma language. The local words for 'group' and 'race', for example, do not map neatly onto the English term 'community', although some overlap clearly exists.

Over time, I realized that I could only grasp the category in the field – descriptively and analytically – if I took individuals' engagements with various forms of we-formation into account. Rather than bestowing on community some sort of positivist reality or deconstructing the category until nothing is left, my aim in this book is to shift the angle of approach: I acknowledge that community (for reasons that can usually be traced historically) feels real to and is meaningful for individuals. Their experiences and their struggles to engage with community are no less real. Through their own classificatory practices, my interlocutors demonstrate that they reason and reflect on symbols and meanings in their own culture as much as anthropologists do. But my approach goes beyond a social constructivist concern over how terms such as community are used, and also beyond a representational approach in which actors are subjected to culture as a system of meaning. Individuals always have the capacity to escape from 'doing "being members"' of a group (see Sacks 1992), at least situationally or temporarily, be it by acting in their own interests or by choosing not to act at all. This is not a return to methodological individualism; I have come to understand the individuals I met as creating themselves in relation to the catego-

---

10. See, for example, Hillery (1955), McMillan and Chavis (1986), Brint (2001), Creed (2006a, b), Esposito (2010), Rosa et al. (2010). In these publications, the authors tend to separate the literature into those asking philosophical questions or having normative standpoints to declare about community versus those who try to research its concrete characteristics, thus again differentiating on a meta-level between community as prescription or idea and community as description or actual social formation.

ries they were born into or have (whether willingly or inadvertently) manoeuvred themselves into. The individual is thus not prior to a *we*, but co-constitutive with it. It is from this perspective that I found it useful to combine an ethnomethodological approach as coined by Harold Garfinkel and others with an existential anthropological approach as advocated by Michael Jackson and Albert Piette, a mix of scholars and directions that might otherwise be seen as unlikely bedfellows.

When I talk about *the work of community* (drawing on Nancy 2015), I reflect on the ways in which individuals accommodate 'community' in their acts of reasoning, meaning-making and symbolization. The way my interlocutors in Yangon see and talk about themselves has a historical context that begins in nineteenth-century England, encompasses British colonial India and later Burma itself, and extends into present-day Myanmar (see Chapters 1 and 2). I then widen the emic perspective of my interlocutors and offer a novel way of describing how a *we* that does not neatly map onto or overlap with a homogeneous social group is generated in various situations. What I call *we-formation* encompasses individual and intersubjective routines that can easily be overlooked, as well as more spectacular forms such as the intercorporeal aspects of the ritual march I described earlier. Attending to such sometimes minute moments of co-existence or tacit cooperation is difficult, but doing so can help us understand how community continues to have such an impact on the everyday lives of our interlocutors, not to mention on our own analytical ways of thinking about sociality. By focusing on individuals and their bodily practices and experiences, as well as on discourses that do not explicitly invoke community but still centre around a *we*, we-formation sensitizes us to how a sense of *we* can emerge.

My co-constitutive approach to individuals who navigate the in-between of a *we*, on the one hand, and 'community' on the other approximates Jean-Paul Sartre's use of 'to exist' as a transitive verb with a direct object: 'I exist my body' (*j'existe mon corps*), he wrote ([1943] 1992: 460), thereby indicating that while our body is not an object of consciousness, we are unreflexively aware of it and can choose to turn our conscious attention to it, thereby turning it into such an object. I seek to grasp what individuals *exist* when they relate to objects or humans in contexts which, from an outside perspective, would normally be classified as 'communal'. Sartre illustrated this by analogy to pain:

first, there is the immediate awareness of 'pain', which leads us to classify pain as 'illness' and, finally, as pathological 'disease'. In this process of incremental abstraction, bodily sensation becomes objectified and – in Sartre's terms – a 'for-itself' (*pour soi*) that takes on a life of its own, so to speak. The same goes for community. We *exist* we-formation, but once we begin to reflect on our doings in abstract or classificatory terms, we enter the realm of community. As with the body and the shift from pain to illness and disease, such a process might lose track of its original source. In contrast to the normative or prescriptive classification of the communal, where community is explicitly invoked by members or observers, what I will call *pre-reflective self-consciousness* has a more immanent association with such practices of we-formation. While community structures the possibilities of how people are socially allowed to (inter-)act and how they can perceive sameness or difference vis-à-vis others, the category would remain meaningless – or would lose much of its naturalistic appeal – without the ongoing, subtler ways in which individuals exist themselves, and by which they come to embody, experience and discursively forge a sense of *we*. I explore how exactly and in what contexts practices of *we-formation* and *the work of community* emerge, converge and diverge, that is, how they relate to one another and in what ways this perspective helps us to shed new light on community as a category that, somehow, seems old-fashioned but never becomes outdated.

A bridging experiment

In this book, I draw on two bodies of theoretical literature that are rarely thought together, let alone brought together: ethnomethodology and existential anthropology. While the former has remained largely unfamiliar to anthropologists, the latter is so recent that not many are familiar with its approach either. Ethnomethodology is the study of sense-making, the investigation of the mundane reasoning of actors and how they manage their daily social affairs.[11] I have found that anthropology

---

11. Ethnomethodology was developed in the 1950s by Harold Garfinkel, a student and assistant of Talcott Parsons, and was further elaborated by sociologists Harvey Sacks, John Heritage, and Eric Livingston in the United States, Jörg Bergmann and Christian Meyer in Germany, and Michael Mair in Great Britain (for an overview of the literature, see Maynard and Clayman 1991; Ten Have 2004; and Bergmann and Meyer 2021).

can learn a lot from ethnomethodology in terms of its rigorous attention to the ongoing accomplishment of (everyday) life. John Heritage defines ethnomethodology as

> the study of a particular subject matter: *the body of common-sense knowledge* and the range of procedures and considerations by means of which ordinary members of society make sense of, find their way about in, and act on the circumstances in which they find themselves. (Heritage 1984: 4; emphasis added)

With roots in both Parsonian sociology and phenomenology, ethnomethodology takes the study of phenomena to a practical level and investigates how people attribute meaning to, interpret, and rationalize their own and others' behaviour. Actors are thus not 'cultural dopes' who always act 'in compliance with preestablished and legitimate alternatives of action that the common culture provides' (Garfinkel 1967: 68). Rather, their 'culture' is understood to be the result of their actions, and not the resource on which actors draw to guide their behaviour (Meyer 2016: 4; see also Meyer 2018). Contra Parsons, Garfinkel argued that norms, rules, and laws always acquire relevance *ex post facto*, as a way of interpreting or explaining concrete interactions. Ethnomethodology is concerned with the mundane obviousness of everyday life as much as with the actors' mundane reasoning about everyday life.[12] As such, it also aims at the de-reification of academic categories as it turns established theories on their head.

Ethnomethodology is important in reconceptualizing community, as it focuses more on the making of *wes* than on the making of *theys* – it can thus be a corrective to both sociological and anthropological theories, in which the making of *theys* and the investigation of the boundary-making that keeps *we* and *they* apart have been dominant (Appadurai 2006; Barth 1969). It advances this project particularly by analysing how members are made.

Existential anthropology is concerned with the situatedness of individual existence and with intersubjectivity. It draws on phenomenological work and is influenced by cognitive approaches to the body and mind that focus on experience. Existentialism is compatible with ethnomethodology's radical empiricism in that it equally centres on

---

12. See also Schütz and Luckmann (2003) on common sense [*natürliche Einstellung*].

investigating how individuals make sense of their world through engaging with others: 'The basic idea of sense-making is that reality is an
ongoing accomplishment that emerges from efforts to create order and
make retrospective sense of what occurs' (Weick 1993: 635). It is with
this view onto the world – a view that is at the same time always a view
onto ourselves – that I see a possibility of bridging from ethnomethodology to existential anthropology, an effort that is spearheaded by
Michael Jackson in the United States and Albert Piette in France.[13]
Drawing on Sartre, Jackson constructs the individual as always embedded in the lifeworld of others. His approach is one that emphasizes
'inter-existence', a notion through which he wants to get at the tension
that always exists between the individual and the communal and the
private and the public (Jackson 2005: 12) or, perhaps more aptly, as he
did in the title of one of his publications, *Between One and One Another*
(2012). Jackson's sometime collaborator, the French anthropologist
Albert Piette, advances a related anthropology that is anthropocentric
and focused on the individual. Piette finds that anthropologists tend to
lose touch with individuals rather quickly in their need to generate statements of generalizable relevance. The exceptions to this rule are mostly
to be found in the realm of autoethnographies and publications with
a strong methodological emphasis on biographies or life histories, but
these are often not intended to contribute to theoretical debates.[14] To
counter this tendency, Piette devotes himself to what he calls 'the minor
mode of reality' (2012), by which he understands empirical attention
to seemingly incidental detail: '[T]he empirical work consists in going

13. I see the work of anthropologists such as Michael Lambek (2017), Tim Ingold
(2000), Joao de Pina-Cabral (2017), Sónia Silva (2017), Thomas Hauschild
(2002), Michael Taussig (1992, 2018), Christoph Antweiler (2012), Tine
Gammeltoft (2014) and others in line with currently emerging existential anthropological thinking, even though the connection is often not explicitly made.
Michael Lambek, in the conclusion of his chapter 'Both/And' in a volume edited
by Jackson and Piette (2017), translated his own work on spirit possession in
Mayotte (1981, 1993, 2010) into the language of existential anthropology, an
exercise he found 'uncertain (sceptical) of certainty'. In his self-observations he
notes, '[B]eginning to look around that neighbourhood it seems to be an interesting if uneasy place to inhabit. ... Perhaps I am an existentialist' (2017: 80).

14. But see the brief, innovative movement towards a 'dialogical anthropology' (Dwyer
1979; Lydall and Strecker 1979; Crapanzano 1980; Tedlock and Mannheim
1995).

always further, in the interval, in the details of which it is made, in the identification and analysis of the rests and of that which remains and of the remains of the remains' (Piette 2012: 103; cited after Deprez 2014). While he acknowledges that '*all* descriptions are inherently "failures"' (Piette 2011: 94; cited after Deprez 2014), the aim should nevertheless be 'to go as far as possible in this work, by intensifying the description and knowing its infinite incompleteness' (ibid.).[15] He calls this type of attention to action in the 'minor mode' a *phenomenographical* approach and draws on photography and video sequencing in his own work on ritual, religion and faith (Piette 1996, 1999, 2017). That the existential-ist anthropologists Jackson and Piette give such emphasis to detail and microanalysis reinforces their compatibility with ethnomethodology.

To summarize: Piette and Jackson urge us to reconsider how we have come to study *anthropos* – namely by recalibrating our ethnographic gaze away from the extraordinary that is often rendered 'typical' and towards the ordinary in all its details and its singularity. While both Jackson and Piette position existential anthropology against interac-tionist and practice approaches such as those of Goffman and Garfinkel, this opposition does not have to be strictly maintained: bridging these bodies of literature allows us to approach practices of *we-formation* and investigate how they relate to *the work of community*. My interlocutors employ what Anthony Smith has called 'participants' primordialism' (1998) and Douglas Medin 'psychological essentialism' (1989), both highlighted by Brubaker (2002: 166), and not without reason: such practices emerge from lived experience and are sustained and even become naturalized. In my case material from urban Myanmar, this oc-curs not only through ethno-religious othering, as when Muslims and Hindus seek to manoeuvre through a majority Buddhist society, but through the ongoing cognitive work of individuals aligning themselves – often bodily and through their senses – with others. This allows first for a re-sensitization of the manifold alternative ways individual beings can *exist themselves* in a situation, and second for a de-naturalization

---

15. Piette's views on the impossibility of complete description reminds me of a quote on the impossibility of complete categorization: '[H]uman beings recognize that the world is actually multiple ... and that any one system of classification is only a pretence at overall orderly encompassment. ... We classify, we categorize, con-scious of the logical impossibility of so doing once-for-all' (Rapport and Overing 2000: 40).

of the category of community that analytically should be exclusively viewed as representational from the actor's point of view, not from that of the anthropologist.

Stagnated subalternity

Beyond sticking 'to the things themselves' and concentrating on people's mundane (and not so mundane) reasoning of their intentional practices, I see value in upholding a complementary analytical perspective to ethnomethodology and existential anthropology that considers structural inequality in the *longue durée*. Ethnomethodology is mostly concerned with strategic action, and while existential anthropology is more reflexive in this regard, it also tends to sideline the question of power. But individuals are not only able to categorize others; they are also always being categorized by others and, in the case of my interlocutors, *as others*. To complicate matters further, my interlocutors have come to draw on and accommodate their own essentialized marginality by and for themselves, and by now identify with particular modes of ethno-religious othering. Just as we cannot ignore the categorical impact community continues to have, we cannot ignore the persistent effects of imperial policies – the structural inequalities and power asymmetries – on contemporary postcolonial societies such as Myanmar. The historical trajectories of my interlocutors' position of marginality vis-à-vis a dominant majority population of Buddhist ethnic Bama help scrutinize how such a position is sustained and continues to shape their very possibility of interacting with others at all.

As members of ethno-religious minorities, my interlocutors are structurally in a position of subalternity vis-à-vis the state and the wider Buddhist Bama population.[16] They are faced with ethno-nationalism

---

16. The term 'subalternity' was originally used by Friedrich Engels in the context of military stratification, where it characterized a subordinate position of soldiers vis-à-vis army officers and later public officials. Gramsci employs it only as an adjective ('subaltern') and only in combination with a certain 'class' (in his early notes) or a 'group' (from 1934 onwards). While he used the term throughout his *Prison Books*, he investigated it in more detail only in 1935, thus towards the end of his writing: 'subaltern' was to characterize 'slaves, peasants, religious groups, women, different races, and the proletariat' (Gramsci 1975, v. 3: 2279–94). Gramsci never quite defined the term, but his notebooks are full of examples and dense descriptions of how he viewed subaltern groups, whose main characteristic

and racial ideologies of superiority by the dominant class on a regular basis. Historically, this positionality grew ever stronger from the moment that the country, called Burma at the time, achieved independence from the British empire in 1948. Burma thus poses an interesting challenge to the general argument made within postcolonial studies, particularly by the Subalternity Studies Group (SSG) that formed in India in the early 1980s around Ranajit Guha, Dipesh Chakrabarty, Gayatri Spivak and others. The aim of this group had been to critically re-evaluate the impact of class in the making of the Indian nation after independence from Britain by drawing on Antonio Gramsci's findings. In doing so, they diverged from his writings in that they argued (1) that subaltern agency could be regarded as independent from that of the hegemonic class; (2) that the subaltern cannot speak 'collectively'; and (3) that they are 'muted' and 'silenced' (Spivak 1988). Whereas in India it was thus assumed that 'the subalterns' ceased to exist as a class once the colonial empire collapsed and the British left the nation to itself, I argue that in Burma, my interlocutors only began to occupy a subaltern position at that very moment – as Burmese Indians.

As a conceptual tool, subalternity requires the investigation of its historical dimensions: how were people of a certain category subjected and slotted into their current positioning, how did they incorporate this positioning into their own subjectivity, and what are the reasons for their ongoing subordination? Massimo Modonesi (2014) has worked out the specificities of the concept of subalternity (which he carefully distinguishes from antagonism). According to him, subalternity exists within a field of domination; its modality is one of subordination, its expression one of acceptance and resistance, its scope always lies within the given boundaries or limits set by a hegemonic counterpart, and its projection is the renegotiation of power over (in contrast to against or beyond) its subordinate position. While subalternity thus incorporates the possibility of resistance in the sense of relative antagonism and for relative autonomy, its practices and activities are never revolutionary:

---

was that they remained in a continuously subordinate position, dominated by a hegemonic class, incapable of being unified unless, so Gramsci asserted, they become the state themselves (see Modonesi 2014: 19; Beyer 2022a; Beyer 2022b). This is why he never used the term as a noun, as it lacks the quality of a homogeneous group.

[T]he specificity of the notion of *subalternity* refers to the subjective formation inherent in and derived from relations and processes of domination, constructed in terms of the incorporation of collective experiences of *subordination*, characterized fundamentally by the combination between the *relative acceptance* and the *resistance within* the frame of existing domination, projecting towards a renegotiation or adjustment of the exercise of the *power over*. (Modonesi 2014: 141; italics in original)

The concept points to the overarching structural inequality that my interlocutors experience and subject themselves to precisely by envisioning themselves as members of a disadvantaged class or – in their terminology – 'race', even though some of them regard themselves as the offspring of the country's intellectual elite.[17]

Subaltern groups have internalized their subordination to such an extent that they themselves will justify it and seek to naturalize their condition when questioned. Gramsci further holds that even when trying to rebel against their domination, striving for (more) autonomy, subaltern classes remain in a continuous state of alarmed defence (Gramsci 1971: 244; see also Modonesi 2014: 17). They are reflexive about their social positioning and might strive to form alliances with other subaltern groups. However, they will not succeed in defining situations according to their own ideologies; they will ultimately be unsuccessful in rewriting the past to accommodate their existence as autonomous vis-à-vis the hegemonic class: 'We can understand subalternity as a condition and as a process of subjective development – of political subjectivation centred in the experience of subordination' (Modonesi 2014: 36). Pandey (2006) has recently come up with a novel term – the 'subaltern citizen' – to prevent 'the easy erection of a barrier between *us* (citizens, the people with history), and *them* (the subalterns, people without)' (Pandey 2006: 4735). He argues that subalternity needs to be thought together with citizenship in order to account for the paradox that subalterns are no longer struggling for recognition as equals, but demand recognition on the basis of their difference.[18] For the case of my interlocutors, however,

---

17. See also Partha Chatterjee (2004) on the paradox of the subalternity of an elite.

18. This aligns with current debates and legislation on indigeneity, autochthony, authentic tradition, and 'culture' (see for example Niezen 2003; Niezen and Sapignoli 2016; Beyer 2019a; Beyer and Finke 2019).

the term 'subaltern citizen' would need to be interpreted differently. Most of them have a very strong attachment to being (good) citizens of Myanmar and in fact usually speak quite highly of 'the state'. Their self-positioning as members of ethno-religious communities in public is always secondary to their sense of citizenship and is often resorted to for strategic reasons, as they know that this is how they are predominantly viewed by the Bama Buddhist majority.

My data confront me with what Modonesi has termed 'stagnation in subalternity' (Modonesi 2014: 150). Subalternity, in the case of my interlocutors, is an overdetermining factor that allows for moments of resistance and relative autonomy, but never transgresses or overturns. It is in these moments that the boundaries of the otherwise free (thinking) individual become manifest.[19] I am particularly interested in how people navigate their individual dispositions and explore their options, all the while essentializing their belonging to a community of cultural (here understood as ethno-religious) *others*. One of the main situational motivations seems to be a desire to avoid having to justify their individual courses of action: acting *as* a Burmese Indian is, in effect, a catch-all account. Such strategic essentialization (Spivak 1993) frees them from having to justify in each case why they are able, in Sartre's words, to choose to live in 'bad faith' (*mauvaise foi*).[20] Sartre credits individuals with the capacity to act even in dire circumstances. To live in 'bad faith' is a choice to opt out of freedom.

I found stagnated subalternity a helpful notion when characterizing the position of 'Burmese Indians' in Myanmar even today: while not wholly disenfranchised from the state, my interlocutors are aware that

---

19. In the context of India, Robert Hayden (2002: 217) has reached the following conclusion after analysing his ethnographic and historical data on shared religious spaces such as shrines: '[T]he warning to minorities [Muslims] not to expect equality of symbolic representation may be distasteful but pragmatic: accepting an inferior status as a group may ensure the continued coexistence of individuals'. Note that I by no means want to advocate that my interlocutors should take on such a 'pragmatic' stance vis-à-vis the Buddhist majority population and the Myanmar state, but my data suggest that they have indeed assumed such a position.

20. Sartre (1992: 800) defined 'bad faith' as 'a lie to oneself within the unity of a single consciousness. Through bad faith a person seeks to escape the responsible freedom of being-for-itself'.

the majority population categorizes them as *other* in various ways, and that they are expected not to dispute the subordinated position this puts them in. In regard to the transversal work of community, I am interested in tracing how individuals reconcile themselves to the fact that they – *qua* their belonging to a wider category of people – are constrained, and even naturalize and incorporate this position. There is thus a conceptual overlap between what the concept of subalternity intends to describe and the category of community: the anthropologist Gerald Creed, for example, has argued that 'the very notion of community may be self-limiting as a revolutionary force because it is defined by (and acquires emotional valence from) its *subordination* to the state' (Creed 2006a: 10; emphasis added). For him, the category is 'an empty, although inherently positive, signifier' (2006a: 7) that facilitates governance and capitalist accumulation in the name of harmony, security, and hope (2006a: 5–6; see also Bauman 2001).

I take this cue from Creed as an empirical question, and in Chapters 1 and 2 of this book I will explore the historical contingencies of 'community' as historically an *other*-making category through which the creation of *theys* became possible, even routinized. The historical perspective provides insights into not only the provenance, but also the changing salience and the shifting manifestations of 'community' (and communities) in Yangon, which are dynamic and susceptible to internal as well as external factors. In Chapters 3 to 6, one of my tasks is to expose the ongoing importance of this process of othering. My other task is to complement the literature on minority groups in urban Myanmar, which have thus far received little ethnographic attention. For this purpose, I concentrate on individuals who are locally recognized as Muslims, Hindus or, collapsing the two categories, as 'Burmese Indians' and show how the category of community is transcended in practices of we-formation. This concept takes into account the fact that, no matter how appealing 'community' might be as it both caters to a 'nostalgic desire for a lost past' and allows for a 'creative reformulation of a postmodern society' (Creed 2006a: 3), it is by *existing themselves* as individuals in interaction with others that all human beings are always trying, albeit pre-reflectively, to surpass the structural constraints imposed on them.

CHAPTER 1

Classifying the Indian Other

'This is our independence minaret!' proclaimed Mukhtar Bhai proudly, waving with his right hand in the direction of the monument erected in the middle of Maha Bandula Square in downtown Yangon.[1] We had met with his family on a Sunday afternoon for a picnic. Mushtari Baji, his wife, had cooked sweet corn for our son and her two youngest children, and while the kids were playing on the well-watered green lawn that has in recent years become a favourite public gathering spot, I listened as Mukhtar Bhai told me about the latest developments going on in the Mogul Shia mosque to which he and his family belong. His statement about the monument stuck with me, as it gives us insight into how public space in Yangon is experienced by a second-generation Burmese Indian man born in Yangon.

To refer to the 50-metre-high obelisk, which is surrounded by two concentric circles of mythical lion-like figures (*chinthe*) that can be found in front of temples and pagodas throughout Southeast Asia, as 'our independence minaret' was not an accidental slip in translation. Mukhtar Bhai was not translating from Burmese into English for me, and he was certainly not seeking to accommodate my interest in the role of Muslims in the making of the Burmese state. As he pointed towards the white pillar, he rather reiterated what it was intended to signify by those who had commissioned the monument: the end of the colonial empire and the beginning of an independent nation-state. But he ap-

---

1. After independence, the park, which had been called Fytche Square (after a former chief commissioner of British Burma), was renamed Bandula Square, after General Maha Bandula, the commander-in-chief of the Royal Burmese Armed Forces, who died a national hero in the first Anglo–Burmese war. The groundwork for the new monument was laid on 4 January, 1948, the day Burma declared independence from the British empire. The pillar that was subsequently built replaced an earlier monument to Queen Victoria, which had been donated by a rich Armenian trader in 1896 and which was escorted to England in 1948.

Fig. 1.1: View from Maha Bandula Square onto the 'Independence Minaret' and the Yangon High Court.

propriated the signifier by calling it a 'minaret' rather than referring to it as an obelisk or simply a monument. His rendering of this particular place in the middle of downtown Yangon was postcolonial, national, and religious all at once, and it was one of many small instances that helped me understand how classifications along ethno-religious lines shape an individual's experience of Yangon as their home.

We were in the direct vicinity of numerous mosques, temples, and shrines, many of them bearing the official names of a group's ethnic origins. Many downtown shops, restaurants, and teashops also indicated through their names historical, even transgenerational connections to people's provenance from southern or northern India, or, more subtly, a Muslim background, such as small signs with the number '786' on them or otherwise identifying the establishment as *halal*.[2] Some Buddhist temples also sport free-standing pillars, but the minarets of downtown Yangon are the more eye-catching landmarks. So when Mukhtar Bhai reframed this important symbol of the independent Myanmar state in terms that expressed his – a Muslim's – sense of belonging and entitle-

---

2. For Muslims from the Indian subcontinent, the number '786' is a numerical form of rendering the expression *Bismillah al-Rahman al-Rahim* ('In the name of Allah, the most gracious, the most merciful').

Fig. 1.2: Sule Pagoda (left), City Hall (right), and the monument to Queen Victoria (centre) at Fytche Square, nowadays Maha Bandula Square. Visible on the horizon (upper right) is the Shwedagon Pagoda. Photograph: Philip Klier, 1895. Courtesy of The British Library, London. Open Access.

ment, it was a striking illustration of the role Muslims have played in the history of the city. To wit: a Shia Muslim had once been the mayor of Yangon and sat in City Hall, a unique, syncretic white building opposite Maha Bandula Square and the current seat of the Yangon City Development Committee (YCDC), the main administrative body of the city. Yangon's first tram line was introduced by a Memon Muslim from India; it connected the Shwedagon Pagoda, the country's most important pagoda and urban centre of worship, with the hotels and magnificent administrative buildings on Strand Road close to the Yangon River. The former brick factories and rice mills, the present-day construction companies and trade businesses, the private schools, the bakeries: many are owned by the descendants of migrants from the Indian subcontinent. In the eyes of these numerically small and structurally subaltern people, Yangon is and always has been their city. Their great-grandfathers and grandfathers had brought not only their labouring hands, but also their businesses, their knowledge, and their ideas and dreams to this place, and their offspring move through the cityscape with an ease and a sense of belonging that those who keep moving in from the many corners of the country in search of jobs, education and a better life have some difficulty acquiring. My interlocutors' narratives, when talking about their city, are not those of marginal people – they are stories of the true 'city-zens' of Yangon. Yet the connection to India is always there.

Most of my interlocutors trace their family backgrounds back to India or other parts of the British empire. Their ancestors crossed the Bay of Bengal and arrived in Rangoon or other coastal settlements as labourers, businessmen, or administrators. (British) India continues to play a role in their conception of self as well as in their conception of community. The theoretical exploration of the category of community that is at the centre of this study is inextricably bound up with the historical development of the British empire. It was in this context that modern social theory took root, including, eventually, publications on community in anthropology and sociology that profoundly influenced nineteenth- and twentieth-century thought and that continue to shape everyday understandings of the category within and beyond academia. In this chapter I also take a closer look at the accommodation of the 'Indian other' following the migrants' arrival in colonial Burma. This historical moment demonstrates how the category of community travelled with the ancestors of my present-day interlocutors across the Bay of Bengal towards old Rangoon, Moulmein, and other port cities as part of the final expansion of the British empire, and how it retained its quality as an *other*-making category that it had acquired in India. The chapter relates the plural ethno-religious landscape in colonial Burma prior to the arrival of 'the Indians' to the ways Burmese politics of ethnicity began to change from the nineteenth century onwards.

The work that 'community' was expected to do in colonial Burma in the nineteenth and the first half of the twentieth century can be understood as an aspect of colonial engineering, and was greatly informed by the British experience in India. According to Mrinalini Sinha, 'communities constituted by castes, tribes, races and religious groups' became the building blocks out of which 'an alternative framework for the constitution of society' could be formed. These communities were 'the products of the complex negotiation between indigenous processes of class formation and the bureaucratic categorizations of the colonial state that together produced a politics of community-based claims' (Sinha 2006: 8). Subsequently, in British India (1793–1947), the predominance of supposed communities led to the new category of 'communalism', a specific label that emphasized people's presumably shared ethno-religious identity and that was conceived of as political from the very beginning of the colonial encounter, administered and orchestrated in a top-down manner by agents of the British colonial state. It later became most prominent in the 1947 partition of India and Pakistan, which was carried out along religious lines, with the distinction between 'Muslims' and 'Hindus' becoming a categorical division that itself had been encouraged and established in its rigidity during colonial times only. While the litera- ture is ambiguous on the issue of whether or not a form of communalism already existed in pre-colonial times and what relation to community it fostered, there can be no doubt that religious identification did play a role in earlier times. The very etymology of the term 'Hindu' attests to this: it can be traced back to Muslim conquerors, who gave this label to the people living along the Indus River who, over time, began to adopt it for themselves (see Talbot 1995: 694). Likewise, supra-local ways of self-identification also existed before modern communications tech- nologies were introduced through the colonial encounter (van der Veer 1994, 2001a). However, it was through the British empire's governance techniques – its divide-and-rule policy, its all-encompassing documenta- tion and administration of the populace, its overemphasis on collective religious identity (and the subsequent regular eruptions of large-scale conflicts that became interpreted along these lines) – that 'communalism' acquired the particular connotation that it continues to carry nowadays. It has proven to be a powerful discourse and an ongoing practice that, in spite of its literal meaning, continues to provide the words and models that are used to divide people.

Thus, efforts that one sometimes finds in the literature to set com- munity and communalism in opposition to one another are certainly too stark and, in the end, too often lead to the idealization of community. For example, Bates contends that

> 'Communalism' is ... related to, but very different from, the idea of 'community'. The solidarity of communities, at a local level, has been an important feature of Indian society since ancient times .... 'Communalism', however is predicated upon a non-local concept of community. (Bates 2001: 1)

I argue that communalism and community in Burma (and argu- ably contemporary Myanmar) are better viewed as intertwined than as analytically distinct. In the words of the historian Sandria Freitag, '[c] ommunalism is the ideology of community organized around religion, combined with the structures through which collective activity could be mobilized' (1989: 197). Freitag criticized the literature on communalism in India for focusing predominantly on institutions and elite actors while disregarding the public participation that made communalism tangible in the first place, shaping it from the inside: 'those interested in the crowd must analyse primarily its actions', she argued (1989: 16). She sought to fill this gap by attending to arenas of mass political participation such as public rituals, processions, and protests. She considered 'crowd behaviour' to be at the very heart of community, but rightly problematizes our methodological access, 'for we cannot know the thoughts of the individuals who make up a crowd' (1989: 14). Moreover, how and when can we determine that a group of individuals have, in fact, become a crowd? At what point are individuals recognized by others as a *they* and at what point do they recognize themselves as a *we*?

I turn to these questions in the subsequent chapters. In this chapter, I seek to shed light on how the British colonial state drew rigid distinctions along 'community' lines for political and administrative purposes.[3] These formal distinctions, I argue, began to strongly determine people's sense of who they were, where they belonged, and how they should relate to one another. What I call *the work of community* throughout this book needs to be understood as a practice of colonial governance that became so naturalized that people of Indian origin in Myanmar still today accept their categorization as primarily belonging to either a Muslim community or a Hindu community. However, we should not uncritically duplicate this taxonomy, which is why in this book I offer a novel sensitizing concept that upholds the conviction that no individual can ever be entirely defined through such acts of categorization. What I call *we-formation* throughout this book is as important in this regard as *the work of community*. To include such practices of we-formation in our methodology, we first need to pay attention to

3.   The literature on communalism in India and on the separation of India and Pakistan in 1947 along ethno-religious lines is vast. I cannot do it justice here, nor is it my aim to provide an encompassing overview of these topics. In the first part of this chapter, I thus draw on the work of Freitag and Appadurai, whose approaches to their historical material are compatible with my ethnographic findings on Myanmar. I refer to other publications on these issues in the footnotes.

the often disregarded or overlooked moments when people come to encounter themselves as *individuals* in their own right. It is from the perspective of the individual that we should understand co-existence and intersubjectivity. At those moments, individuals become a *we* that is situational, contextual, and non-dependent on communal identity, but that still contributes to individuals' sense of self in interplay with the societal taxonomies.

Moreover, any discussion of the development of community and communalism must take the role of the colonial state in India and academic discourses in Europe at the time into account, as I do below with reference to Henry Sumner Maine and J.R. Seeley. I should note that some commentators are of the opinion that any use of this terminology is problematic, as when Rajat Kanta Ray argued that to discuss relations in India at the time in terms of communalism would be 'pejorative', and that it would be 'best to leave the term "communalism" alone' (2003: 26).[4] While I could easily follow Ray's injunction, as the term itself never gained great traction in Burma/Myanmar, the tension between community and communalism is still analytically generative and therefore useful for my purposes. It is precisely in the situation of the colonial/ imperial encounter that we need to locate their ongoing relevance – for the institutions that impose them as much as for the people who are subjected to them (see Chidester 1996; van der Veer 2001b). The colonial encounter thus did not mark a complete rupture from 'indigenous' processes not yet much influenced by Western models of belonging (such as nationalism), but was rather a crucial stage of their transformation, in the course of which relationships were forged anew, with consequences that continue to have an impact on the present-day political landscapes of India and Myanmar, as well as of Great Britain.

After discussing the roles of Henry Sumner Maine and J.R. Seeley in reifying 'community', I will move on to more concrete cases from India proper, beginning with a court case from 1809 in which colonial

---

4. For further literature on the different connotations of communalism in colonial and contemporary India and the relation to (village) communities see, for example, Chandra (1984); Chatterjee (1993); Pandey (1990); Prakash (2002); Münster (2007); Rao (2003); Ray (2003); Sinha (2006). The term 'communitarian(ism)' has sometimes given way to 'communal(ism)' in a number of Indian publications to avoid the negative association with ethno-religious strife. For an in-depth discussion of communitarianism in East Asia and beyond, see Brumann (1998).

authorities intervened in a fight over public space in Banaras in Uttar Pradesh. This is one of the earliest well-documented cases in which the category 'religion' became linked to the category 'race', in effect creating communalism and cementing 'the Muslim–Hindu divide'. This set a precedent for future conflicts to escalate precisely along these same lines that continues in India and Myanmar today. I subsequently draw on an extended ethnohistorical study from Tamil Nadu by Arjun Appadurai (1981), which moves away from the state-centred perspective by showing how, in this colonial setting, Indians began to adapt to and creatively make use of the category of community that, over the course of the century, had come to acquire an ever more 'natural' character. Particularly important for my analysis here are Appadurai's findings on how the category of 'the Tenkalai community' came into being and what role the colonial courts played at the time, as this ethno-religious category from India will become relevant in my ethnographic data on present-day Myanmar (see Chapter 4).

An empire of village communities

What was the task of 'community' in colonial India, long before the term was used as broadly as it is today? What was the work the British expected the term to do that eventually turned it into a category? I will focus on Henry Sumner Maine's work in answering these questions, as he is often referred to as the founder of legal anthropology. Maine was a comparative jurist and a practising lawyer who became interested and invested in Indian political institutions, kinship systems, and law when he was serving as a member of the council of the Governor-General of India (1863–69). While there, he was in charge of developing a universal code of law and was tasked with ending religion-based personal or family law. Although he was ultimately unsuccessful in getting his propositions accepted by his superiors in London and his inferiors on the subcontinent (see Chatterjee 2011), his work is important in that it shows how anthropology and empire-building were entangled in colonial Britain. It was through figures such as Maine that 'community' entered the vocabulary of colonial engineering.

When he wrote *Village Communities in the East and West* (1871), Maine regarded the village community as 'the true proprietary unit of India' (1871: 106) that would 'determine the whole course of Anglo-

Indian administration' (1871: 62).[5] Maine deemed a study of the customary law of 'the East', particularly India, important for understanding more about 'the ancient proprietary system of the Teutonic races' (1871: 21) because, in his view, the Indian villages of his time resembled those of ancient Europe: '[T]he East is certainly full of fragments of ancient society' (1871: 12), he claimed. '[T]he Indian and the ancient European systems of enjoyment and tillage by men grouped in village communities are in all essential particulars identical' (1871: 103). He portrayed India as 'the great repository of verifiable phenomena of ancient usage and ancient juridical thought – of Roman law' (1871: 22). In making these claims, he was continuing an argument he had laid out earlier in his 1861 *Ancient Law*:

> If by any means we can determine the early forms of jural conceptions, they will be invaluable to us. These rudimentary ideas are to the jurist what the primary crusts of the earth are to the geologist. They contain, potentially, all the forms in which law has subsequently exhibited itself. (Maine 1861: 3)

Maine's arguments about the inextricability of (village) community and law grounded his work firmly in the theory of social evolutionism as developed by August Comte, Edward Tylor, Lewis Henry Morgan, and Herbert Spencer. He stated that the Indian society exhibited 'earlier stages of human society' than the English one, detected 'phenomena of barbarism' (ibid.) in India, used the general term 'existing savage races', and spoke of 'the minds of men who are at this stage of thought' (1871: 16, 111). His firm belief in the existence of separate kinds of people comes out in his warning of 'using that language on the subject of *common race* which has become almost popular among us', as he thought that only ignorance on the part of the researchers who had not sufficiently investigated Eastern societies could lead to such a claim (1871: 14; emphasis added). Expecting the colonial encounter to ultimately destroy all things 'native', he understood that, once codified, customary law would inevitably be displaced by English law (1871: 37). His interest in the codification of customary law (including what later came to be called Burmese Buddhist law) was grounded in a distinction between 'civilized' and 'wild' races, as well as in the special personal status laws

---

5. See also the work of Karuna Mantena (2010).

for Muslims and Hindus, which the British had already begun to codify starting in the early nineteenth century.[6]

Maine's agenda to codify and institutionalize customary law was grounded in his belief that different 'races' required different laws; proper English law was inappropriate for the Indian in his community. In his 1871 text, he used the term 'community' almost exclusively in the conjoint plural of 'village communities', which he defined as 'a group of families united by the assumption of common kinship, and of a company of persons exercising joint ownership over land' (1871: 12). Maine regarded these village communities as the backbone of Indian society within which caste was integrated – a view, as will be shown, that is not too far removed from uses of the term 'community' in the context of present-day Myanmar. He considered caste to be an ancient version of class:

> Caste is merely a name for trade or occupation, and the sole tangible effect of the Brahminical theory is that it creates a religious sanction for what is really a primitive and natural distribution of classes. The true view of India is that ... it is divided into a vast number of independent, self-acting, organised social groups – trading, manufacturing, cultivating. (Maine 1871: 57)

Village communities were held together by 'tradition', which was 'kept steady by corresponding practice' (1871: 59) – what Maine termed 'custom'. He declared that 'each individual in India is a slave to the customs of the group to which he belongs' (1871: 13–14). In general, he saw little to no agency residing in the Eastern individual, whose lack of power to even dispose of his own property (1871: 41–42) proved his complete subordination to the group. He considered each village community a stratified, self-sufficient, 'little society' (1871: 175), with organized bodies of representation and authority, and with people carrying out a wide range of occupations so as to be completely independent. But in contrast to Europe, Maine argued, the village community displayed elements of egalitarianism alongside elements of feudalism. While some offices were in the hands of dominant families, other tasks could only be decided communally. The gravest error of the English, according to Maine, was that they failed to understand that Indian forms of property were based on 'the Village Group as the proprietary unit' (1871: 183–184). Instead,

---

6. See also Ilyse Morgenstein Fuerst's (2017) work on the racialization of religious identities in colonial India.

they imposed their own understanding of property rights on the Indians, thereby turning members of those superior families into 'landowners'. In doing so, they introduced a market-oriented rule whereby land could be rented out or sold in a competitive way. Moreover, '[t]he partition of inheritances and execution for debt levied on land are destroying the communities – this is the formula heard nowadays everywhere in India. The brotherhood of the larger group may still cohere, but the brethren of some one family are always wishing to have their shares separately' (1871: 113).

Besides directly imposing colonial laws, the English attempted to grapple with what they considered to be customary law, which proved quite resistant to codification and sanction (Cohn 1965, 1983). Nevertheless, they began writing down what they learned, a rudimentary form of codification that started to deprive these laws of their flexibility and capacity for ad hoc adjustment.[7] Moreover, despite village dwellers unwillingness to accept higher authorities, the English began entrenching a strict hierarchy and, with the possibility of addressing courts with grievances, established 'the sense of legal right' in the individual villager to be used against his co-villagers: 'Unfortunately for us, we have created the sense of legal right before we have created a proportionate power of distinguishing good from evil in the law upon which the legal right depends' (Maine 1871: 73), lamented Maine who, throughout his work, was quite critical of the whole colonial enterprise. In his fourth lecture on 'The Eastern Village Community', he argued that the establishment of individual property rights is 'the point at which the Indian village community is breaking to pieces' (1871: 112). To put it briefly, under British rule the word 'community' acquired the characteristics of a category that was expected to do a certain type of work for the colonial apparatus, mostly by classifying people into distinct ethno-religious groups. It was based on false assumptions and, as such, was saddled with its own contradictions and ambiguities from the very beginning.

The two-empire theory

Following Maine, I turn to J.R. Seeley for a contrasting view regarding the intricate relationship between academic theory-building around the

---

7. The same approach was pursued by the Russian empire in its conquest of Central Asia (see Beyer 2016).

category of 'community' and the colonial enterprise. Seeley borrowed from the legal and political theories of Maine, but then turned his reasoning in the opposite direction: while Maine never questioned that India was to be included in the British empire and only struggled with how it could be governed, Seeley wanted to keep India separate from the rest of the empire (Behm 2018: 32). Whereas community was the backbone of India for Maine and the arena where he felt English engagement was necessary (but misguided), for Seeley, India's separateness became a key notion. His arguments are worth citing for their insightful agenda.[8]

According to Seeley, 'modern English history breaks up into two grand problems, the problem of the colonies and the problem of India' (Seeley [1883] 2010: 175). When Seeley spoke of 'political community', he was first of all referring to England and its 'colonies'. By 'colonies', he meant only those overseas in America and Australia: 'By a colony we understand a community which is not merely derivative, but which remains politically connected in a relation of dependence with the parent community' ([1883] 2010: 45). He further specified: 'The modern idea of a colony is that it is a community formed by the overflow of another community' ([1883] 2010: 178). He argued that '[t]he chief forces which hold a community together and cause it to constitute one State are three, common nationality, common religion, and common interest' ([1883] 2010: 13). India, according to him, lacked all three forces. Indians were of different 'blood' and adhered to a different 'religion', unable and unfit to join progressive nations:

> For besides the colonies, we have India. … India is all past and, I may almost say, has no future. What it will come to the wisest man is afraid to conjecture, but in the past it opens vistas into a fabulous antiquity. All of the oldest religions, all the oldest customs, petrified as it were. No form of popular government as yet possible. Everything which Europe, and still more the New World, has outlived still flourishing in full vigour; superstition, fatalism, polygamy, the most primitive priestcraft, the most primitive despotism; and threatening the northern frontier the vast Asiatic steppe with its Osbegs and Turcomans. (Seeley [1883] 2010: 204–205)

---

8. For an opposing view on the role of British India as a part of the colonial enterprise, see *The Rise and Expansion of the British Dominion of India* by Alfred Lyall (1894).

For Seeley, the separation between Hindus and Muslims was a pre-colonial fact that divided Indian society, 'for we come as Christians into a population divided between Brahminism and Mohammedanism' ([1883] 2010: 214–215). Conquering India was 'unintentional', 'unnatural', 'an accident' even, and this conquest relied on the fictive upholding of a categorical difference on the basis of religion through which the 'infinite confusion', as Seeley called it, between notions of property and government became mediated. It was very much through competition over the administration of religious property – land grants, rights to erect shrines, etc. – that colonial governance was exerted locally, incidentally establishing groups around these properties and then cementing differences between them on the basis of religious adherence, which came to be merged with what foreign administrators and scholars understood to be 'caste'. Muslims, however, had a special position since, according to Seeley, 'the Mussulmans who formed the bulk of the official class under the Great Moguls, have suffered most and benefited least from our rule' ([1883] 2010: 227). Even before the arrival of the Moguls in the sixteenth century, the majority of rulers in India had been Muslims ([1883] 2010: 238). This, for Seeley, was one of the key justifications for arguing that India as such had not even existed prior to British conquest:

> But what is a man's country? When we analyse the notion, we find it presupposes the man to have been bred up in a community which may be regarded as a great family, so that it is natural for him to think of the land itself as a mother. But if the community has not been at all of the nature of a family, but has been composed of two or three races hating each other, if not the country, but at most the village has been regarded as a home, then it is not the fault of the natives of it that they have no patriotism but village-patriotism. (Seeley [1883] 2010: 238)

Both Maine and Seeley were children of their times, replicating theoretical assumptions about societal evolution and class that had been prevalent from the 1820s onwards in Europe, which echo old distinctions between modern people in society and traditional people in community (or tribe or caste), of mechanical and organic solidarity.[9] But according to Nicholas Dirks, even Louis Dumont ([1966] 1980) continued with

---

9. By arguing that India could never have self-governance and by emphasizing the difference between settler colonialism and imperialism, Seeley echoed the work of John Stuart Mill.

this trend when he 'reinstall[ed] caste once again as the major symbol for Indian society. This symbol was a powerful reminder of how that society is organized by religious (read Hindu) rather than secular values' (Dirks 2001: 57). Dirks has elaborated the ways in which the category of caste was tailored to fit colonial interests. Caste, for him, is a colonial form of power and representation that transported 'a vision of an India in which religion transcended politics, society resisted change, and the state awaited its virgin birth in the late colonial era. Thus, caste has become the modernist apparition of India's traditional self' (Dirks 2001: 60). Caste continued to be viewed as a mainly religious phenomenon and eventually became conjoined with the growth of communalism, which had also been conceptualized along ethno-religious lines. In keeping religious aspects (of caste), particularly the question of untouchability (in official terms, 'scheduled castes'), separate from social, political, and economic issues, Dumont ended up reproducing colonial ideology and diminishing both the role of the (colonial) state and the role of the individual in society:

> In Dumont's view, caste not only subordinated the political, it also reduced the individual to a position of relative unimportance. The individual only has ideological significance when placed outside society, or to put it in Dumont's terms, as 'the individual-outside-the-world'. (Dirks 2001: 59)

Ethnohistorical and anthropological studies have pursued a different perspective by focusing on how individuals began to self-identify with these newly demarcated ethno-religious groups, claiming a corporate identity that had not existed earlier in order to pursue tactical aims. By way of example, I summarize the work of the historian Sandria Freitag (1989) on early nineteenth-century northern India and of the anthropologist Arjun Appadurai (1981) on southern India.

On the making of communal identity in Banaras[10]

When Hindu worshippers erected a stone foundation in a public square in Banaras in 1809 on which a statue of Hanuman[11] could be placed,

---

10. The case is summarized and analysed in Freitag (1989). Banaras (also Benares) is a city in Uttar Pradesh that is today officially called Varanasi.

11. Hanuman is a divine monkey and the companion of the god Rama, but is worshipped as a deity in its own right. See Lutgendorf (2007) for a detailed account of this 'second generation deity'.

Muslims removed it. Prior to that day, all statues had been built on mud foundations, thus making them temporary. With the exception of religious buildings, up until that moment people had never placed symbols of their religious faith and belonging to a 'religious community' in public. In removing the Hanuman statue and destroying the stone foundation on which it had been placed, the Muslims also damaged other sacred objects. Hindu representatives brought the British Acting Magistrate and the *kotwal* (another representative of the state) to the site to complain about the damage, but once these authorities had left, some Hindus retaliated by destroying a nearby *imambargah* shrine of the local Shia, where ceremonial items for the annual Moharram processions (see Chapter 6) were kept. The Shia, in response, armed themselves with swords and sticks usually used for self-flagellation and marched – procession-like – through the city. The colonial government intervened by bringing some of the rioters to court, assuming that they had instigated the violence 'purely upon religious principle' (Boards Collections No. 9093, cited in Freitag 1989: 43) and that they had acted on behalf of their entire community.

Freitag, in analysing this case, argued that the existing 'communal identities' at the time of the riot were based not on religion alone, but on 'caste, occupation, place of origin of immigrants to the city, even mother tongue' (Freitag 1989: 41–42). People drew on religious symbols because it was through these that they could navigate public space, that is, 'the realm in which status had come to be defined' (ibid.). Religion was an 'idiom in which competition was expressed and through which adjustments were made in the social and cultural fabric'. The process was more intense during periods of change, particularly change initiated by alterations in the relationship between the state and its constituent communities: 'The conflict itself thus expressed not so much timeless hostility between immutable communities of Hindus and Muslims as the readjustment of power relationships in an urban site undergoing significant political change' (Freitag 1989: 51). Freitag then analysed a second riot in 1810–1811 during which the population – irrespective of their religious orientation – had collectively rallied against the state over the issue of housing taxation. By looking at these two events side by side, she was pointing out the shortcoming inherent in the predominant focus on 'communal' violence (that is, violence between religiously divided groups) in Indian scholarship, to the neglect of other events where religion did not play a role. The legacy of these early riots and how they were handled has proven to be multifaceted and long-term. Pandey, for example, has argued that '[w]hat applied to a particular city – the experience of "convulsions" in the past and the "religious antagonism" of the local Hindus and Muslims – now applies to the country as a whole. Banaras becomes the essence of India, the history of Banaras the history of India' (Pandey 1990: 28; cf. Freitag 1989a: 203).

The long-term effects can be summarized as follows. First, the colonial state began to intrude into people's ways of local self-governance. But instead of directly participating in public life to gain legitimacy as pre-colonial governance carried on, it began to work through local intermediaries, whom it labelled 'natural leaders', thus distancing itself from direct interaction and accountability while remaining firmly in control. It is important to emphasize that British modes of 'non-interference' and indirect rule through representatives shifted in significant ways during the nineteenth century and varied by region. Official permission from these new indirect leaders was made mandatory for carrying out religious activities such as processions, construction work on religious buildings, and even charity-related actions, thus particularly in the realm of colonial patronage of religious institutions (see also Chatterjee 2011). Second, local power structures were disregarded, and a policy of 'evenhandedness' was put in place. When people complained about their rights not being recognized, the state argued that rights 'could only be affirmed or denied by the courts' (Freitag 1989: 56).[12] By bringing individuals before a court in their role as religious representatives, the colonial state placed the emphasis on only one possible dimension of ethno-religious identification, which may well not have been the dimension that was most important to the people themselves, let alone their only one. But the concept of indirect rule and the categorization along religious lines were familiar to the British, especially as the latter had been part of their own European socialization. Throughout the British empire, the colonizers fostered a protectionist policy of ethnic pluralism or of 'racial-cum-ethnic "communities"' (Kahn 2008: 263), a policy culminating in the so-called personal status laws in the eighteenth century

---

12. See also Cohn (1983). I deal with the repercussions of these interventions in Chapter 4.

for Hindus and Muslims and the Race and Religion Laws in present-day Myanmar (see Chapter 5). It was not, however, an accurate reflection of how rural Indian society was set up. Nevertheless, over time, the categorizations caught on: 'The broad terms "Hindu" and "Muslim" denote but the most obvious of these categories. As time passed and certain groups received rewards or penalties by virtue of their supposed identities, the labels came to possess a persistent institutional reality they had lacked earlier' (Freitag 1989: 61). Individual case studies today continue to reveal how the naturalization of such labelling played out concretely, and how the colonial subjects began to engage with the categories that were imposed on them, as the next section demonstrates.

On establishing communities in southern India

At the same time as the riots became communalized and 'religionified' in the northern provinces, similar developments were taking place in the southern province of Tamil Nadu. In his *Worship and Conflict under Colonial Rule: A South Indian Case*, Arjun Appadurai (1981) investigated the various points where British rule intersected with local politics revolving around the Śri Partasarati Svami Temple, a Hindu temple devoted to Śri Vaisnavism. Appadurai's ethnohistory goes back even further than Freitag's, starting in the pre-British Vijayanagara period around the fourteenth century, the time when adherents of Śri Vaisnavism became 'an intellectually divided community' (1981: 82).

Appadurai first showed how, over the course of several centuries, two sects emerged as a result of a scholastic fission within 'the Śri Vaisnava community' (Appadurai 1981: 71). They split into two schools over the role that was to be attributed to the Sanskrit tradition in religious study and missionary work: the northern Vadakalai, for whom caste was fundamental to the social ordering; and the southern Tenkalai sect, for whom caste restrictions did not matter. The Tenkalais' use of Tamil as a religious language of instruction and prayer was inclusive: '*Prapatti* (surrender), according to them, can be done by all persons irrespective of caste, community or status' (ibid.). The Vadakalais' emphasis on knowledge of Sanskrit, on the other hand, meant that only Brahmins were able to shape religious discourse.

English merchants acquired the temple in 1639, and it, as well as the adjacent village of Triplicane, became British territory in 1676 (Appadurai

1981: 105). The colonial state took over the governance of the temple from those they understood to be the temple's 'hereditary trustees' and their hitherto 'immemorial usage' (1981: 60). By approaching the temple and its administration with the Western idea of a 'trust' in mind, the colonial authorities intended to deal with disputes that emerged in the everyday temple affairs only when they concerned 'civil' matters, refusing any involvement in 'religious' affairs, for which they established a separate judiciary in 1842. Not only did the temple lose its autonomy to the state, but in a 'paradoxical affirmation of the ideology of "non-interference" at all levels of government' (1981: 152), 'religion' became separated from other types of temple affairs. This entailed a 'shift from a unitary model of the Hindu king as judge-cum-administrator to an institutional structure in which the supervision of temples was divided between bureaucracy and judiciary' (1981: 162–163), transforming 'previously ritually constructed privileges into bureaucratically defined ones' (1981: 165). We see the same dynamics motivated by similarly changing conceptualizations in colonial Burma a century later.

Subsequently, and importantly for my discussion of ethno-religious othering in general and the emergence of 'the Tenkalai' in particular, 'a new meaning began to apply to the term Tenkalai: it lost its pan-regional, sectarian, and ritual connotations and began to acquire the status of a local socio-political category that designated the political constituency of the temple' (1981: 139). Up to that point, the term 'Tenkalai' had referred to people who 'preferred to rely on specific roles, rights, ranks, or caste affiliations. Thus, the petitioners (in their appeals to courts) described themselves variously ... [but] [i]n no case did a petitioner justify his interest on the basis of being a "Tenkalai" or of representing Tenkalais' (1981: 155). This gradually changed. Appadurai traces how litigants began to present themselves as 'Tenkalai', as people of the 'same sect and caste' as their predecessors. Noting that '[t]his tacit reference to his Tenkalai affiliations is the first explicit and self-conscious invitation to the British to formalize the sectarian ideas as a principle for local temple control' (1981: 155), Appadurai pointed out how, in the court documents, the term Tenkalai had acquired a new usage. He concluded that in approaching the state (courts) for protection in this way, people showed that they had learned how to address 'the Leviathan that has all but abolished them' (1981: 61).

In their studies, both Freitag and Appadurai emphasize ethno-religious othering as an instrument of colonial governance and stress how, over time, this led people to self-identify primarily along the lines of 'Hindu' versus 'Muslim' in some contexts, and as 'ethnically' distinct or different in others. However, while scrutinizing communalism, neither Freitag nor Appadurai investigates the use of the category 'community' that went hand in hand with the developments they described. Rather, they both employ the category rather uncritically. In his work on transversality, Félix Guattari (1984, 2015) has cautioned against assuming that 'the main purpose of the group is the mutual reinforcement of "togetherness" or some kind of "faux" ideal collegiality' (cited in Cole and Bradley 2018: 3), yet this tendency seems difficult to avoid even in the very publications that intend to show how, in India, communalism took centre stage in politics and people's everyday lives under the conditions of the colonial encounter.[13] Drawing on Guattari's concept, I suggest approaching community as a transversal category that cuts across other categories such as 'race', 'class', and 'religion'. In contradistinction to these categories, community might appear less fraught, less divisive, and less politicized while, in fact, it contains all these characteristics.

The uncritical application of the category 'community' has continued unabated from the imperial conquest right up to the present, not because modern-day authors have failed to notice its complex and conflicted history, but because the category still 'does' some work: it is still evocative, still a helpful shorthand, still a useful contrast, still a way to paraphrase many things without having to explicate them. It is, in brief, a common-sensical category. In tracing its development in key works of the British empire, this chapter has thus far highlighted the historical context through which people came to see the colonial Indian state as

---

13. To cite another example of this blind spot in the scholarship from a different regional context: In a recent edited volume on the principles of transversality (Cole and Bradley 2018), Mark LeVine and Bryan Reynolds applied Guattari's principles to a case of what they call 'resistance pedagogy' of 'the Zapatista community'. To them, a transversal approach is exemplified by the Zapatista exercises 'in community creation, identity, and solidarity' (2018: 158) that led to 'achieving unity through the radical acceptance of the "Other"', a concern they argued was also central to Deleuze and Guattari's later oeuvre (ibid.). My point is that 'community' does not radically *accept* such an *other*, but actually *creates* it in the first place.

organized in communities. In the next part, I will trace how the category travelled across the Bay of Bengal along with the so-called Indian *others*, who came to Burma in search of labour or to settle on land that the British had offered them as part of the final stage in the expansion of their empire.

Migrating across the Bay of Bengal

The Indian Ocean is often depicted as a 'shared communal space at the interregnum of several world orders' (Moorthy and Jamal 2010: 3–5). Sunil Amrith has calculated that 'from the beginning of organized Indian emigration in 1834 until 1940, well over 90 per cent of *all* Indian emigrants went to Ceylon, Burma, and Malaya. Put simply, the Bay of Bengal region accounts for nearly the sum total of India's emigration history in the age of empire' (2013: 104, emphasis in original). The reasons for migration varied. British forces needed labourers and preferred non-Burmese of Indian origin over the local population. For Indian labourers, migration to Burma provided them with new employment opportunities. For low-caste people, it was a chance for upward social mobility. For moneylenders and businessmen, it opened up new markets (Amrith 2013: 119–122; Charney 2009: 10; Satyanarayana 2001). Finally, retired military officers received land grants in Burma as a reward for their service in the imperial army. By the 1880s, Burma had become the number three destination for Indian labour (behind only British Malaya and Ceylon), and it would attract between 12 and 15 million labourers from 1840 to 1940 (Amrith 2013: 104).[14]

While through the First Anglo-Burma War (1824–1826), the northern provinces of Arakan, Tenasserim, Assam, and Manipur were brought under British control, the following years also saw the expansion of British presence in lower Burma, where Rangoon had already been briefly occupied. The First Anglo-Burma War started over the disputed border area of British Bengal and the Brahmaputra River valley where Assam and Manipur are located (see Fig. 1.4). After initial successes for the Burmese, the war was likely decided for the British when they assaulted the port city Yangon (later Rangoon) and fought towards the

---

14. The exact number of people who migrated across the Bay of Bengal to reach Burma cannot be accurately determined, as migrants regularly travelled back and forth (see Jaiswal 2014).

capital Ava from there. Soon, King Bagyidaw surrendered. The colonial powers forced a treaty on him in which he had to accept new borders, ceding the disputed north-western territories as well as southern Tenasserim to British India (see Fig. 1.4). Rangoon only became a part of the British holdings after the Second Anglo-Burma War (1852–53); it had been under Burmese rule for less than one hundred years, ever since King Alaungpaya seized it – when it was still called Dagon – from the Mon in 1755 with the help of Muslim sailors (Yegar 1972: 9–10). It was this king who renamed the at-the-time still quite small city, calling it Yangon, which means 'the end of strife'. In 1795, a British officer who visited the city on his way to the Court of Ava wrote that he could hear 'the solemn voice of the Muezzin, calling pious Islamites to early prayers' (Symes 1955: 160). In 1804, the number of Muslims living in Rangoon was recorded as 5,000, compared to around 500 Christians, most of whom were non-Europeans. The number of Europeans, in comparison, was just 25, as the civil surgeon of Rangoon, B.R. Pearn, has noted (1939: 78). Thus, Rangoon was just a small provincial town of little significance to the Burmese empire prior to the arrival of the British, occupied mostly by ethnic Mon fishermen. The city's overall population estimates in 1823 range from 9,000 to 30,000. In 1856, there were 46,000 people living in the city.[15] In 1852, Pegu and lower Burma were annexed and Rangoon became the capital. After the Second Anglo-Burma War, the aim of which had been to secure exemption from Burmese law for European traders in Rangoon, the East India Company, which had developed into a 'military-economic complex' (Noor 2016: 158–161), was absorbed into the British state, with its desire to be exempt from local regulations as strong as ever. Upper Burma was added to the British empire in 1886 after the Third Anglo-Burma War ended with the banishment of the last Burmese king. It was at this time that massive migration across the Bay of Bengal began. The government encouraged immigration as the only means of ensuring the cultivation of the land and, at the turn of the century, nearly 30,000 immigrants, mostly from Madras and Bengal, entered the country.[16]

---

15. See Yin May (1962: 32); Zin New Myint (1998: 69) cited in Kraas et al. (2010: 27).

16. *Report on the Administration of British Burma during 1881–82* (Rangoon: Government Press, 1882), India Office Library and Records (IOR) V/10/497, 20; cited in Heminway 1992: 269.

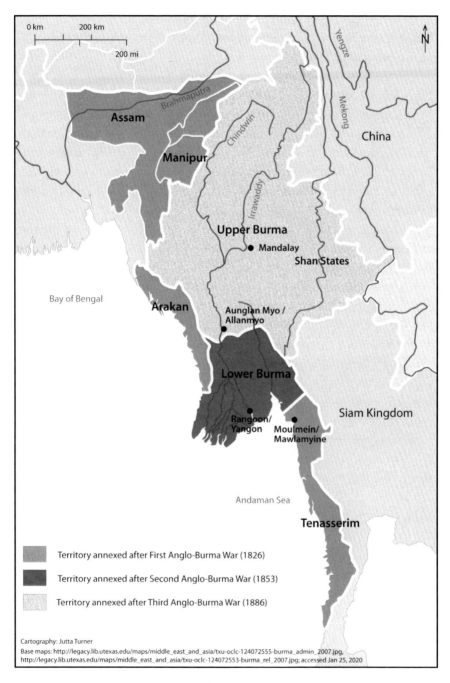

Fig. 1.3: The British conquest of Burma.

When speaking of 'Indian migration', however, we need to remember that these were diverse people who moved in different ways for a variety of reasons. Most of them would not have recognized themselves as belonging to one and the same category, and would not even have been able to communicate across group lines. Some, looking for work, came only for a few months, planning to return to their families in India again; others relocated permanently to make use of parcels of land that were given to them as a reward for their service in the colonial apparatus or in the Indian army; others again took up positions in the higher echelons of the administration in Burma – Burma was, after all, a part of India.

Burma poses an important counter-example to the rest of the British empire. Although she does not mention Burma specifically, Amanda Behm (2018) informs us that the British long sought to curb immigration from the 'coloured' colonies to 'the West', with sophisticated justifications for this institutional racism. At the same time, however, they moved hundreds of thousands of people across the Bay of Bengal as settlers. Particularly with the growth of rice as an important cash crop after the First Anglo-Burma War, the king could no longer control exports or even impose trade restrictions as he had done in previous times. For this economic enterprise, which effectively turned Rangoon into a major hub for global trade, new labour and foreign investment were needed: 'Initial attempts to employ indigenous Burmese and Chinese laborers had met with limited success and therefore, the attention of the British administrators turned to the peasant-cultivators from the Madras and Bengal presidency in India' (Mazumder 2013: 65–66). Mazumder mentions Fielding Hall's half-admiring account of the 'lazy' Burmese who refuses to 'turn himself into a machine, because he will retain his liberty', whereas the Indian is described as always 'trying to hold at arm's length disease and want and death, never escaping from them' (1906: 22–31, cited in Mazumder 2013: 66, fn. 68; see also Pearn 1939), and is therefore more compliant and more willing to work harder and subjugate himself.

For the labourers, boarding a steamship to Burma was made attractive through government subsidies for ticket fares and the comparatively high wages that could be earned in the rice mills, as domestic servants, or on the shipping docks. The steamships had begun to criss-cross the

Bay of Bengal from the mid-nineteenth century onwards: from Calcutta to Chittagong and Akyab, as well as to Rangoon and Moulmein, mostly transporting rice in one direction and migrants in the other.[17] The British India Steam Navigation Company introduced regularly scheduled trips between Rangoon and Madras on a fortnightly basis. These intense migratory activities occasioned descriptive poetry: 'As the great rivers Kaveri, Krishna, and Godavari spilled into the Bay of Bengal, so the sons of their valleys crossed it, pouring in their thousands into Burma and Malaya' (Amrith 2013: 108–109). The 'sons' to whom Amrith refers were mostly male labourers who came for several years to Burma to work in the rice mills and on the plantations. They migrated across the Bay of Bengal from Telegu-speaking areas north of Madras (present-day Andra Pradesh), from the Tamil region, from Orissa, and from Bengal. They also came overland from Chittagong (Amrith 2013: 119).

In general, migration followed seasonal patterns, as it was closely related to agricultural labour. These migrants were categorized by the British bureaucracy as 'domestic' and 'free' after Burma had become part of British India in 1886. However, criticism of the indentured labour system that had been set up in contrast to earlier slavery in Africa, long outlawed by this time, was voiced once it became obvious that people had been labouring in abysmal health and working conditions (Tinker [1974] 1993; Carter 1996; Kaur 2006; see also below). The demand in Burma for seasonal labourers was immense, and specialized agents of Telegu origin, the so-called *maistry*, scouted and recruited suitable candidates, paying their fares in advance.[18] Trying to understand the mo-

---

17. Until the 1880s, the monopoly lay with the British India Steam Navigation Company (BISN), which was then joined by the Asiatic Steam Navigation Company (ASNC), with the competition resulting in a decrease in travel fares (Cheng Siok-Hwa 1968, cited in Mazumder 2013: 78–79).

18. The *maistry* were established labourers who cultivated an unequal relationship with their dependents, who entered into a patron–client contract relationship with them. In the literature on south Indian labour migration in the nineteenth and twentieth centuries, the *maistry* have been compared to the *ka(n)gany* (Kaur 2006; Satyanarayana 2001; see also Andrew 1933: chs. 8 and 12). Heidemann (1992) has described the changing roles of the *kagany*, particularly their contribution to the formation and administration of the plantations, as well as how their presence has altered what counts as a 'caste' in the cases of Sri Lanka and Malaysia. In his account, the *kagany* is remembered nowadays 'as a diabolic slave-trader who recruited innocent people from South India to the plantations and extracted the

tivation of individual migrants rather than analysing official documents, Mazumder turned to Bengali novels as a potential historical source. In her book, she recalls the story of a man who had travelled to Rangoon to pursue a legal career, but instead became a famous writer of semi-autobiographical stories about a high-class Bengali Brahmin protagonist who seeks his fortune in Burma – a place 'where Bengalis were at such a premium that they were lifted bodily from ships carrying them the moment the latter touched the shore, and carried away by Englishmen to be showered with jobs, money, power and prestige' (Chattopadhyaya 1993: 109, cited in Mazumder 2013: 86).[19] The predominantly male migrants' purpose in coming to Burma was to earn a livelihood.[20] Women seldom featured in archival accounts of migration and, if they did rise to the level of notice, it was with reference to prostitution (see Mazumder 2014: 510). In more recent historical work, the voices of individual migrants have gained a more prominent place than in earlier accounts of the role of Burma in the British empire. Parthasarathi Bhaumik (2022: 1), for example, has traced the 'complex network of power, subjugation, and resistance' in Bangla-language autobiographies, travelogues, poems, and journals. These textual sources reveal the fragmented and diverse representations of colonial Burma that motivated Bengali migration. Likewise, Arash Khazeni examined microhistories of Indo-Persian travellers across the Indian ocean and particularly to Burma. Combining historical work with observations from visiting contemporary Myanmar,

---

maximum labour out of them, but also as a benevolent patriarch who upheld law and order and gave justice to all' (1992: 7). While Heidemann has provided a detailed account of the *kagany*, the *maistry* have been investigated by Satyanarayana (2001) in direct comparison to the '*kangany*' [*sic*] in order to argue that 'it is impossible to make any fundamental and clear-cut distinction between free and unfree migration' (2001: 5). The literature is divided, as the migration of south Indian labourers has been portrayed both as a 'new system of slavery' (Tinker 1993) and as a 'rational and deliberate choice on the part of migrants' (Emmer 1986, 1990).

19. For a vivid account of passengers waiting for the ships at the port of Calcutta, the medical examinations by white doctors for signs of the plague that they had to undergo before they were allowed to board, and the intense situation on and below deck during the five- to six-day journey, see Mazumder (2013: 87–94).

20. The sex ratio of immigrants was as high as 250 men to one woman (Mazumder 2014: 510), as wives and families were left in India or young men left before establishing families.

Khazeni (2020: 173) finds what he calls 'imperial debris of the past' as well as ruins that hark 'back to times before European colonialism, to an age of contact between the Indo-Persian Mughal world and the Buddhist kingdoms of Southeast Asia'.

In contrast to the educated Indian elites – such as lawyers, clerks, and officials – who settled in Upper Burma and who had already served under the king in earlier times, the *chettiar* moneylenders and indentured labourers from India settled in Rangoon, turning it into an Indian city or – in the eyes of some British observers – 'an asylum for fraudulent debtors and violent and unprincipled characters from every part of India' (Pemberton 1835: lii).[21] As of 1881, only 49 per cent of the city's population had been born in Rangoon. Of all inhabitants, 44 per cent were Indian. Chakravarti notes that '[b]etween 1852 and 1900, Rangoon thus developed from a small town into a city of about a quarter million people – and looked Indian in appearance' (Chakravarti 1971: 8). By 1913, a total of approximately 290,000 immigrants had arrived from Indian ports. The census of 1901 shows that 'Indianization' increased in the coming years: of a total population of 293,000 in Rangoon, 165,000 were Indians (56 per cent), compared to 90,000 Burmese (31 per cent).

In the early 1920s, Rangoon was more heavily populated by immigrants than New York City. Some 300,000 seasonal migrants were arriving annually (Harvey 1934: 501–502) and, according to Amrith (2013: 146), between 1926 and 1929, 400,000 Indians arrived in Burma, making migratory labour 'the most economically important segment of the Indian Ocean world' (2013: 30; Andrew 1933). Employment was readily available in the port and in the rice mills and sawmills of Rangoon. Housing conditions, however, deteriorated further with the influx of settlers from Upper Burma looking for job opportunities in the south (Charney 2009: 6). The Scotsman Alister McCrae described his impressions of Rangoon as an Indian city in 1935: 'Lower Burma had been flooded with Indian clerks, servants, labourers and others after the 1852 annexation, and the legacy in 1933 was that half of Rangoon's population of 400,000 was Indian. ... Hindustani was the lingua franca of Rangoon, imported with the influx of Indians' (McCrae 1990: 70).

As time went on, the Indian migrants began raising their voices against adverse colonial measures regulating public health, policing, and

---

21. See also Tinker (1993) and Turnell and Vicary (2008).

housing. Increasingly fearing violent responses from squatters if evicted from their settlements, colonial administrators in Rangoon had to work their rules and regulations around the fact that they simply could not handle the number of people they had invited to live in the city. In the following chapter I discuss how the problem of housing in particular has exacerbated the portrayal of evolving conflicts in Rangoon as being of a 'communal' kind.

CHAPTER 2

Making oneself a(t) home

On a street in downtown Yangon stands a four-storey house that is like many in the area, but has its very own story to tell.[1] In this house live Auntie Amina and Uncle Ghaffar, an elderly Muslim couple in their seventies with their adopted children.[2] Auntie Amina has raised more than ten adopted children in her house so far, among them Buddhists, Muslims, Christians, and Hindus; all of them are grown up already. Although busy with her family and the businesses she runs, she prays every morning for one hour, reads the *Qur'an*, and goes for a walk in nearby Maha Bandula Square. In December 2013 she was contemplating wardship of three young children from Burmese families in the northern part of the country whose parents had died, and when I returned in 2015 two young girls whose mother could no longer take care of them were living with her. Uncle Ghaffar, who passed away in 2021, taught English and was an active member of several Muslim organizations, but closest to his heart was his work for the Yangon Memon Jamaat, the 'Memon community'.

Along the covered pavement in front of the house – a rudimentary portico of sorts – tea stalls and small makeshift eateries provide temporary rest and offer *mohinga* (Burmese fish noodle soup) and *dosa* (Indian pancakes) to passers-by. The ground floor opens towards the street and is divided into one-room shops where various services are available. Beyond the main entrance, an old, stained wooden board on

---

1. Some of the ethnographic data in this section have appeared in a previous publication (see Beyer 2014).

2. All conversations with Auntie Amina and Uncle Ghaffar were in English – which they both spoke fluently. With each other and their community members, they speak Memon. Some of the community members, however, have a better command of Urdu. Members of the younger generation of Halai Memon increasingly use the Myanma language, but there is an expectation that people speak Memon within the family.

the wall to the left lists the names and owners of the businesses that used to be based here. About twenty people had their private companies in this house, as indicated by the abbreviation 'Ltd.' after their names. Some wooden plates have been removed from the board, rendering the stories of some former inhabitants invisible. Climbing the stairs to Auntie Amina's flat on the second floor for the first time in February 2013, I ducked beneath hanging laundry and passed by storage boxes in the shared hallway. I noticed the tiny golden Buddha statues and fresh flowers, placed on altars installed above the doors. Each door led into a maze of flats and rooms, of which only a small part was visible from the stairwell. I continued to the second floor and, before entering my hosts' apartment, I passed through another, shorter hallway, from which a number of tiny rooms branched off to both sides. There was one shared toilet for all the inhabitants of these rooms. Before I could reach my hand through the iron gate at the end of the hallway to knock on the door of Auntie Amina's flat, her daughter opened the door: 'Please, come in.' Auntie Amina's flat was light and spacious. I took off my shoes and sat down on a divan, and while waiting for coffee to be served, my eyes wandered along the walls of the living room: a large picture of the *ka'aba*,[3] a copy of the *hadith* (the sayings of the Prophet Muhammad [a.s.]) resting on a piece of cloth, various family photographs, a large clock, a cupboard with festive china, a *Qur'an* on the side table, next to it an old brochure about yoga. Auntie Amina waited patiently for me to orient myself and, while her daughter served coffee and brown sticky rice with coconut ('Burmese chocolate'), she explained what I had been looking at with the simple proclamation, 'We are Muslims.'

In this chapter I draw on ethnographic and oral history data I collected from this Muslim family and their house in downtown Yangon, along with colonial-era publications for the time before 1950, to illustrate the different stages of housing regimes that were implemented in the city, including their consequences for residents. In doing so, I also retrace the development of Rangoon/Yangon from a small fishing village to a metropolis of several million inhabitants, keeping a focus on the role of 'Indian' Muslims and Hindus in shaping the city, which from the very beginning was characterized by ethno-religious diversity and plural-

---

3. The *ka'aba* is the sacred building in Mecca that all Muslims face when undertaking their daily prayers.

ity. The angle I have chosen allows me to focus on changes in national policies and laws concerning housing through the lens of individual experience. It is through the interlinkage with housing that Burmese ethnic politics and the marginal positionality of 'Indian others' became manifest – in a material, thus literal, sense, but also conceptually. These housing policies were developed and partly justified on the basis of a certain understanding of 'community', and also served to solidify that understanding among both policy makers and the members of the communities. This chapter also probes the various partial and tentative ways in which Muslims and Hindus were (or were not) allowed to belong to the Burmese Buddhist body politic. A general problem is that scholarship on (ethnic) minorities in the country is often only concerned with those groups who resided in the country prior to British occupation, which means that 'Indians', who only came to the country with the British in the nineteenth century, rarely feature in this body of literature. One exception is Moshe Yegar's *The Muslims of Burma* (1972), which provides a historical account of Muslims in Burma, but only up to the 1970s (see also Berlie 2008). Many other earlier works do indeed invoke 'community', but they do so uncritically, which means that they occlude the specific processes by which colonial categories continue to shape present-day sociality. But attention to fine differences in categorization in Myanma, the officially recognized state language, reveals the ways in which community as a category functioned from early on as a marker of otherness.

To understand the relations between the majority Buddhist population, the state, and Indian migration, a focus on housing is particularly promising. During the colonial era, as well as under the various later Burmese governments, housing has presented a constant challenge in a city where land, living space and labour have been scarce or have remained in the hands of the powerful few for a long time. Such a focus on housing as a very material problem sheds light on what has generally been conceptualized as racial antagonism in the literature on colonial Rangoon. Struggles over housing are intrinsically related to a series of conflicts that have come to be characterized as 'communal'.[4]

---

4. Saberwal (1981: 27), for example, argued that 'the growth of communally homogeneous neighbourhoods in the metropolitan centres' has led to the rise of communalism during the colonial period in India.

By tracing the personal struggles of owners, tenants and squatters of one particular house in downtown Yangon, I provide an example of a Muslim household's response to broader trends and patterns in Yangon, with a degree of applicability to the rest of the country. We will see how key historical turning points, such as the granting of land to immigrant settlers at the beginning of the nineteenth century, the disposal of land after the Second Anglo-Burma War, land speculation at the beginning of the twentieth century, the nationalization campaign of the 1960s, and finally the recent introduction of new land laws and foreign investment laws, have played out in the concrete life story of an elderly Muslim couple and their house. I show how state policies on land and housing, designed by, in succession, colonial, socialist, military, and current regimes, have impacted my interlocutors' everyday lives and how, historically, problems related to housing have been framed in terms of problems between ethno-religious communities. Through the lens of housing, we can gain a better understanding of how ethno-religious classifications have come to manifest themselves, particularly in regard to how the state and Bama Buddhists have over the years related to the Burmese Indians, who played such a significant role in building the city from the ground up, continue to own construction companies, consider themselves to be part of the educated class, and are often not only influential in certain arenas, but also wealthy.

The buildings I am concerned with (houses with or without an explicit 'religious' usage) all have an unsecured property status. Instead of delving into legalistic debates about who really 'owns' a building, which in many instances could not be unambiguously answered anyway, throughout this book I focus on how the buildings are used (i.e., what or who is 'housed' in them) and how my interlocutors negotiate the insecurity that comes with not knowing or being able to prove whose property a certain building really is.

Whereas property can be a relation, a good or a right (see Benda-Beckmann 2001; Benda-Beckmann et al. 2006), I understand housing to be first and foremost a practice, which often puts people trying to secure their mode of residence at odds with the state and other powerful actors. In the anthropological literature, housing has long been viewed predominantly from the perspective of citizens demanding their rights from the state, or from the perspective of the state trying to plan citizens'

Fig. 2.1: 'How much land does a man need!' Slogan spray-painted on corrugated iron in downtown Yangon. The wall separates a new construction site from farmers selling their produce. Yangon, January 2014.

lives. Alexander, Bruun, and Koch (2018) have described housing as 'an essentially contested domain where competing understandings of citizenship are constructed, fought over and acted out'. Questions regarding maintenance or securing of housing are as pertinent as ever in Yangon, especially as, according to the Yangon City Development Committee (YCDC), the city has tripled in area in the last thirty years (from 210 to 790 square kilometres) and doubled in population in the last twenty years, with now around seven million inhabitants. Most of the newly arriving are unregistered and live on the outskirts in expanding squatter villages.

Since about 2011, the housing context in Yangon has been marked by an increasing need for land on which to build apartments and other housing units. With the end of international sanctions and until the attempted military coup in 2021, new foreign investments poured into the country. Alongside tourism and real estate purchases by people who are locally called 'cronies' (businessmen on good terms with the military establishment), this led to skyrocketing land and property prices and rental rates, the launching of modernization projects, and the general development of the city. Elizabeth Rhoads and Courtney Wittekind

(2018: 196) have argued that, whereas urban land used to be rented out to tenants for a small but steady income, nowadays investment in land is a capital accumulation strategy, and affordable housing is becoming increasingly hard to find. The YCDC has calculated that each year 30,000 new housing units (for an average family size of 4.2 people) would be needed to accommodate the population growth. The downtown area is densely populated with 30,000–40,000 people per square kilometre,[5] and has recently become a flashpoint for tensions, with tenants being forcibly removed so that land can be sold to foreign investors or prestigious new high-rise buildings can be constructed. All the religious buildings that I am concerned with in this book are located in prime downtown locations, and are thus potentially highly valuable. Although legally most of these buildings are on 'sacred property', that is, on land that is 'non-transferable', there is significant leeway in how the rules are applied. This has caused heightened tensions especially among the trustees who administer these buildings, as internal conflicts have emerged and outsiders' interest in these properties has grown exponentially.

Rangoon: Land grants, sacred property, and allotted housing

Before the annexation of Burma, '[t]he Burmese Government [i.e. the Burmese king] had never given land to foreigners and rarely permitted permanent buildings to be erected; anyone who erected such a building did so at his own risk and by the custom of the country was liable to see it destroyed or appropriated at the discretion of the Burmese authorities' (Pearn 1939: 180). In the First Anglo-Burma War (1824–1826), the city was razed to the ground by British forces that arrived by ship and surprised the local population and the Burmese army, as the war with the British had to that point been limited to the north-western border area of British Bengal. After the war, foreigners still needed the express sanction of the king to buy property in Yangon (Pearn 1939: 147). Relations between the king and the governor of India deteriorated over a housing dispute in 1840, when the city governor demanded that

5. All figures cited in this paragraph come from an official presentation in December 2015 by U Kyaw Latt, who, in his capacity as architect and city planner, was working for the YCDC at the time and kindly provided me with his Powerpoint presentation.

an assistant to the British colonel, who preferred to live in Yangon rather than in the capital Ava, should vacate the house in which he was living at the time. The assistant left not only the house, but also the country, following his colonel.

While Yangon was becoming a military hub as it prepared for yet another war with the British (Pearn 1939: 151), houses were not being renovated and new buildings were not being constructed because the inhabitants were under 'the impression that the town might be entirely removed by order from Court [of the king of Burma]' (1939: 152). Instead, after a big fire in 1841, the king issued an order to fortify and expand the city, and even stayed for a year to observe the construction process. As Burmese flocked to the newly built quarters, the foreign mercantile community was left alone in the area near the riverside, isolated from the king's new city (1939: 156–158). The British finally annexed Yangon and the rest of Lower Burma in the Second Anglo-Burma War in 1852, and turned into an imperial port proper, now called Rangoon.

Rangoon was populated first by Indian soldiers. Montgomery, Fraser, and Dalhousie, the three British colonial administrators responsible for the development of the city, designed a town plan that was to accommodate 36,000 people. It was based on 'a general British philosophy of colonial urbanism' (Heminway 1992: 34) and did not take any pre-war arrangements into account. It was oriented towards the river and the sea, set up to function as a port city of significant commerce and as an example of successful colonial modernization. Lord Dalhousie, who was Governor General of India from 1848 to 1856, was responsible for the naming of streets, among them Mogul Street, named 'after the Muslim merchants who settled in that quarter of the town' (Pearn 1939: 188; see also Chapter 5). When the new rulers of Rangoon planned the city, they declared all land government property, which was later to be distributed to private citizens under the auspices of the government. Land and property soon became a commodity:

> It is to be distinctly understood that all persons now occupying houses and land in Rangoon only occupy and hold the same on sufferance; present permission gives them no legal right to the property. ... All these matters will be arranged after peace has been restored either by British Commissioners, or the Burmese authorities, as the case may be. (Laurie 1853: 148–149; cited in Pearn 1939: 176)

In a letter to Dalhousie, Phayre declared that '[n]o buildings now existing or which may hereafter be built without sanction from the authorities will be considered to entitle the occupants to property in the soil they cover' (dated 25 December 1852; cited in Hall 1960: 11). Dalhousie and Phayre did away with traditional property rights, assuming that only when a Burmese person occupied a plot of land and thereby had physical possession of the property did he or she intend to keep it.[6] Europeans residing in Rangoon demanded the recognition of existing occupancy, and Persians, Armenians, and Indians demanded the safeguarding of former rights they had acquired to land, although the authorities rejected these claims (Pearn 1939: 191). No such requests from the Burmese appear to have been recorded. Captain Phayre, who became commissioner of the new province Pegu (Bago), in which Rangoon was to be incorporated, proposed to sell outright all freeholds in the town at fixed rates. He preferred this method of disposal because it would be fairer to the poor than sale by auction (Pearn 1939: 191).[7] An annual land tax should be imposed, and there should, in addition, be a monthly municipal tax based on the value or size of the land. The Governor of India accepted Phayre's views about the propriety of selling the land regardless of former occupancy, but the prices, which Phayre wished to fix, were considered much too low. In 1854, Phayre introduced the renting of town lots because, up until then, no Burmese had bought even the least expensive lot. By 1855, 823 lots had been rented by the same Burmese and non-Burmese squatters who had been living on the lots before (Heminway 1992: 77). In 1855, Dalhousie noted that 'the land [that the squatters had occupied] has been readily disposed of either by sale or lease, and the price or rent has been promptly and easily paid' (Pearn 1939: 197). Hindu, Christian, Jewish, Muslim, and Chinese representatives received free land grants to build their places of worship.[8] This land is still referred to as 'religious land'

---

6. Heminway (1992: 94) reports that, at one point, Phayre discussed 'follow[ing] Burmese practices in property law. However, this attempt was certainly not made in Rangoon, where all land was assumed to be government property and previous rights of tenure were disallowed.'

7. For a recent analysis of the long-term consequences of this policy, see Rhoads (2018).

8. Government [of India] to Phayre, India Political Proceedings (IPP) 200/38, 16 September 1853, No 124. The exact basis on which land was granted to religious 'communities' is unclear.

(*thathana myei*) or 'sacred property' (also known as 'green land', from its colour on zoning maps), and forms a separate type of non-transformable and non-transferable land that exists along with ten other categories of land known in Myanmar. According to the Land and Revenue Act (India Act II 1876, Part II 4 h), 'land belonging to the site of any monastery, pagoda or other sacred building, or of any school, and continuing to be used for the purposes of such monastery, pagoda, building or school' cannot be possessed by any person.[9] Part III ('of Revenue and Taxes') under A ('of land-revenue') specifies that 'land which, on the 1st February, 1879, belonged to the site of any monastery, pagoda or other sacred building, or of any school, and which continues to be used for the purposes of such monastery, pagoda, building or school' was exempt from land-revenue taxes. The Upper Burma Land and Revenue Regulation (Regulation III 1889) specified that 'sacred property' was not to be classified as 'state land' and was also exempt from taxation.[10] In addition, some minorities, such as Christians and Muslims, bought land for graveyards.

Nowadays, some of these places of worship only have copies of these land grants, made by the Yangon City Development Committee (YCDC), while others have no documentation at all, a lack they take care to conceal. This continues to pose a problem whenever trustees want to pursue any sort of permission-requiring alteration to their religious buildings, be it restoration, renovation, modernization, extension, renting, or selling, as any such applications would normally have to be accompanied by complete documentation of ownership rights.

Accommodating the Indians

After several visits to Auntie Amina's house, I came to appreciate the history of her family's arrival in Myanmar in 1905 and the coming about of one of Yangon's smallest Muslim organizations: the Yangon Memon Jamaat. The ancestors of both Auntie Amina and her husband came from the port city Thatta, which used to be the capital of the Indian

---

9. 1 February 1879; substituted by Act II 1945. The clause contains an exception stipulating that '[t]he President of the Union may from time to time, by notification, exclude any other land from the operation of this Part or of any section thereof.'

10. Art 27, 6a; see also The Lower Burma Town and Village Lands Act (1889/1899), Ch 1, 3c and Ch 6, 22a.

province of Southern Sindh.[11] The city is located close to Karachi in present-day Pakistan. Uncle Ghaffar recalled the story of conversion and forced migration of the Halai Memon:

> *Halai Memon came to Burma from India, but actually they are from Sindh, Pakistan. They had a partition ... so, we are from Thatta. Thatta is a town, 70 miles from Karachi. So, our ancestors were Hindus. Our ancestors became Muslim under some saint; I don't know the name of that saint.[12] So he made us Muslim. At that time, since we changed our religion, most of the Hindus became our enemies, because they don't like their religion to be changed by anyone. Maybe there was some massacre ... so some ran away. Some remained there. Those who remained there, they are called Sindhi Memon. Because it is in Sindh province in Pakistan. Those who ran away up to Kutch in Rajastan in India, they were called Kutchi Memon. Most ran as far as Gujarat [province], they are called Halai Memon. In Gujarat, there is a sub-province called Kathiawar.[13] Those people who ran away to Kathiawar are called Halai Memon. From Kathiawar, the British took over India, Burma, everything. And Burma was a very fertile country ... so our forefathers, I don't know – my grandfather or her grandfather [nodding towards his wife] – they came to Myanmar; at that time, it was Burma. And they spread throughout Burma. So actually, we are from Pakistan, but you can say we are from India. Whatever, so this is the real history. We are Khatiawar, this is why we are called Halai. Halai in the Sindh language means 'I leave you' – meaning 'gone'. Halai means 'gone' in Sindh. Our ancestors' houses were burnt, people were killed, everything. Here, also you must have heard, Rakhine people [meaning Rohingya], they ran away ... because when it comes to your life and your property, you throw away your property and you run away. Now these Rakhine people they run ... as far as Australia ... by boat or anything they can get – they also go away.*

Memon are often described as a merchant class or sailor businessmen whose extensive networks spread across the Indian Ocean. Despite their

---

11. Sindh is said to be the ancient Patala, conquered by Alexander the Great (see Burnes 1835: 27).

12. A saint called Pir Yusuffuddin Saheb converted the trading-class Lohanas from Lohanpur in Sindh to Islam in the fifteenth century. There are various versions of the etymology of the word 'Memon', including that it comes from the Urdu word *Momin* (lit., 'the one who believes in God'). See, for example, the Chicago Memons (2014) and Ebrahim Moomal's account of the Kuch Memon community in South Africa (1996).

13. Now a province in western India on the Arabian Sea coast in the state of Gujarat.

conversion to Islam in the fifteenth century, Memon living in India were classified as Hindu by the British colonial power, for example when it came to the application of personal status laws regarding matters of succession and inheritance (Rankin 1939: 101–102). Auntie Amina recalled what her grandfather had told her from the early days of his arrival:

> *My grandfather was a lord in India and he was brought here by force by the British. My family settled in Aunglan Myo in Upper Burma, where they were given land. My grandfather took cottonseeds from India and was the first to introduce cotton to this country. My family were businessmen and knew how to start a business. They started with a small factory, but were soon prohibited to engage in trade. When the Prince of Wales visited Aunglan Myo in 1906, my grandfather gave him a rousing welcome, as he was from a family of lords and knew how to welcome royalty. He was then permitted to work as a businessman with cotton. He traded for and with the Steel Brothers Company and the Bombay Burmah Company, which were the two biggest companies at that time. He started with cotton but then expanded to other crops.*

During the British occupation of Burma (1824–1948, as discussed in Chapter 1), some of the Burmese Indians who arrived were highly educated and served in the colonial administration as bureaucrats or officers, or were private merchants. Like Auntie Amina's grandfather, many had had businesses in India and managed to re-establish themselves in Burma. Muslims from India, like the families of Auntie Amina and Uncle Ghaffar, were by no means the first Muslims to arrive in the Buddhist country.[14] As time progressed, the migrants, particularly those from India who had been brought to Burma to augment the labour force, refused to subordinate their interests to the colonial measures regulating public health, policing, and property.

In contrast to this seemingly uncontrolled and uncontrollable population dynamic, the history of the Yangon Memon Jamaat, the religious organization to which Auntie Amina and Uncle Ghaffar belong, provides an alternative vision of how Indian Muslims organized themselves and

---

14. A general problem in assessing the situation of Indian Muslims is that many publications on the 'British Indians' or 'Burmese Indians' do not differentiate between those who were Muslim and those who were Hindus. The religious orientation of Indians who came to Burma was often not explicitly discussed in the literature.

even helped others.[15] The Jamaat was founded in 1909 and was located downtown, not far from where Auntie Amina and Uncle Ghaffar live today. After its establishment, the first thing the trustees decided was to provide *kafan* and *dafan*[16] for poor Muslims who did not have family in Burma. The Jamaat still provides these services for all Muslims who request them, not only Memons. Another tradition, one that continues to the present day, is the support of poor children from both 'pure' Memon families and those who have intermarried with non-Memons.[17] The Jamaat opened a *madrasa* (Islamic boarding school) in a neighbouring building and offered Islamic studies and Urdu language lessons to all Muslim children up to the fourth grade. Both buildings were purchased by the organization through donations from its members.

Returning to my historical material, the next section illustrates how notions of racial antagonism between the urban (and sometimes rural) residents of Burma arose in the early twentieth century and, most notably, how these notions found their way into British governmental reports, where violence subsequently became interpreted in communal terms.

Crisis, class, and the emergence of racial antagonism

Three interrelated developments directly impacted the life course of Burmese Indians residing in Rangoon at the time, including the family of Auntie Amina and Uncle Ghaffar. First is the so-called 'footwear debate' at the beginning of the twentieth century, which concerned Burmese Buddhists, Indian Muslims, Hindus, and foreigners (particularly colonial officers); second, from 1929 onwards, conflicts between Burmese Buddhists and Muslims in Rangoon; and third, from 1930 onwards, conflicts between Bama Buddhist party members, on the one

---

15. The following account is based on a letter written by one of the established community members for a fellow Memon residing in Karachi (Pakistan) who had inquired about the history of the Yangon Memon Jamaat for a journal article. The document is from 2003; I received it directly from Uncle Ghaffar.

16. After-death rituals including washing, wrapping, and burying the body of the deceased. The terms are Arabic, but are also used in Urdu.

17. The trustees of the Memon Jamaat have come up with an elaborate way of calculating the racial 'purity' of their members in order to define who deserves what kind of social and financial support from the organization, thereby mirroring colonial ways of 'sorting out', as Leach ([1954] 1964: 2–3) put it.

Fig. 2.2: Uncle Ghaffar in his living room with the author's son Constantin. February 2020.

hand, and the offspring of British personnel and 'Indians', on the other hand. I suggest that the dominant perception of communal conflict and racial antagonism in the nineteenth and twentieth centuries needs to be understood in light of the overall economic and housing crisis and an emergent class struggle.

The first key event took place at the beginning of the nineteenth century. Alicia Turner (2014) in particular has elaborated how the self-granted European exemption of not having to remove one's footwear before entering pagodas – behaviour that was locally interpreted as disrespectful to the Buddha – led to an internal schism when a famous monk began to enter the pagodas himself without removing his sandals in order to provoke debate among Buddhists about the importance of mental intention over action (Turner 2014: 122). But then the 'footwear debate', as it is known in the literature, turned into a nationalist narrative once public attention focused on Muslims, who were also not removing their shoes when entering pagodas, despite the fact that they did when entering mosques. The debate culminated in the perception that 'English and Muslim customs may actively denigrate Buddhism' (2014: 125). In 1916, Buddhist lawyers and the Young Men's Buddhist Association (YMBA) lobbied to rescind the European exemption because it 'tend[ed] to arouse racial feeling and disturb the harmony' (cited in Turner 2014: 129). The British, in turn, saw this as a threat to their colonial authority, to which they responded with a military resolution that phrased the issue in terms of a lack of respect towards European customs. Was it not enough that Europeans removed their hats when they entered pagodas? Turner argues that this reflects a Western Christian understanding of religion that sees local traditions as subordinate to European ones, which always remained hegemonic. In contrast, Burmese asserted the strictly universalist argument that their religious laws applied to non-believers as well as to believers.

A decade later, a second event that further paved the way for a distinctly Burmese Buddhist identity in contradistinction to Muslims occurred in Upper Burma and led to riots between Burmese Buddhists and members of a Burmese Muslim population that had been living in the country long before the Indian Muslims arrived. In 1929 (or 1931, depending on the source), a Burmese Muslim, Shwe Hpi, wrote and published a document that contained highly disparaging references to the Buddha, although it was not noted by the local press until 1938.[18] In a mass meeting at Rangoon's Shwedagon Pagoda, it was declared that, should the government fail to act appropriately, 'steps will be taken to treat the Muslims as Enemy Number 1 who insult the Buddhist community and their religion, and to bring about the extermination of the Muslims and the extinction of their religion and language'.[19] Note how the two categories – community and religion – are mentioned alongside each other in this official document. Community, at this time, had already begun to acquire a distinct 'racial' connotation. After having

---

18. Maung Shwe Hpi was a teacher in Myedu, a village in Shwebo district whose population was mainly Muslim. Their ancestors had been deported from Thandwe (Rakhine) by the Burmese king in the middle of the sixteenth century. They were most likely not ethnic Bama (personal communication with Uta Gärtner, 27 June 2014).

19. Final Report 1939: x, appendix xi.

clashed with the police, the Young Monks Association attacked Muslims and looted Muslim shops in Rangoon. Over one hundred mosques were set on fire (Final Report 1939: 286). There were also violent attacks against Indian Hindus:

> Soon the whole country was ablaze with encounters between Burmese and Indians augmented by mass attacks on unarmed isolated Indians. Although a few Hindus tried to save their lives on the basis of religion, it is doubtful whether any appreciable number of them were spared by the frenzied mob of Burmese. (Mahajani 1960: 79)

In this quote it is now obvious that it was not religion alone that was targeted, but 'race' – it was 'Burmese' against 'Indians', and it was not important whether the latter were Muslim or Hindu. As a result, hundreds were wounded and killed. Yegar (1972: 37) speculated that the official numbers given in the Final Report of the Riot Inquiry Committee (1939) might not contain all the casualties sustained. Mahajani noted that '[t]he Indian National Congress registered its feeling of grave concern over "the danger to Indian life and property in Burma"' (1960: 80). A member of the Indian Legislative Assembly, to whom the riots had been reported, noted that they needed to be seen as 'a design to turn out all Indians from Burma' (1939: 203–7, cited in Mahajani 1960: 81).

It is important to emphasize that these 'inter-communal' conflicts were emerging at a time of global economic depression. Ethnonationalist politics, new immigration laws, and erupting violence against minorities need to be seen in connection with the Great Depression, during which Indian *chettiars*, who could lend money to farmers, became de facto land holders when farmers could not manage to pay back their debts. World War I also had a significant detrimental impact on sea-borne trade and influenced the reorganization of the trading companies. With the economic depression setting in, envy directed against the Indian labourers, who made up almost 90 per cent of the unskilled and semi-skilled labourers of Rangoon, rose as they competed with the Burmese over labour opportunities:

> [O]n the 26th May [1930] fighting began between Burman and Indian coolies, and grew into a serious communal riot which did not cease until the troops were called out four days later. Many deaths occurred during the rioting; … Scandalous to relate, although at least 120 deaths occurred, not a man was convicted, not a man was even brought to

trial, for his part in this affair: such was the complete breakdown of the system of law and order. (Pearn 1939: 291)

While the aspect of 'inter-communality' has been emphasized in all publications, the fact that this was *also* a class struggle is barely noted in the literature. But these riots started out as a protest movement of Indian dockworkers (the so-called coolies; for an account of the riot, see Carter and Torabully 2002; Breman 1989; Collis 1955) who demanded higher wages and labour rights. Likewise, the so-called Saya San rebellion in 1930, during which unskilled Burmese left their villages in search of employment in the cities, 'was exploited by certain politicians to create tensions between Indian and Burmese labour' (Chakravarti 1971: 43). I argue that we need to look at these structural inequalities as an issue of class. The concept of class is often narrowly understood as concerning economic issues only, but the Subaltern Studies Group (SSG) in India took a broader view, using the term 'subaltern' to include not only economic inequality, but experiences of inequality in everyday life. Mazumder (2013) has argued that the dockworkers were blamed by 'upper class elites' of Burmese, European, and Indian origin for 'the scarcity of housing in Rangoon, marrying indigenous Burmese women and then abandoning them upon their return to India, and also causing the shortage of jobs for [the] native Burmese working force' (2013: 8–9). She shows that debates about nationalism and immigration evolved less along the lines of 'race' than along the lines of class, gender, and religion (2013: 8). She also speaks of 'subaltern migrants' (2013: 15) and 'subaltern life histories' (2013: 16), thus bolstering my argument that the positionality of non-Buddhist minorities in Myanmar can be fruitfully conceptualized as 'subaltern' (see Introduction).

The third development that was crucial to naturalizing a conception of racial antagonism has been elaborated by Kei Nemoto (2000), who has shown how, in the context of Burmese party politics from 1930 onwards, the terms *dobama* ('we Burmese') and *thudo-bama* ('those Burmese') became key to reinforcing categorical differences between Bama Buddhist party members leading the nationalist agenda at the time, on the one hand, and the offspring of both British personnel and of Indian ethno-religious minorities on the other: 'The party pamphlet [from 1936] admonishes the Anglo- and other mixed-blooded Burmese to identify themselves as Burmese citizens at that propitious time when Burma is to realize its destiny as a strong and fully independent nation' (Nemoto 2000: 222; see also Nemoto 2014). While refraining from criticizing the British empire, the party pamphlet accused the 'snobbish or mixed-blooded Burmese who did not respect the Burmese language and culture and who denigrated the *lower-class* Burmese who had acted so commendably in the riots' (2000: 8, emphasis added). They thereby forged an alliance across classes and against people of non-Bama, non-Buddhist background. In 1936, elections for the House of Representatives were to be held, and again the *Dobama-asiayoun* party distributed leaflets. The following passage, also cited in Nemoto's article, shows not only the differentiation between the concepts *dobama* and *thudo-bama*, which are the focus of Nemoto's interest, but also that the accusation that the Bama Buddhist party members held against the *others* was related to their strategic manoeuvring in the political arena:

> If there exist *dobamas*, there also exist *thudo-bamas*. Be aware of them. *Thudo-bamas* do not cherish our Buddhism, do not respect it, they go into councils, they try to dominate monks whether directly or whether indirectly, they take advantage of the law, accept bribes, they pretend towards voters as if they are good citizens. (Cited in Nemoto 2000: 5)[20]

Taken together, these three developments – the 'footwear debate', emerging conflicts that became phrased as conflicts between Buddhists and ethno-religious minorities, particularly Muslims, and the way in which 'we Burmese' has been set in opposition to people of 'Anglo-Burmese' and 'Indian Burmese' origin – have contributed to the by now taken-for-granted assumption that ethno-religious communities are naturally opposed to one another, engaged in a fierce competition not only over economic resources, but over religious and racial superiority.[21]

---

20. After the war, independence leader and soon-to-be martyr Aung San tried to mend one of these rifts and allay a history of suspicion in the well-known speech 'An address to the Anglo-Burmans' (see http://www.aungsan.com/angloburmans.htm), in which he said: 'Let me be perfectly frank with you – your community in the past did not happen to identify yourselves with national activities; on the other hand, you were even frequently on the other side. Now you have to prove that you want to live and to be with the people of this country, not by words but by deeds. So far as I am concerned, I am perfectly prepared to embrace you as my own brothers and sisters.'

21. According to Foxeus (2019: 666), Burmese nationalism originated first as an anti-Indian response against Hindus and Muslims and later turned anti-colonial.

I have also suggested that we should not forget the colonial responsibility for this situation and the intricate relationship it had at the time to the scarcity of housing and labour. It is in this context that I return to the discussion on communalism in India from the previous chapter (see Chapter 1) and show how the categorization of ethno-religious *others* played out linguistically in the Myanma language.

'Community' as a non-indigenous category

Along with the differentiation into upper- and lower-class people, whereby 'Indian elites' could be positioned against Indian *chettiars*, or into *dobama* and *thudo-bama*, we encounter the figure of the 'mixed-blood Burmese' – *kabya* – also referred to as 'Eurasian' or 'half caste' in the colonial literature, who is positioned against a 'racially pure' (*than-sin-hmu*) type.[22] According to local understanding – then and now – *ka-bya* are the offspring of an intermarriage in which, typically, the father is 'Indian' and the mother 'local' (that is, putative Bama Buddhist). The term is relational in that it requires a 'racially pure' counterpart, which is envisioned to be encompassed in the category *tain-yin-tha:* ('indigenous') or *tain-yin-tha: lu-myo:*. *Tain* is an administrative division; *yin* means 'closely related'; *tha* means 'son'. *Lu-myo:* is a compound noun that is nowadays usually translated into English as 'race' or 'ethnicity', although *lu-* means 'people' or 'human' more generally and thus the term can be translated as 'type of person'. Then there is *tain-yin-tha: e-pwe-e-si* – officially recognized 'ethnic groups'. The number of these *tain-yin-tha:* in the country stands at precisely 135, the so-called 'national races'. It is important to note that the category *tain-yin-tha:* evolved as a colonial-era classification over the course of the various censuses.[23]

---

22. Roger McNamara (2006: 219) has noted that the English were deeply suspicious of the 'Eurasians' and that the 'Eurasians' likewise maintained an uncomfortable relationship with the English. George Orwell brought this discomfort to the fore in his essay *Shooting an Elephant* (1936), in which the relationship between English and 'Eurasian' police officers during Britain's colonization of Myanmar is mentioned. For a fascinating account on the way encounters with animals were mediated through imperial discourse see Jonathan Saha's (2022) *Colonizing Animals: Interspecies Empire in Myanmar*.

23. British census data differentiated between nine races: Burmese, other indigenous races, Chinese, Indians born in Burma, Indians born outside the country, Indo-Burman, Europeans/allied races, Anglo-Indians, and other races. Instead of reli-

It became a term of state in the 1940s and was institutionalized in the 1960s (Cheesman 2017: 467) when, in a specific interpretation of the term, it was used to unite *us* against all *others*.[24] In another way, it served to specify national races as subsections of a community, differentiating the 'advanced' from the 'primitive' ones, the latter being the so-called (Christian) 'hill tribes' (see Cheesman 2017: 467). Over time, *tain-yin-tha:* increasingly took on the meaning of 'Burmese' (Bama), thus further strengthening the majority ethnic group.[25] The notion of *tain-yin-tha:* formed the basis of the country's 1982 Citizenship Act, which codified via legislation a general differentiation between those who belonged to the nation and those who did not. The arbitrary number of 135 'national races', however, was only established and made public in 1990.[26] Since then, it has been stable, but only because all 'new' ethnic groups that have tried to gain official recognition in the meantime have simply been added to the ethnic Bama majority group, thereby enlarging it further.[27]

In effect, the English word 'community' has no single equivalent in Myanma. Rather, there is a range of concepts with a variety of possible translations depending on who is speaking, who is listening, and what the context is. The different connotations that these Myanma terms encompass are asymmetrical – from the all-inclusive *e-su* to the most exclusive *tain-yin-tha*. While 'community' as it has been understood in its historical, imperial context pathologizes others by rendering them 'communal' via religious and ethnic identification only, in the Myanma language we have a more nuanced taxonomy that also includes general

---

gion or caste, language – i.e., 'the speech of a particular community' – became the key factor according to which the British grouped individuals (Lowis 1902: 112, cited in Ferguson 2015: 7). See also Appadurai (1998) on 'enumerative strategies' in India and Cohn (1987) for an earlier analysis.

24. See also de Mersan (2016) and Robinne (2019).

25. See also Carstens (2018) on the new category *Buddha-bha-tha-lu-myo* ('Buddhist ethnicity').

26. See the Myanma-language newspaper *Workers' Daily*, 26 September 1990, p. 7.

27. This happened, for example, in March 2016 when the roughly 60,000 ethnic Chinese Mone Wun, who do not speak Myanma, became 'Mone Wun (Bama)' by decree of then-president Thein Sein and received new identification cards in May of that same year (Ye Mon 2016; Htoo Thant 2016).

'groups'.[28] Thus, not only is context important, but there is a certain semantic imprecision to all of these terms, which is why one will often find within the same text or transcript different words that are used synonymously. This is also why the English term 'community' is prevalent throughout the country, even in Myanma-language texts – its meaning is clear: it refers to an ethno-religious group that can be separated from all others along ethnic and religious lines.

In his widely influential work *Colonial Policy and Practice*, J.S. Furnivall (1948) described the inherently unstable character of what he called the Burmese 'plural society'.[29] He laid out three characteristics of this type of society: first, '[t]he society as a whole comprises different racial sections'; second, 'each section is an aggregate of individuals rather than a corporate or organic whole'; and third, 'as individuals, their social life is incomplete' (Furnivall 1948: 306). The problem, in Furnivall's understanding, was precisely that individual will was more important to the people living in Burma than community interests (or so he assumed), and custom and tradition were of no value because everyone was striving for individual economic gain and interacted only in the market place:

> In Burma, as in Java, probably the first thing that strikes the visitor is the medley of peoples – European, Chinese, Indian and native. It is in the strictest sense a medley, for they mix but do not combine. Each group holds by its own religion, its own culture and language, its own ideas and ways. There is a plural society, with different sections of the community living side by side, but separately, within the same political unit. Even in the economic sphere there is division of labour along racial lines. Natives, Chinese, Indians and Europeans all have very different

28. There are other words that are more 'neutral', but they are usually not used when speaking about ethno-religious minorities. These are *e-thine-a-wine* ('crowd', 'environment', 'the people around you'), *nain-gan-de-ga a-thine-a-wine* ('international community'), *e-pwe-e-si* ('a group of people'); *lu-e-pwe-e-si* ('society'), and, most generally, *e-su* ('group').

29. Furnivall developed his model of a plural society in Burma in line with Fabianism, a socialist theory that had its origins in the 1880s in London. Early members such as George Bernard Shaw, Sidney Webb, and the suffragette Emmeline Pankhurst were influenced by John Stuart Mill's *Principles of Political Economy* (1848) and advocated a slow transition to socialism, in contradistinction to Marx's revolutionary approach. Furnivall adopted Fabianism's five states of development and applied them to Burma.

functions, and within each major group subsections have particular occupations. (Furnivall 1948: 304)

Furnivall's 'plural society' was in fact a parallel society, stuck in equilibrium. And while he was critical of colonial capitalism, he still found foreign colonialist intervention to be necessary to overcome the problems inherent in the uneasy co-existence of ethno-religious groups. Colonial administration was needed because 'the natives are slow to assimilate western values' (Furnivall 1948: 304). To address this, he advocated 'a western superstructure representing an outpost of Europe and not rooted in the soil' (ibid.).[30] It is in this context that we encounter the key term for 'Burmese Indians' more generally: *kula/kala/kalar*. According to *The Anglo-Indian Dictionary*, the term *kula* is defined as

> [The] Burmese name of a native of Continental India; and hence mis-applied also to the English and other Westerners who have come from India to Burma; in fact used generally for a Western foreigner. ... But the true history of the word has for the first time been traced by Professor Forchhammer, to *Gola*, the name applied in old Pegu inscriptions to the Indian Buddhist immigrants, a name which he identifies with the Skt. Gauda, the ancient name of Northern Bengal, whence the famous city of Gaur.[31] (Yule and Burnell 1903: 495)

Whenever we read about 'the true history' of a word, we should take it with a pinch of salt: words change meanings over time, as people put them to use in different contexts for different purposes. The term *kala* has acquired a pejorative meaning since the early colonial period, and has often been translated as 'black', referring to the skin colour of 'Burmese Indians', particularly those from the south of India. Yegar mentions that in the days of the Burmese Kingdom, the descendants of Arab, Persian, and Indian Muslim traders were referred to as 'Pathee or Kala' (1972: 6) or, alternatively, the Muslims as 'Pathikula' and the Hindus as 'Hindu-kula' (Yule and Burnell 1903: 669). Yegar also notes that the earlier translation of the term *kala* was understood to mean

---

30. Needless to say, much of what Furnivall regarded as 'western values' had been known throughout the Indian Ocean world at much earlier times. Engseng Ho (2006), for example, drew a picture of the sixteenth-century Muslim trading ecumene, in which Hindus, Jews, and Christians existed alongside Muslims, and liberalism, free trade, and the rule of law were cherished principles.

31. Gaur was the capital of the Bengal Sultanate.

simply 'to cross over', thus indicating movement across the Bay of Bengal rather than the ethnic or religious identity of a group of persons. In his glossary, Amrith defines the term *kala* as a 'Burmese term used to describe Indians, originally a term denoting "foreigner", but it assumed pejorative connotations' (Amrith 2013: 287).[32] Together with all other people from India, no matter which class, caste, or religion, they are referred to as *kula lu-myo*. It is important to understand that all these local terms that have come to take on a derogatory meaning can also become entwined with the words that are often translated into English as 'community'. While I have sometimes encountered expressions such as 'the Buddhist community' (Nyi Nyi Kyaw 2018a; see also Carstens 2018), 'community' is usually reserved for ethno-religious *others*, specifically urban minorities.[33] Or, if one speaks about 'the Bama community', then a non-Bama *other* needs to be present for this expression to make sense. 'Community', in Myanmar, is therefore not only underdetermined, but it is also far from being a neutral category: it is racially charged and highly political.

Returning to the oral history of Auntie Amina and Uncle Ghaffar, the next section details how World War II led to the mass departure of Burmese Indians from Rangoon and traces the the long-term effects of colonial engineering even after Burma became independent in 1948.

From independence to 'Burmese socialism'

On 23 December 1941, the Japanese launched their first air attack on Rangoon, which was, according to Amitav Ghosh, partly aggravated by the withdrawal of the Indians from the city:

> There was a general breakdown of law and order and the Indians, already wary after the riots of the past decade, began to panic. The perception was that the British were about to withdraw from Burma, and that in

32. Christians were formerly referred to as *feringies* ('foreigners'), a term that is also familiar in the African context. The term itself stems from the Arabic *afranj*. 'Foreigner' continues to sometimes be translated as *kula phyu* in Myanmar – the white *kula*.

33. Nyi Nyi Kyaw (2018a), who looks for definitions of both 'religion' and 'community' in Myanmar's Constitution and other official texts, argued that '[a]lthough "community" is not defined, the framing of Buddhism as the religion adhered to by the majority people by the 2008 constitution effectively creates a majority Buddhist community' (2018a: 3).

their absence, Burmese mobs would have free reign to terrorise the Indian population. Suddenly, the Indians began to move northwards. But without the Indians the city simply could not function: they made up almost the entire working class of Rangoon. The dockworkers were the first to abandon their jobs. This meant that essential supplies could not be unloaded from the ships in the Rangoon docks. Many of these vessels became sitting targets for Japanese bombers. (Ghosh 2011)

While half of the Indian population began what Tinker has called 'a forgotten long march' (1979) from Burma to India via the hill tracts, the other half of the Indian population decided to stay in Rangoon.[34] Auntie Amina recalls the situation at the beginning of the war:

> When the Second World War started, the Steel [Brothers] Company and the Bombay Burmah Company were closed. There were bombings. My grand-father passed away due to his age around this time, but business continued in the family. My family started a rice mill in Taikkyi – about 40 miles from Rangoon. I was born in Taikkyi in 1948. My father was active in politics during the war and got arrested. When he got free, he decided to move all of us to Rangoon, where he had received his school education. The rice mill exists even today, but it is closed now and people are trespassing there although it is still in my family's property. Between 1945 and 1957 my family had businesses in Rangoon, in different smaller houses.

Rangoon was severely damaged during the war: half of the public and commercial buildings and one third of the houses were ruined. About 80 per cent of the city had to be rebuilt (Charney 2009: 58). The Yangon Memon Jamaat continued performing *kafan* and *dafan* for those Muslims who had died during the war. They also continued their charity work, opening a free medical dispensary on their premises staffed 'with doctors who saw people of every caste or creed'. Medicine was given free of charge.

The country became nominally independent under the Japanese occupation in 1943. When the British re-occupied the country in 1945, they devalued the newly introduced Japanese currency (the 'Japanese rupee'). As a result, riots broke out, and poor rural civilians sought shelter in the city, much of which had been deserted over the course of the war. As in former times, 'Rangoon was a veritable metropolis of matting and thatch' (Appleton 1947: 514, cited in Charney 2009: 59). The country

---

34. For a first-person account of a Muslim family that fled from Rangoon to Calcutta, see Afsheen (2011).

declared full independence on 4 January 1948, and Muslims from India who were still living in Burma could apply for citizenship along with other minorities. The alternative was to receive a foreign registration certificate (FRC), or become stateless. Auntie Amina recalled:

> *Most Indians who had come to Myanmar were low-class workers. What did they know about citizenship? They did not even register after the government announced in the newspaper that whoever registered within a certain time would receive citizenship. After 1955–1958* [she did not remember exactly], *nobody could become a citizen of Burma and received an FRC instead. My family and the family of my husband were educated and registered – others did not even know how to read and did not register.*

After the country became independent in 1948, the demand for moneylenders' services re-emerged due to the banking system's inability to provide the peasantry with credit and because the Indian *chettiars* had left the country (Taylor [1987] 2009: 279). This demand was filled by 'the class of indigenous moneylenders' (ibid.), meaning non-Indian Burmese. This group, however, 'remained dependent upon the state, regardless of who controlled it, just as it had been before the war' ([1987] 2009: 280). The Indians who had remained in the country and the city played no further role in the urban development from the 1950s onwards. While Taylor attributes to the Burmese middle class a 'growing sense of ... communal consciousness', he tells us nothing about the perspective of the now racialized 'Indian class'. But Auntie Amina had a lot to say about this period. More than a decade after the war, in 1957, her father, together with two partners, bought a piece of land in downtown Rangoon, close to the river. The house that had been on this land was damaged beyond repair during the war; after tearing it down, they built a new house on the same plot:

> *My father, together with two partners, bought the land. Each had their own businesses, a nylon factory and a weaving factory. After independence, the business went up and it was impressive. In 1959, the new building was finished and we moved in: on the ground floor there were offices for rent to other businesses, on the first floor there were our own offices, on the second floor there were four apartments (two for my father, two for one of the two partners), on the third floor there were also four apartments, all of them taken by the third partner since he had a big family. We owned the house only until 1962. Everyone was very happy.*

These years were also prosperous ones for the Yangon Memon Jamaat, which opened a Young Men's Memon Association, located in the *madrasa*. The club brought old and young men together over sports such as table tennis, billiards, and *carrum*.[35] A library was opened with books in Gujarati, English, and Urdu. Debates and religious sermons (*viaz*) were held in the building, and the cricket and scout teams of the association competed with other clubs in the city. The *madrasa* relocated to a new and larger building, and the curriculum was expanded. In the evenings, bookkeeping, type-writing, and other vocational skills were taught to adults who had to work during the daytime. Wealthy members who owned factories built four mosques in Yangon so that their factory workers would have a place to pray.

The overall political situation, however, deteriorated when the government under U Nu sought to declare Buddhism the state religion in 1961, a move much protested by Christians and Muslims. The same year, anti-Muslim riots occurred in Rangoon again (Smith 1965: 322). When General Ne Win seized power in a military coup in March 1962, he suspended the Constitution, but the State Religion Promotion Act failed to cement Buddhism's status as the state religion.[36] Ne Win dismantled some Buddhist institutions and proclaimed that Burma was to be turned into a socialist state. From 1964 onwards, the only political party would be the Burmese Socialist Programme Party (BSPP) – all other political parties were declared illegal. Private businesses, regardless of size, including general stores, department stores, brokerages, wholesale shops, and warehouses, were nationalized, beginning with foreign businesses (Chinese, Indian, and 'Eurasian'[37]). This ended the dominance of foreign commercial interests in Burma's economy at the time (Ooi 2004: 58), which was certainly one of the main aims of Ne Win's coup. Thus, while the well-being of Muslims was threatened in 1961 during the riots, their property rights came under attack by the socialist regime when they became targets – not because they were

---

35. A table game common in South Asia (also spelled *carom*).

36. The 1947 Constitution recognized 'the special position of Buddhism as the faith professed by the great majority of the citizens of the Union'. The second paragraph of the Constitution declared that '[t]he state also recognizes Islam, Christianity, Hinduism and Animism as some of the religions existing in the Union at the date of the coming into operation of this Constitution'.

37. Meaning Anglo-Burman in this context (see Charney 2009: 81–82).

Muslims, but because they were 'foreigners' owning businesses and property. Ten years after the event Yegar writes, in regard to the Muslim population in Burma, that '[v]ery little is known as to how deeply the Muslims in Burma were affected by the military rule of General Ne Win … and to what extent their organisational life and religious and cultural activities were affected' (Yegar 1972: x). This is, to some extent, still true today, as it was difficult for foreigners to pursue field research well into the 2000s, and Burmese scholars during the time of the military regime did not study this recent history of Muslims in the country. Before I was introduced to Auntie Amina by a local friend of mine, I asked whether her family was rich, knowing that they owned a house in downtown Yangon. My friend answered, 'Not as rich as she should be.' When I later asked Auntie Amina about the 1960s, I understood his comment. She said, 'Everything was nationalized. The army came at noon and took the key and closed the offices. We had to leave immediately. We could only keep the apartments to live in.' A similar fate awaited the *madrasa* run by their community organization: the school was nationalized and taken over by the government, like all other schools, in 1965. At least one of the four mosques of the Halai Memon community was closed or, as Auntie Amina put it, 'martyred' (Arab., *shahid*), in the Ne Win era. Auntie Amina recalls how her father managed to secure an income after he was deprived of his business:

> *My father found work as an accountant in a governmental position since he and one more person were the only ones that could properly do the job. The other accountant was Mr Chaudry, a Bengali. From 1964–66, every 15 days a steamer named* Monguadi *came and took every Indian who had an FRC [Foreign Registration Certificate] and a birth certificate with them – the Hindus were the first to emigrate. The capacity of people per ship was 2,500. There were two steamers, one going one direction, the other the other direction. These two steamers came for two years on this 15-day schedule: India took back all its citizens [mostly to Orissa and Madras]. Others pretended to be Indian and went also. Most of them were Oriyas. The steamer came until 1972 regularly, but not every 15 days. After that, migration became less.*

Uncle Ghaffar recalled the impact this change in policy had on his immediate family:

> *I had seven brothers – all of them left. The first two in 1966 to India, the second two left in 1971 to Bangladesh, and the last three went between 1980*

and 1983 to Pakistan.[38] My family had a 300-acre rubber plantation which was nationalized in 1966.

The 1980s are remembered as particularly hard times. In 1971, the Memon Jamaat trustees provided service to the refugees from the Bangladesh Liberation War who had fled to Burma via Arakan. These were Pathans, Punjabis, Mahjirs, Sindhis, and Memons. Although the funds of the Jamaat were meagre in those years, the organization hosted refugees in four apartments that were allotted to them. In the letter addressed to fellow Memons in Karachi (see fn. 15), the writer described that they were properly clothed and fed until their papers were cleared to proceed to Pakistan: 'We are very proud to say that only the Memon community could stand high in doing this Yeoman Service [loyal help] in the name of Islam and humanity.' The Memon's *madrasa* was appropriated by the state and turned into a state school. Moreover, their application to renew the licence of their men's association was denied, and so it was closed in 1974. That same year, the 1974 Constitution was introduced, and in article 161 it was noted that:

> Every citizen's income, savings, property and residential buildings lawfully earned and acquired by his diligence and manual and mental contribution, instruments of production permitted to be owned within the framework of the socialist economic system, and other lawful possessions shall be protected by law. (Constitution 1974, art. 161)

However, while personal property was thus formally protected, other articles in the earlier Constitution that had guaranteed the right to private property (arts. 17(I), 23) had been removed. It was during these years that Auntie Amina and Uncle Ghaffar were married in an arranged marriage, after which they moved into the house they lived in during the time of my fieldwork. Uncle Ghaffar recalled: 'Amina and I got married in 1971 and moved into the upper floor [the third floor] of this house. The floor beneath us was occupied by the Andaman Islanders.'

---

38. The family had connections to other South Asian countries through his brothers' wives. In his comparative work on diasporic 'communities', Egreteau (2011a) has listed the countries in South (East) Asia and beyond to which the Burmese Indians emigrated, paying particular attention to those who have 'returned' to India (Egreteau 2011b, 2013, 2014; see also Bhaumik 2022, Chatterjee 2021, and Amitav Ghosh's blog [amitavghosh.org], where he collects oral history accounts of Burmese Indian 'returnees').

Finding a home in Auntie Amina's house

When the British government established a permanent detention colony in 1857 on the Andaman Islands, located at the juncture of the Bay of Bengal and the Andaman Sea, Burma began sending prisoners there who had been sentenced to life in prison.[39] After independence from Britain in 1947, the Andaman Islands remained under Indian administration. It took almost twenty years for the Burmese government to agree to accept the offspring of those whom they had sent to the Islands. When in 1966 several hundred native Burmese people, all of them born on the Islands, speaking only Urdu, were repatriated to Burma, many of them were placed in vacant flats or other confiscated property that had been nationalized but never been put to use. One of these was the house of Auntie Amina's father. She explained:

> When the Andaman people arrived in Burma, they spoke only Urdu, they used to play only Indian songs in the beginning. There are two or three older ladies living in this house who still speak Urdu, but the rest of them are all 'Burmanized'. Some went back because they could not stand the 'city life' in Rangoon – although in those times, between 1966 and 1988, you would not see a car within five minutes – there were only busses in downtown Rangoon. Our neighbour [Ma Mala] was a child when she came from the Andaman Islands to Rangoon; still, she is inclined to go back. She says, 'My parents made me come here.'

When I met Ma Mala the following week at Auntie Amina's house, she told me about her grandfather, who had been sent to the Andaman Islands in 1900. She repeatedly mentioned how much she would like to return to her family's spacious house on the island, where curries tasted good and the air was fresh, not like in Yangon. She showed me the tiny, dark flat she calls home. Leaving Auntie Amina's place, we passed through the common hallway where many inhabitants from the second floor had gathered around a TV set, watching the South East Asia Games. When I returned to Auntie Amina's flat, I shared my thoughts with her about the living conditions I had seen: the small rooms, the low ceilings, the lack of light and air, and the obvious poverty. Auntie Amina remarked, 'And she is more of a citizen than us', indicating that no matter how much of a citizen she, the well-off businesswoman, is, her Muslimness still set

---

39. See Anderson (2016) for details on this, and Heidemann and Zehmisch (2016) for an overview.

Fig. 2.3: Watching soccer in the common hallway in Auntie Amina's house. Yangon, February 2014.

her apart from individuals such as Ma Mala, who had been born abroad and who did not want to stay. Nothing – not the fact that she had made a deliberate decision to stay in Burma in the 1960s when she could have gone 'back' to India, a place she did not know; not even the fact that she possessed the right kinds of documents to prove her citizenship – would ever change that. She then told me how in 2004, she and her husband moved from the flat on the third floor to the second floor. Auntie Amina was able to do this only after buying her own property back from the people who had been put into her family's house in 1966. With her money, several Burmese families from the Andaman Islands moved out, but many more are still there.

It is not only the house that has been carved up into tiny quarters; as noted earlier, the covered pavement out front has also been divided into little stalls, with vendors, some from the Andamans, claiming usage rights to a particular space on the pavement. Auntie Amina expressed sympathy for them, as they lacked a regular income and could not afford to rent a place. She buys food from them, allows them to live for free in her house on the first and second floor, and invites some of them regularly to her apartment. This complex arrangement cannot be analysed by resorting to the labels 'legal' and 'illegal', nor could it be adequately portrayed by discussing property in terms of 'private', 'state', and 'communal'. Neither tenants nor squatters, these people share their lives with Auntie Amina door-to-door in a form of neighbourliness that is based on fateful circumstances and Auntie Amina's conviction that the poor deserve to be helped.

Renovation, rent control, and religion

Having relocated from the third floor to the second, Auntie Amina joined forces with an ethnic Chinese businessperson in 2015 and turned the vacated third floor into a guesthouse. I asked her how she had proved to the authorities that the third floor was actually her property, a prerequisite when trying to obtain a permit to renovate and open a business such as a guesthouse. She explained that in cases like hers, people present tax receipts showing that they have been paying fees to the Yangon City Development Committee every month. Initially, they thought that only Chinese tourists would take advantage of the central location of the guesthouse, but increasingly, Western tourists, mostly backpackers, have been showing up on her doorstep, too. In the last decade, a massive influx of foreigners – investors, NGO representatives, and tourists alike – have entered Yangon. The notorious lack of living space in the city has once again created a problem for those who need a place to sleep, be it for a night, a week, or a year.[40]

Besides her guesthouse, Auntie Amina owns an import–export business, exporting broomsticks to Saudi Arabia and tea leaves to India. In terms of bureaucracy, in her opinion, it has become easier because the paperwork has been reduced over the last few years:

> In former times it took so long to file the necessary documents that by the time you had obtained everything, the ship had already left. Now it's easier, but it's a lot of work, still. Eventually I will hand over the tea-leaves business to another friend.

She also runs a travel agency located in one of the houses of the Jamaat, to which she pays a small monthly rent. At present, the Yangon

---

40. Prior to the lifting of heavy international sanctions, Burmese military generals invested in property. Many hotels and large businesses are in the hands of (former) military personnel. For example, in 2014, UNICEF reportedly paid $87,000 per month for a villa owned by a former military general in an exclusive neighbourhood in Yangon (see Kyaw Hsu Mon 2014).

Memon Jamaat owns eight buildings in downtown Yangon. Most of the tenants are Buddhist Burmese, but they pay no rent to the Jamaat. Uncle Ghaffar explained:

> *We do not have proper rent control here, and most of the tenants are Myan-mar Buddhists. We cannot go against them. And we do not have the time. We [would] have to go to court and go after them. ... As it is, we get enough money from our donations.*

The Yangon Memon Jamaat continues working through charity, which currently includes, for example, stipends to 'old-aged Memons and mixed Memons, even to widows of Memons or mixed Memons, for their upkeep' as it was put in the aforementioned letter written by one of the established community members for a fellow Memon residing in Karachi (Pakistan).[41] The elderly also receive food aid in the form of rice and cooking oil every two months. Stipends are also given to poor children of Memon and 'mixed Memon' background to cover educational expenses from kindergarten up through postgraduate study. Medical aid is given for free to the needy, and 'houses are purchased or leased for Memons who for unforeseen disaster are immediately in need of it', as this letter also stated. Moreover, those who have failed in starting a business may receive start-up grants. Finally, Islamic studies is taught in one of their *madrasa*s to about 250 non-Memon students in both Myanma and Urdu. English and Arabic language lessons are also offered. They celebrate Eid-ul-Fitr together and hold an 'Urdu symposium' during the winter months, at which prizes are given to talented poets. Covering the expenses related to these events is part of the philanthropic work of members. Despite these wide-ranging activities, Uncle Ghaffar emphasized that they take care to keep a low profile:

> *Muslim organizations have to stay low-key. We should not come before the eyes of the government, otherwise they will say, 'From today, it is closed until further notice.' And what will we do? What should we do? This is a phase, you know.*

In 2006, the trustees of the Memon Jamaat encountered difficulties exercising their property rights when they wanted to renovate the head-quarters in downtown Yangon. The second floor hosts offices and meet-ing rooms, and the third floor is used as a hostel for male Muslims from

41. See also footnote 15.

all over Myanmar, who can stay there for a minimal charge. Sometimes the entire floor is rented out to poorer members or outsiders for weddings or other functions, also at a low price. The ground floor is owned by a non-Memon Muslim. The entire building is in need of renovation. To be granted a permit to renovate, the property would first have to be reclassified as 'damaged'. This is a common procedure that does not specifically target buildings owned or administered by Muslims. However, despite the fact that the trustees presented all the necessary documents, the city authorities did not grant the reclassification of the property. While no official reason was given, renovation measures usually have to be agreed to by all tenants or parties, and Jamaat representatives suspect that the owner of the ground floor of the building may have refused to agree. The members have repeatedly tried to buy the ground floor from the owner, but have not succeeded thus far.

Towards the end of one of my evening visits to Auntie Amina's house, Auntie Amina told me that the YCDC intended to demolish the portico in front of the house to make room for parking spaces. As part of recent reforms, the government has embarked on road-widening initiatives that displace sidewalks and the covered passageways, as the pillars take up valuable space that could be used for parking. Auntie Amina showed me the letter from the YCDC announcing that the portico would be removed. As we went outside onto the roof of the portico that serves as a balcony for the second-storey flats, where Auntie Amina's family cooks in the dry season, hangs the laundry to dry, and tends the plants, she explained: 'For us, we will manage, but they [pointing towards her neighbours whose part of the balcony is separated by a brick wall] will suffer. They live there with fifteen people in one small room. What they will do without the outside space, I do not know.'

Peering across the balcony to the far left, I could see the four lanes of Strand Road and, behind it, the Yangon River, where container ships depart for the Andaman Sea, dwarfing the ferries and small wooden boats criss-crossing to Dala, a small town on the other side of the river. We talked about the many new parking spaces that had recently been built to accommodate the influx of imported cars. 'But they want more', Auntie Amina said. As I uttered a quiet curse, she hastened to add:

> *Don't feel sorry. We are used to it. The government has taken much, much more than this from us. In 1964, they took our factory, our shops, everything.*

We had nothing to eat. We survived only barely, but we survived. So this is nothing new ... gradually, it will change. There is pressure now from so many countries, but actually, they [the government] do not care about the world. The previous head of government [General Than Shwe] said, 'The world can go to hell! We have enough rice, we can survive.'

The parallel she was drawing between the military government's behaviour and the 'democratic' government that was in charge during the time of my fieldwork was illuminating, providing historical context for the wide range of new laws regulating housing, land, and property, in line, it would appear, with current government's policy of 'opening up' the country to foreign investment, tourism and general democratic change. The new state laws, however, apply only to a small proportion of de facto existing properties.[42] Auntie Amina's house is a case in point: starting from the sidewalk and moving up to the unoccupied fourth floor, several different types of ownership arrangements come into play. The one thing they all have in common, however, is that the right of possession cannot simply be proven by a standardized bureaucratic act. Instead, the 'bundle of rights' in place in Auntie Amina's house ranges from customary regulations such as the distribution of space on the sidewalk for tea stalls and how access to and use of the common hallway is determined, to state laws that are still in place from the socialist era enforcing expropriation and state resettlement policies that led to the loss of her rights to control or dispose of the family property. But the 'bundle of rights' is also shaped by the personal decision-making processes of Auntie Amina, evident in the way she tried to 'make do' under fateful circumstances and how she related to the 'Andaman occupants'. She also reacted quickly when state legislation allowed for the development of tourist infrastructure in response to the end of international sanctions and the influx of tourists.

---

42. For example, the Condominium Law, enacted on 16 January 2016, is directed at buildings that are erected on freehold land or land that was granted to the residents. The majority of buildings in Yangon, however, continue to be built on leased land, meaning that the owners of the condominiums do not own the land the building sits on. While the new law specifies that all owners of housing units in a condominium complex (up to 40 per cent of whom may be foreigners) will be considered collective owners of the land on which the building is built, this does not apply to condominiums built on state land or land administered by a state institution. As such, the new law actually creates further uncertainty and insecurity.

If we return to the concept of property as a 'bundle of rights', she has enlarged the bundle by now, also owning a jointly-run guesthouse. Diversification of ownership might be a tactical move, especially considering the fact that the current governing regime is often as unpredictable as its predecessors had been when it comes to property. Although the 2008 Constitution now guarantees private property again (art 37c) and the right to ownership as well as the use of property (art 372), complaints about land grabs are common, not only in Yangon, but also in neighbouring Dala across the river.[43] In Yangon, approximately 10 per cent of the inhabitants live in slums (Gómez-Ibanez et al. 2012: 9), and many of them have been evicted in the course of 'modernizing' the city in the last two decades (see Skidmore 2004). The demolition of the portico will not only violate Auntie Amina's ownership rights, but also the Andaman Islanders' usage rights of their part of the portico, as well as the customary rights of the tea stall owners, who will lose both their established locations and their regular customers once the sidewalk is gone. As it turned out, the YCDC announcement had been much ado about nothing: as of 2020 the portico was still there, a fact appreciated by the tenants, but the threat of its removal still underlined the fundamental precariousness of housing in a situation where not even public proclamations are reliable.

Uncle Ghaffar joined us on the balcony to say goodbye to me as the *muezzin* started calling all Muslim men to evening prayer. He had heard what Auntie Amina told me about the city government's plan to demolish the portico and added:

> We live here, because most Memons are here, our mosque is here. We cannot move because the government does not allow the building of new mosques. We want to be near our culture.

To be 'near our culture' has become especially relevant in recent years, as the country has witnessed an increase in ethno-nationalist rhetoric in which Buddhist supremacy is often coupled with demonizing Muslims as the 'dangerous *other*'. The general atmosphere in Yangon during some periods of my fieldwork was tense in the sense that the downtown areas,

---

43. Article 37a of the Constitution stipulates that 'The Union is the ultimate owner of all lands and all natural resources above and below the ground, above and beneath the water and in the atmosphere in the Union', indicating that, when push comes to shove, customary land regulations will not hold sway.

Fig. 2.4: 'Every day, an opportunity': street vendors chopping ice for sugar cane drinks in front of another downtown construction site of a future luxurious mall. Yangon, 2016.

as well as other quarters, had become religiously segregated, with ethnonationalist plaques and stickers posted on restaurants, taxis, and above street signs indicating which places were 'Buddhist'. Not only Muslims, but also Christians and Buddhists expressed their insecurity and confusion in light of these developments.

When asked directly about the waves of anti-Muslim violence in the northern Rakhine state, Meikhtila in the central lowlands, and in other places since 2012, my Muslim interlocutors stressed that 'Yangon is different' from the other parts of the country. They were, however, very much aware of the deteriorating situation, as Uncle Ghaffar's historical account of the flight of the Memon indicated. He directly linked the persecution of his own community to the situation in present-day Rakhine state, arguing that people will leave their property behind if they feel that their lives are in danger. The Memon Jamaat in Yangon has set up internal modes of taking care of its members and other Muslims, providing social security, education, and even alternative forms of dispute resolution, such as a get-together for all male members of the community where they discuss problems. These measures are efforts to remain as independent as possible.

Conclusion

Since British colonial times, housing, land, and property regimes in Yangon have been both complex and fragile, mirroring the country's political processes of transformation that produced them. This chapter focused on Auntie Amina and Uncle Ghaffar, who have to 'make do' with changing laws and policies amidst insecurity and injustice. Since colonial times, Myanmar has undergone constant transformations of housing, land, and property regimes, initiated first by the colonial administration and later by the independent Myanmar state. While the role of the state in guaranteeing or distributing these bundles of rights has lessened over the years all over the world, in the case of Myanmar, many changes in government, especially throughout the twentieth century, have affected or were directly aimed at housing, land, and property regimes. These changes have ranged from the initial free land grants to religious communities to forcing owners to give up their business properties to opportunities to invest in the booming property market after the country 'opened up' in 2011. Violence that did emerge and that was couched in ethno-religious terms needs to be situated in a historical context that was defined by rapid societal transformations caused by factors such as war, shortages of housing and employment, and the fact that many Indians occupied strategically important economic niches that often made them wealthier than the Bama. To speak of communal conflict in these contexts would be to ignore the political and economic realities in which these conflicts were embedded. The fact that they have been and continue to be understood locally as such, however, shows how quickly the classification of individuals as members of ethno-religious communities has caught on and how deeply ingrained it has become.

Indian, Hindu, Muslim, and Burmese Buddhist have become naturalized identity categories that continue even today to be related first and foremost to race and religion rather than to class. For my interlocutors such as Uncle Ghaffar and Auntie Amina, who self-identify as 'pure Memon', the possibility of bypassing the state or even openly protesting against its policies or laws has been and continues to be greatly limited and comes at a high risk. In their case, we can see how a family of high-class origins (the grandfather having been 'a lord in India') that owned plantations in Myanmar not only became dispossessed in the 1960s, but never really felt quite welcome or at home. While they were born in

Burma, became citizens in the 1960s as children, and insist that they do not belong anywhere else, they are at the same time painfully aware that they are viewed as *others* by the Burmese Buddhist majority population. This became particularly clear to me when Auntie Amina referred to the Burmese woman who was born on the Andaman Islands as 'more of a citizen' than she would ever be.

However, there are other ways in which my interlocutors manage to retain an image of themselves as the true *city-zens* of Yangon. I end this chapter with a story about public transportation. In 2017, the Memon Jamaat, of which Uncle Ghaffar and Auntie Amina are members, co-funded the first line of renovated public buses that began to circle through downtown in an effort by the Yangon City Development Committee (YCDC) to ease the city's notorious traffic jams. It was one of the Memons' ancestors, Adamjee Hadji Dawood, who had single-handedly financed and realized the first tram lines in Yangon in 1884. Neither this nor the Memons' present-day involvement in public transportation is common knowledge in Yangon. By continuing their charitable support of infrastructural development, the Memon Jamaat was not offering donations in a religious sense – be it Islamic or Buddhist or Hindu. They were consciously 'doing being *city-zens*', which entails an understanding of self and of their community as the founders and enablers of Yangon. For this, they did not need to rely on public awareness and acknowledgment of their contributions. That they were financially supporting the trams was known to administrators within the YCDC, but not advertised in the newspapers or on television, and not even publicized on the community's Facebook page. It was a gesture that only Memons knew about, a gesture only they could understand. It is in line with their subaltern positioning, whereby they do not intrude in the public sphere outside the 'religious' and the 'traditional' realm, but nevertheless engage in subversive acts that, rather than challenge 'the state' or demand a fair deal vis-à-vis the majority population directly, call the existing hegemony into question. From their point of view, they are doing so through their own (financial) means and thus, on their own terms. They were and are the ones who keep on running the city.

CHAPTER 3

Caught by the Goddess

A year had passed since the Śri Kāmāchi Amman Temple on Bogyoke Aung San Street had been thoroughly renovated. The temple is located on one of Yangon's busiest downtown streets, opposite the old Scott Market,[1] where locals as well as tourists flock in the thousands every day. The temple's colourful exterior, with hundreds of statues and ornaments adorned with electrical lights in the evening, has recently been further illuminated by a large Kentucky Fried Chicken sign – the first restaurant of its kind in Myanmar, and one that quickly became a magnet for the young and well-to-do (see Fig. 3.1). 'They do not bother us', Amit Kumar,[2] one of the temple trustees, said politely of KFC's patrons, but when talking to men and women who visited the temple on Tuesday and Friday evenings when it was open to the public, I often heard more direct criticism: the consumption of meat in such large amounts 'next door' was in fact offensive. Within the temple facilities, the temple cooks prepare only vegetarian dishes, which are then handed out for free to whoever needs a meal or happens to be in the temple at the time. For *pujas*,[3] temple staff sell trays with bananas, an apple, a

---

1. Scott Market was named after former municipal commissioner Gavin Scott (see Pearn 1939: 284). After independence in 1948, the market was renamed Bogyoke Aung San Market, in honour of the recently killed founder of the army, Major General Aung San, who is worshipped as a hero of war and the person who made independence from the British colonialists possible. He is also the father of Aung San Suu Kyi, the country's state counsellor until the military attempted a coup on 1 February 2021 (see Girke 2018 on General Aung San's legacy in contemporary Myanmar). Both 'Bogyoke Market' and 'Scott Market' are commonly used.

2. When we first met in 2015, Amit Kumar initially introduced himself with his Burmese name, and gave me his Indian name only at a later stage when we had known each other better. As with all my collaborators, I consciously addressed him using the name by which he was addressed by others in his everyday life.

3. A *puja* (Sanskrit for 'reverence', 'worship') is an elaborate prayer ritual that is usually carried out inside the temple compound by the temple priests (*pujari*), who

coconut, a candle, and a small pouch filled with red vermilion powder (*sindoor*) to mark people's foreheads, usually for 2,000–3,000 *kyat* each.[4] The items are bought wholesale at local markets and then sold at a profit. With the money, the trustees manage the running expenses of the temple, including salaries for the priests and the staff, food, and maintenance of the premises.

The 'Viswakarma community', as the temple's ethnic Tamil trustees refer to themselves and as the electronic display above the temple entrance states, is responsible for the administration of the temple. While the sign's English version reads 'Śri Kāmāchi Amman Temple. All Myanmar Viswakarma Community', the Tamil version reads 'Visvakarma Camūkattinarkaḷ', the second word of which, while often translated as 'community' in English, is understood to indicate 'caste' in the Indian context.[5] Finally, the Myanma version says 'Śri Kāmāchi Amman Paya-Chaung',[6] thus completely avoiding the term 'community', for which there is no direct translation available (as I have laid out in Chapter 2). Its meaning is clear: it refers to an ethno-religious group that can be distinguished from others along those same lines. Amit Kumar explained to me that 'Śri Kāmāchi is Shiva's wife', adding that 'her name is English, Tamil, and Burmese. Amman means Lady.' He thus immediately embedded 'her', the temple and the community in a field of associations characterized by linguistic plurality.[7] In the academic literature, the group has come to

---

chant mantras from the ancient Vedas and Agamas. They do so for worshippers and on festive occasions, but also if no audience is present; in some temples in Yangon this is done twice daily, at sunrise and at sunset. *Pujari* offer rice, ash, oils, saffron, milk products, white *abil* and red *sindoor* powders, coconut water and rosewater to the gods and goddesses. After rounds of offerings, one of the priests or a helper rings a bell inside the temple, and a lamp or fire will be held up before the deity. Priests and worshippers then begin prayer or prostration.

4. In 2016, €1.00 was worth approximately 1,400 *kyat*.

5. I thank Thomas Lehmann from the University of Heidelberg for helping me translate this and other Tamil excerpts that I rely on in this chapter.

6. In this case, I would translate the Myanma term *paya-chaung* as 'temple'. *Paya* has a range of meanings – it can refer to the Buddha, to a pagoda housing his relics, or to a pinnacle on top of a religious building. The word *paya-chaung* is nowadays generally understood to mean 'church'.

7. There are several temples with the same name in Tamil Nadu and in South India more generally.

be described either as a caste or as a community whose members trace their genealogy back to the Hindu deity Lord Viswakarma, the divine engineer or architect of the universe. Its members belong to one of the five Viswakarma occupational subgroups: blacksmiths, carpenters, coppersmiths, goldsmiths, or sculptors.[8] That their often-claimed Brahmanic origins in India are disputed does not play a role in Myanmar. The Viswakarma community members' knowledge about these historical categorizations is limited. Amit Kumar, for example, explained to me that 'in former times', Viswakarma were 'goldsmiths, carpenters, or sculptors', but that in their community people had all kinds of jobs; he himself was working as a truck driver. How unimportant employment in these artisanal spheres was to the members' connection to Viswakarma is illustrated by the fact that they did not renovate their temple themselves.

In 2016, the trustees had managed to secure permission to renovate the entire premises by directly applying to U Thein Sein, the president of the country at the time, and by 'convincing' the Yangon City Development Committee (YCDC) that the renovation was necessary.[9]

They had spent about 5,000 *lakh*[10] for the renovation, and had flown in an engineer from Chennai in Tamil Nadu to help them renovate

---

8. The anthropologist Jan Brouwer has written extensively about the Viswakarma (see Brouwer 1995), whose position in Indian society he characterized in a published interview as follows: 'Historically, the Visvakarmas have no point of reference in the indigenous sociological theory of *varna* categories. They responded by claiming either the Brahman or Kshatriya status. This response I see as one to an opportunity/threat from outside. For in society they are not recognized as having a clear status. The others do not really know how to classify them and hence not how [sic] to behave with them. In many situations they are often avoided even in such modern institutions as universities' (Brouwer 2016).

9. I will not address corruption any more directly than in this way. While it dominated the politics and economics of religious buildings as much as the interaction of trustees with the state and – more generally – a great deal of the general interaction between citizens and state representatives, I have no direct data on these practices apart from people's narratives. I do, however, consider such narratives to be highly plausible, as often there was no stigma involved when reporting how one interacted with the state, namely as 'the way things get done here'.

10. *Lakh* is a commonly used unit that goes back to the Indian numbering system and equals 100,000 of whatever unit is being discussed (but is used most commonly with reference to money). Amit Kumar thus said that they spent roughly the equivalent of €350,000 on the renovation of the temple.

'according to religion'; they even brought in paint and painters from Chennai. When I tried to find out why it had been necessary to bring people and even paint from India, the reply was always the lack of specialist knowledge in Myanmar and the need for 'authentic' materials that were required for a proper renovation. One year after completion, two priests from Chennai brought a new statue of the goddess Kāmāchi to replace the old one, which people deemed to have been in the temple for about 100 years. The two priests were responsible for an 'auspicious water-pouring ceremony', conducted to invite the goddess to come and dwell in the new image, while the local priests carried out the *puja*. An acquaintance of mine who has been going to the temple since his early childhood explained to me:

> The one [statue] from India is more important now because they brought it from India and there they do all the ceremonies very knowledgeably. Myanmar people [including himself] do not know what to do or how to do it. The Indian people know how to do it. So they did all the ceremonies to give life to the statue. This image is now alive.

Amit Kumar later reiterated this view, saying, 'There are two *pujari* [priests] from India here. After the ceremony, they will go back home. Because our people don't know what to do – so we brought them from India.' While acknowledging their lack of religious knowledge to properly animate the new statue (and the skills to renovate the temple), temple administrators, trustees, and staff were expertly preparing for Kāmāchi's inauguration and the one-year anniversary of the completion of the renovation. They had already been busy for several days setting up a stall on the boardwalk outside the premises, where they sold small amulets with images of various deities to be worn around the neck on a red woollen thread. The money thus generated would be used for further maintenance of the temple. They also printed a large poster announcing, in the Tamil language, the three-day long festival, the highlight of which was to be a procession through downtown. The poster was affixed on the outside walls of the temple for everyone to see but, as it turned out, not for everyone to read.

On the first night of the celebration, I befriended a pair of elderly sisters who had been visiting the temple since their early childhood. They lived in the immediate neighbourhood and worked as private tutors of English and Hindi. One of their Indian pupils, an 18-year-old girl, had

Fig. 3.1: Under the watchful eyes of the temple president (lower left) and Colonel Harland Sanders, the founder of KFC, young men in white T-shirts, indicating their membership in the temple, bring out the old statue of the goddess Śri Kāmāchi. 29 January 2016.

come to the temple with them for *pujas*. When I asked Aadita Auntie, one of the elderly ladies, if she could translate the sign on the outside of the temple wall for me, she said, 'We don't know what it says either. We are Gujarati. We do not speak Tamil.' It turned out that they knew Amit Kumar by sight and that 'he is in charge of the temple', but they neither knew his name nor had ever spoken to him. 'Previously, this temple was very small. Now it has gotten bigger', said Aadita Auntie.

> *The priests and the staff speak in [the] Tamil language. From my childhood onwards I have been coming here. My father was born in India and my mother in Moulmein. They moved to Rangoon and I was born here. I have no parents anymore and I am not married. We are pure Hindu – we can't marry another caste. We are Gujarati, so if we go to another caste, they cannot prepare vegetables for us. The Bama eat meat, too, so there is an eating problem. Veena [her sister] is also not married. We can only marry those who also eat no meat. I now look after my brother and my sister.*

'But this is the temple of your childhood?' I ask. 'Yes, but it is entirely from the Myanmar Tamil community. They are organizing this event.'

We continued speaking about India, and it came out in conversation that, while I had visited their father's birth country, they had not. 'We have never been to India, but we would like to go and see the birthplace of Krishna, visit the temples. But we have no money', Veena Auntie said. I later realized that those who had openly criticized the consumption of meat 'next door' at the American fast-food chain were classified differently from those who administered the temple; Aadita Auntie and Veena Auntie did not, it turned out, belong to 'the Viswakarma community'. Thus, neither was their common Hinduness nor their continuous temple attendance over several decades sufficient, in their own view, to turn them into members of this community. This is a frequent pattern across temples in Yangon: temple ownership is classified according to a sometimes quite narrow ethnic categorization, and temple administration runs within family networks.

During the three days of celebration, I noticed that another makeshift canopy was being set up just outside the main entrance to the temple. It partially blocked the view of the Tamil-language sign, and impeded access to the smaller stall where temple staff sold their religious paraphernalia. Taking turns, women and men would stand underneath the new canopy, which was decorated with small prayer flags and larger posters depicting Buddha, lotus flowers, and the dharma wheel. Holding plastic alms bowls in one hand, they positioned themselves right in front of the main entrance and were asking for donations for the Buddhist *sangha* (order of the monks). Several tourists stopped to give money, as did local passers-by. Throughout my fieldwork this had been a frequent occurrence: Buddhists trying to attract donations (*dana*) by pitching a tent right outside or in the direct vicinity of non-Buddhist temples and mosques. During the day, the temple trustees and their daily visitors blithely ignored their presence, but at night, when the stall was deserted, the administrators and others brought their food outside and used the table and the chairs that had been left behind. Later I asked Amit Kumar what he thought about the practice of Buddhists occupying a prime spot so close to 'his' temple. He tilted his head slightly to the left and right – a common gesture among Indians in Myanmar and, indeed, throughout the world – and made a dismissive gesture with his right hand, but did not say a word. 'I couldn't care less', I read into his body language, but I also read a 'Can't talk about it' into his silence.

When I reached the temple in the afternoon of the third day of the celebrations, I saw six cows waiting opposite the temple along the board-walk of the main road, resting under the few remaining trees that had not fallen victim to tsunami Nargis in April 2008 and the ongoing renovations of the downtown area. The owner, a man from Yankin township further north who identified himself as Hindu, made sure his animals had enough water. He also held at bay the tourists who wanted to pet and photograph them, as they were a very unusual sight in the middle of downtown Yangon. Once the sun had set, the pace picked up and kept me going in and out of the temple many times in order to keep an eye on all of the activities and developments. Donors arrived, and each took a tray of offerings, stashed some paper money in among the bananas on the tray, and took the tray inside. Once inside, they handed the tray over to the president of the temple, while one of the seven temple trustees announced the name of the donor and the amount of money through a microphone, and then passed it on to yet another trustee. The tray was then passed over to one of the temple priests, who was standing next to the Kāmāchi statue. He, in turn, blessed the offering, cut open the co-conut and gave the donor a taste of its water, anointed him (there were only men) with the white *abil* and red *sindoor* powders, and 'poured' incense smoke over his head, which the donor accepted with open hands. Another trustee again announced the amount of money given and the donor's name through a microphone, while yet another member of the staff filmed the whole transaction (see Fig. 3.2).

With these transactions going on, the young men in white T-Shirts imprinted with the name and date of the inauguration festivity, indicating their membership in the Viswakarma community, brought out the old Kāmāchi statue from its inner sanctuary and placed it on a lion throne and then onto a wooden structure that was so heavy and unwieldy that the men had problems navigating it out of the temple and onto a cart. Then a second statue was brought outside: Ganesha, the elephant god, who himself was sitting on an elevated throne in the shape of the elephant god Ganesha. Finally, a Buddha statue, resting on a gold-coloured serpent throne, was carried out of the temple. While the men were placing the three statues on their respective carts, which by then had been decorated with lights and flowers, a group of dancers and musicians began their performance inside the main hall. Two men acted out the *poikāl kutirai āttam* performance – the 'False Horse' folk dance of Tamil Nadu – while another man performed a form of *karakāttam*,

Fig. 3.2: The temple president (centre) passes the monetary donation from a donor (right) to a trustee, who offers a garland of flowers in return. The transaction is announced via microphone and documented by camera (left). 26 January 2016.

Fig. 3.3: Performing the Tamil *poikāl kutirai āttam* ('False Horse Dance') and the *karakāttam* ('Decorated Pot Dance'), accompanied by Tamil tavil drums and oboes (*nātasvāram*). 26 January 2016.

which involved balancing a pot, decorated with a cone of leaves and flowers and topped with a small figure of a parrot, on his head (see Fig. 3.3.). They were accompanied by two men playing *tavils* (drums) and one playing a *nātasvāram* (oboe), both regarded as traditional Tamil instruments by the temple trustees and the priests whom I later quizzed about the names of all these objects.

On the basis of this description it would now be possible to proceed directly to a Durkheimian analysis of the various elements that people employed during this effervescent event in order to celebrate their community. We have all the elements necessary for a good socio-anthropological analysis in terms of 'structure', 'culture', 'relationships', and 'meaning', and even economics, exchange, reciprocity, and 'the gift', depending on our theoretical inclinations. There are practices that centre on ritual festivities and the strong symbolic character of the dance and the *pujas* that are being publicly performed. We can reflect on emic rationalizations of the need for 'authenticity', trace translocal connections between Myanmar and India, note the social stratification according to status groups, with individuals clearly divided into administrative trustees on the top, religious experts in the middle, and lay practitioners on the bottom, scrutinize the various public and mediatized performances of economic transactions that bind patrons to the temple and the temple trustees to the patrons, or engage in a materialist analysis of the statues, the musical instruments and other ritual tools, and their usages and respective histories, to just name a few options. But instead I will focus on a specific situation that caught my eye because, to me, it stood out even more than the colourful dance, the arranging of statutes, the *pujas*, or the general hustle and bustle. Sensing that there was something of even greater 'relevance' to observe, I switched focus, allowing all other ongoing activities to fade into the background of my attention and my inner commentary regarding what might be 'valuable' data.

Processing possession

A young man belonging to the white-clad helpers was 'caught by the Goddess' (Tamil *pudiccikkiradu*): he 'became' Kāmāchi, as Amit Kumar later put it. The man's entire upper body started convulsing uncontrollably. His limbs were shaking, his arms flew in the air and his chest was pushed upwards. Some of the younger men from his age group who were standing around him must have noticed immediately what was going on and tried to keep him down, with several clinging onto his shoulders and holding his arms tight. Several women then formed a second circle around the inner cluster of men, thus keeping themselves at a distance while at the same time remaining present in the situation (Fig. 3.4). I had missed the very beginning of this commotion and thus have no data

Fig. 3.4: The priest arrives (shirtless man in upper left, behind the horse dancer), carrying a tray of incense and other items. The woman in purple helps to hold the possessed man down (central magnified circle). Others observe the struggle; a woman in orange touches her head, looking down. 26 January 2016.

Fig. 3.5: The woman in purple acknowledges the arrival of the priest (central magnified circle). 26 January 2016.

on how the bystanders came to realize that there was 'something' going on; in any case, 'being caught' seemed to be nothing out of the ordinary, and triggered a certain seemingly routinized behaviour that everyone present seemed familiar with. As soon as I became aware of the unfolding dynamic, I started video-recording the situation.

The priest who had seen to the new Kāmāchi statue that the helpers had placed inside a shrine in the middle of the temple was called by one of the men attending to the possessed. He hastened towards the scene with a tray of incense and candles. Dipping a finger of his right hand into the white *abil* powder, he reached for the forehead of the young man, who, thrashing about, kicked the priest's tray and almost knocked it out of his hands, but one of the women reached over and steadied it (Fig. 3.6). The very moment the priest managed to touch the man's forehead with his finger, the man fainted and collapsed. He was dragged to the side by two men while others hurried to bring water and fan him with one of the metal offering trays (Fig. 3.8). The priest left the room immediately, returning his tray to the inner temple area where the new statue resided, only to return once more to check on the man who was slowly regaining consciousness. All the while, the dancers and musicians had carried on with their performance.

The priest moved in only when called upon and moved out once he had managed to touch the possessed man's forehead. He returned briefly,

Fig. 3.6: The priest's first attempt to touch the forehead of the possessed man fails as the possessed kicks wildly and almost knocks over the tray. The woman in purple reaches out and prevents the tray from falling (magnified circle). 26 January 2016.

to check on the young man from a distance, but did not get involved and then left again. While one could argue that it was his touch that allowed for the transition from possessed to unconscious human, most of the work before and afterwards was done by others. The trustees and the temple president remained marginal, too, watching from a distance, and

Fig. 3.7: The possessed then kicks the man in the red shirt, whose cell phone falls to the floor (which the young man to his left indicates with his left index finger). The man turns his head away as he reties his longyi. 26 January 2016.

Fig. 3.8: Once the priest succeeded in touching the possessed man's forehead, the man collapsed. The priest immediately left the situation. When the young man lost consciousness, he was dragged away. 26 January 2016.

only after the young man's unconscious body had already been dragged to the side. There was an absence of spoken communication, as the individuals' actions were all body-centred. The only person uttering words was the woman in the purple *saari* – she was also the one who had steadied the priest's tray and touched his arm. She displayed behaviour that was different from those who kept their bodies to themselves and did not speak. She was, in a way, mirroring the possessed as her arms reached out, and her mouth opened and closed. While the men in white, the priest, and the woman in the purple *saari* were moving about quite a lot, the other individuals stood rather still, as if bearing witness. The atmosphere was suffused with calm a certain competence in handling the situation, despite the physical struggle and the loud music that continued playing throughout.

None of the individuals backed away or exhibited what I would have interpreted as shock or dismay; in fact, some of the men were even smiling as if slightly overwhelmed or bemused by their friend's behaviour. I noticed two Western female tourists and a young local boy also standing by. Together with some other younger men they formed a third semi-circle to my right, remaining further removed from the action than the others, yet still present.

As I watched the video sequence over and over, I noticed a particular type of behaviour right after the possessed had lost consciousness and the priest had left the situation, thus, at precisely the same time that the Goddess 'left' the possessed man's body, as I later discussed with Amit Kumar. It was at that moment that the bystanders, almost in unison, appeared to unconsciously draw into themselves, crossing their arms in front of their chests, touching their faces or their heads, covering their mouths, or keeping their arms close to their sides (Fig. 3.8).

People continued to come into the room to observe, enlarging the crowd of bystanders. After a while, everyone dispersed and began to engage in other activities, and the behavioural convergence ended.

To make sense of these data, a common approach in sociocultural anthropology would be to employ 'situational analysis' as originally developed in the Manchester School around Max Gluckman. His idea was 'to arrive at the general through the dynamic particularity of the case' (Evens and Handelman 2008: 1). Moreover, according to Kapferer, who draws on Gluckman, 'individual action, including the inner conflicts and tensions integral to individual motivations, have their effects and realize their potential in and through the socio-historical contexts, processes, and structures within which they are born' (Kapferer 2014: 151). This approach demands an investigation of situations, institutions, and practices as embedded in the *longue durée*, particularly in relation to the (colonial) state. In the case at hand, it would mean reading the celebrations and the spirit possession in light of its postcolonial context, where the very existence of the Hindu community needs to be understood as the outcome of a century-long process of British cultural engineering, as I have laid out in Chapter 1, and of which a possession such as I describe here would be one among many different possible displays of historical as much as of contemporary Hinduness.

Gluckman was among the first in anthropology to focus on individual action and historically developed structures; in his view there is no situation that cannot be harvested for its *socio*logical relevance: 'The logic, Gluckman would maintain, is in the practice – in the various situations of practice – and not merely a product of abstracted theories that were independent of the actual social actions to be comprehended' (Kapferer 2014: 6). In line with how sociocultural anthropology continues to understand its object more broadly, individuals are of interest particularly in their role as members of collectives. Likewise, to the present day, in ethnographic accounts from around the globe, possession continues to be treated as 'an essentially social and cultural reference, enabling us to consider it as a category of sociocultural analysis' (Strathern and Lambek 1998: 3). It centres on extraordinary individual action, but usually gets interpreted in terms of relationality or collectivity. Brac de la Perrière (2017b), for example, has analysed spirit possession in Myanmar among Burmese Buddhists as an autonomous field of practice that is constituted through asymmetrical relationships: on the one hand, between a 'chosen' individual who gets possessed by a spirit (*nat*) and is expected to undergo 'an apprenticeship in embodiment by letting the entity enter him or her (*nat win-*) when it appears' (2017b: 73), and, on the other hand, between the spirit medium and his/her clientele who, during public festivals, approach him/her to earn merit. Thus, spirit possession in Burmese Buddhism is, according to Brac de la Perrière, a 'form of sociability analyzable with reference to clientelism' (2016: 26). Janice Boddy interrogated possession rituals in the Zar cult in southern Sudan as 'an alternative view of the world in response to an elites' implicit domination of discourse' (Boddy 1989: 157). Both authors thus discuss possession in relation to social stratification, particularly to class. Michael Lambek (1981, 1993, 1998) has investigated spirit possession alongside Islam and cosmology on Mayotte, an island of the Comoro archipelago, as ultimately incommensurable forms of embodied and objectified knowledge that still blend into each other, but are fundamentally inconclusive and change over time. In another essay, he emphasized that his argument about the interrelation of knowledge and practice was 'resolutely social' (Lambek 1997: 132), where 'the person', rather than 'the individual', stands in the foreground. Thomas Kirsch has likewise discussed spirit possession within African Christianity as 'essentially social' (2002: 57), with bureaucratic authority and charisma providing 'mutually enforcing roles' for a community's religious leaders. Both Kirsch and Lambek emphasize personhood – of the spirits and of the individuals involved with them – in light of the broader social community in which they are embedded. Willford and George have investigated possession in Hindu temples in Malaysia in terms of status empowerment and debates around authenticity, interpreting the act of possession as 'a moment of mimicry (of orthodoxy) and an evacuation of self' (2005: 61). Corin (1998) has argued that spirit possession in Congo can be viewed as a locus of individuation. These latter authors thus consider possession in light of transcending body and self, as subjects are repositioned within a larger collective context, a context that is presupposed to exist. Following from this brief overview of the anthropological literature on possession, it seems that it is still rather uncommon to interpret and analyse possession without embedding individuality within some form of 'community' or 'sociality' as a background foil.

Anthropologists often seek to document people's everyday lives, but are at the same time trained to spot and are possibly even incentivized to highlight the extraordinary. Accordingly, my ethnographic gaze during the ritual was focused on the more sensational aspects of the possession, and my own material is in line with how anthropologists gaze at sociality more generally. But at the same time, my visual data allow me to gain insights into aspects of the situation beyond the relationality of the possessed. Thus, the common anthropological approach to possession brings with it a mismatch between where we look and how we observe, on the one hand, and what it is we intend to describe, on the other. It only focuses on one side of the equation. In the case of possession, we know that these practices are a well-known phenomenon across religions, including among Hindus in South Asia (see Kapadia 1996, 2000; Sax and Weinhold 2010; Sax and Basu 2015). However, by analysing such events through a focus on the possessed individual and their relation to others, rather than on the overall situation, observers tend to extrapolate from the extraordinary to the general. This risks overlooking situational processes of *we-formation* that do not presuppose the existence of community beforehand, or that cannot be viewed as representations of collectivity or as an indication of the evolving relationality between individuals.

Minimal integration behaviour

Had I not videotaped the possession, the behaviour of those individuals around the possessed young man would certainly have escaped my attention. I would have been fascinated by the possessed, and maybe the actions of the priest. I realized only later that I had been the only one filming the actual possession, even as the temple trustees had ordered one of their members to document the three-day ceremony on video and, indeed, both the monetary transactions and the artistic perfor- mances had been filmed extensively. While I used my own photographs and video recordings as an *aide mémoire* to reconstruct the situation afterwards, their filming of patrons offering donations and of the Tamil dance and music performance can be understood as enlarging the (at least hypothetical) audience by producing material that might allow witnessing after the event. The act of videotaping can even be seen as substituting for an audience altogether, as neither the donation activi- ties nor the performances were well attended by others. In his article on Max Gluckman's reliance on photographs during and after fieldwork, Wingfield argues that photographs, like ceremonies, initiation rites, or other rites of passage, 'can function in a similar way to a scar pro- duced through a technique of bodily incision, and become a visual, as well as a bodily, focus for memories of the event' (2012: 73).[11] In my

---

11. Gluckman was a 'participant-photographer' (Morton 2005) who used his photo- graphs from his fieldwork among the Zulu in South Africa to 'provide evidential support' for his writing and his texts (Wingfield 2012; see also Engelke 2008).

case, however, it seemed that the objective was not so much to create a memory, but to provide an additional means of bearing witness to the orchestrated set pieces of donation and dance. Technically speaking, of course, the temple staff's camera was actively recording and not in 'stand-by mode', but its function was similar to that of the individuals 'standing by' during the possession, which was only filmed by me. The body analogy is thus fitting, as individual bodies were there to bear witness rather than to document an event that could later be reviewed for the sake of enhancing one's memory.[12]

This leads me to argue that we can discern several ways of 'standing-by' in this situation. From an ethnomethodological perspective, it is a practice that needs to be actively pursued. A competent audience needs to display that they are 'doing "being present"' (Sacks 1992) in a given situation. The individuals who formed what I will call the 'first-order group' around the possessed were engaged in an intercorporeal activity that involved touching another person's body, using physical force to restrain that body's movements, coordinating their behaviour without much (or any) talk and, finally, removing the unconscious individual from the centre of the temple to the sidelines. The 'second-order group' stood to my left in a semicircle around the group of men and consisted of elderly women and elderly men who remained at a distance but watched attentively and made sure that enough space was given for the first-order group and the priest to do their work. Only the priest and the woman in the purple *saari* actively engaged in intercorporeality, touching the possessed, preventing the priest's tray from toppling over, giving directions by pointing and speaking, and thus also claiming space for themselves. They helped by moving out of the way and preventing accidents from happening. I would argue that for the first- and the second-order groups, we could fruitfully speak of displays of 'competent membership' in Sacks's usage of the term.[13]

---

12. The video recordings that the temple staff produce often end up on social media and are distributed within networks of friends and friends of friends, and can therefore be watched by yet a larger number of people, who then become additional bystanders.

13. Sacks held, somewhat convolutedly, that 'if a member sees a category-bound activity being done, then, if one can see it being done by a member of a category to which the activity is bound, then: see it that way' (Sacks 1995: 259).

In a 'third-order group' to my right stood male youths, the two female tourists, and a small boy holding his mother's hand. These individuals, too, became part of an observing audience, but remained passively watching for most of the time. Only when a man in the first-order group lost his cell phone did one of the youths from the second-order group actively engage, drawing the man's attention by pointing to the cell phone on the floor (Fig. 3.7). Once the possessed man had lost consciousness, the young men from the third-order group joined the second-order group in that they also began to display increasingly convergent behaviour, namely 'closing their bodies off' by crossing their arms or holding objects close to themselves once the Goddess had left the possessed person's body. The situation had, in that moment, turned from one connoted by religion, where knowledge had been key to 'reading' the situation and performing appropriately, to one without religious connotations, where individual expressions could be observed which then were mirrored across the two outer semicircles. The two tourists and the child, however, still did not join in. How were these degrees of membership constituted?

Reynolds (2017) criticized ethnomethodologists for having 'largely not yet explored the intersection between embodied work and membership'. His own approach as well as recent ethnomethodological work on intercorporeality (see Schegloff 2007; Tanaka 2015; Meyer et.al. 2018) can be fruitfully applied to investigating the (re-)production of membership in embodied action. Taking the example of observing others train at the gym, Reynold holds that '"observation", "glances", "looks" or "staring" is *action*, and accountable action at that' (Reynolds 2017: 100, emphasis in original). People in a given situation will recognize the other's gaze, and there is only a certain period during which one can observe without having to account for that act of observation. Overlong observation may call other parties to account or reframe the orientation to a person's body (Kidwell 2005; Heath 2006, cited in Reynolds 2017: 100). Sharrock and Turner (1980: 28) argued that '[m]embers can, then, be faced with the task of managing the observability of their own observational work'. I argue that this is what we see happening in the case at hand: it was only after the possessed person lost consciousness, thus after the Goddess had left their midst, that the observers began accounting for their individual bodily reactions to the possession. This, however, was done by replicating and copying or displaying common patterns of behaviour that all centred on 'closing off' one's body, such as the crossed arms. Garfinkel, however, conjoins two quite different aspects of accounting practices when he characterizes them as both 'reflexive' and 'incarnate' (Garfinkel 1967: 1). I would argue that these two dispositions should not necessarily be lumped together. Whereas reflexivity points towards implicit knowledge (rather than explicit norms) that then might lead to (ill-defined) shared behaviour (as with Jörg Bergmann's 'structural sense of uncertainty' [*strukturelle Sinnungewissheit*]; see Bergmann 1988: 40), 'incarnation' is more bound up with the 'body' and thus not necessarily with knowledge (implicit or not). While I would argue that *we-formation* does not have to be conscious as claimed in phenomenological work (see Walther 1923; Calcagno 2012: 98), I also do not locate it in 'a deep psychological structure of habit' (2012: 89). Rather, I would turn to 'situated co-existence' of individuals, as Albert Piette terms it (2015: 104), with the videotaped possession sequence serving as an exemplary case.

Ethnomethodologists argue that members feel a sense of belonging to one another because their practices are understood and perceived as orderly by co-members. But Piette holds that individuals not only manage 'the collective aspect necessarily implied by the interaction in which they are participating', but are also capable of 'managing their own singularity through gestures, movements and thoughts that are specific to each of them', thereby introducing 'the individual detail against a backdrop of coordination' (Piette 2015: 40). Here, Piette does not contrast ethnomethodology with existential anthropology (as he otherwise likes to do), but acknowledges that they can be, in fact, two sides of the same coin. He would, however, not go so far as to argue that all kinds of by-standing are actively being 'managed'. Piette's distinction between three different types of what he calls 'minimal integration behaviour' – 'the social minimum', 'the minimum of human presence', and 'the minimum of remains' (Piette 2015: 189–190) – can fruitfully complicate ethnomethodological approaches towards (competent) membership. What he terms 'the social minimum' concerns 'the execution of what is expected in a situation with several people against a backdrop of rules, laws and habits'. This would characterize the first-order group in my case and is very much in line with Goffman's 'focused interaction', which 'occurs when persons gather close together and openly cooperate to sustain a single focus of attention' (Goffman [1963] 1966: 24).

'The minimum of human presence' I would align with the second-order group in my example. It refers to 'cognitive engagement [that] can be very economical' while 'inner engagement' may be unnecessary (Piette 2015: 190). This would align with Goffman's 'unfocused interaction' – which 'occurs when one gleans information about another person present by glancing at him, if only momentarily, as he passes into and then out of one's view' (Goffman 1966: 24). In this second-order group, only the woman in the purple *saari* stood out as she oriented herself more towards the first-order group, thus partaking in coordinated action. The young men who were initially standing by rather passively and were restrained in their movements also began to change their orientation and engaged more with others by mirroring the behaviour of other grown-ups once the Goddess had 'left'. On the other hand, there were men from the first-order group who subsequently moved out into the second-order group (e.g., the man who had dropped his cell phone and needed to regain bodily composure), distancing themselves from the coordinated action.

Finally, there is 'the minimum of remains', which Piette describes as 'those that stay on the sideline ... those very remains that link together the continuity of existence' (Piette 2015: 190). I have argued previously that 'standing by depends on not fully knowing; it also smudges the distinction between full members and people who think of themselves merely at the side-lines' (Beyer 2019b). Likewise, Vered Amit has recently posited the notion of 'indifference' as 'a measure of civility between strangers' who might assume 'a stance of watchful – and therefore self-conscious – indifference to the co-presence, activities, and occasional infringements of other people' in shared public space. She terms this modality of by-standing 'staying apart together' (Amit 2020: 63). I would assign the role of the bystander to the two tourists and the child who, at no point, changed their positions in the situation. Although Goffman would probably lump these individuals into the 'unfocused interaction' group where, according to him, 'sheer and mere copresence' (Goffmann 1966: 24) are managed, I would argue that in the case of the tourists and the child, to speak of 'managing' co-presence would be attributing too much intentionality to their existence in the situation. I would thus downplay the conscious aspect which Amit foregrounds in her analysis of joint commitment.

When taken together, these three different types of minimal integration behaviour can account for the breadth of human existence in a given situation, ranging from coordinated interaction at its centre to passivity and minimality on its outer fringes. While by-standing might not go unnoticed and certain individuals might step up and intervene in the actions of others, such self-organizing instances of *we-formation* should not be viewed as active interventions entirely. We need to acknowledge that, at least for some individuals, they can be an unintended side-effect they themselves might not even be aware of, while others can be co-present but not become participants at all. What we see in the case of the possession is the simultaneous co-existence of three different types of minimal integration behaviour that, while binding all individuals to the situation in practices of *we-formation*, they do not lead to an overall structuring of groups, let alone to communality or community.

Moreover, once the Goddess had left, we can recognize a reshuffling of group boundaries, as religious knowledge was no longer necessary for an implicit account, i.e., for legitimizing action and inaction, and the individuals were then left to their own devices. By aligning their postures with one another, a new competent group was formed that now also included the youths, who might have known how to indicate their positionality prior to this experience, but felt the need to restrain themselves due to their young age or lower status in the presence of elders. There is, thus, a certain flexibility within a situation regarding where individuals locate themselves: they can move in and out of coordinated action or individual presence. On this point, I think, Goffman, ethnomethodologists, and Piette would all agree. But this is also the point where ethnomethodological analysis reaches its limit, because not only do we need a *longue durée* approach when it comes to understanding how situations are emically judged to be of 'relevance', but we also need to follow the actors over extended periods of time to learn about their ways of behaving and being in the world from one situation to another. While I thus can only speculate as to why the youths only started to display competent behaviour in mirroring the adults' bodily gestures after the Goddess had left, it is important to note that the two female tourists and the child did not. Besides my camera and the camera that the temple trustees had designated for filming situations that they considered to be of relevance, these two Western women, too, had cameras, which they only pulled out and began to use once the original tripartite group formation had dissolved and some people had already left the situation entirely. Placing their cameras between their own bodies and the collapsed figure on the ground, they started taking pictures. They had not displayed such documentary interest only a couple of seconds earlier, although there had been much more 'action' going on. Rather, they had remained in a mode of passive co-presence, bearing witness to the possession. They stood by, at best mirroring the small child next to them rather than the adults. I interpret their renewed interest in their cameras at the very end, when the possessed man was about to regain consciousness, as suddenly reawakening to their role as 'tourists', for whom taking photographs is an expected and thus accountable type of behaviour.

Pierre Bourdieu has accused ethnomethodology of seeking 'to explain everything that occurs in an experimental or observed interaction in terms of the experimentally controlled characteristics of the situation, such as *the relative spatial positions of the participants*' (Bourdieu [1972] 1977: 81–82, emphasis added). The ethnomethodological approach leaves little room for the human capacity to stand by without attributing a particular underlying logic or even reflexivity to the existence of an individual. Idle bystanders are thus rarely mentioned in either ethnomethodological or ethnographic accounts. In moments of heightened attention, anthropologists tend to ignore them, and practice theorists tend to assume strategic behaviour. In his work, Albert Piette has criticized Goffman and ethnomethodologists for their 'inability to consider distraction outside of its relevant or incongruous impact' (2015: 31). He complained that 'all of the details Goffman observed are in fact reincorporated into issues of relevance, incongruity or strategy' (2015: 32). This, however, was very much in line with how the social sciences had dealt with individuals in general. In anthropology, for example, Raymond Firth, in his foreword to Leach's seminal study *The Political Systems of Highland Burma*, argued that 'individuals are continually faced by choices between alternatives for action. When they make these choices, Dr. Leach believes their decisions are made *commonly* to gain power' (Firth [1954] 1964: vi, emphasis added). This might be true for the antagonists most directly involved in one of these classic arenas, but it helps little with understanding the role of the bystanders and of audiences more generally. While I think that it is thus unfair to criticize Goffman for ordering his data in this manner, I consider Piette's approach worth recognizing. In his work, Piette has made the radical decision to treat 'details' as important data precisely 'because they are not relevant' (Piette 2015: 39). By focusing on what he also refers to as 'leftovers' or the 'non-relevant' ways of human existence, he develops an anthropocentric approach in which the individual remains at the centre of anthropological inquiry at all times: 'existential anthropology's task is to undertake observations characterised by an intensive methodological detailism centred on individuals, and a theoretical perspective that sets its sights on humankind as a species' (Piette 2015: 68). On the basis of his empirical material from religious life in French Catholic parishes, Piette developed a theoretical concept he calls the 'minor mode' (Fr. *mode mineur*), which draws particular attention to a '"lesser" way of performing actions' (2015: 40) that is 'not relevant, not noticed or barely noticed' (ibid.). He argues that the minor mode disappears once there is intention, strategy, or rationality involved in an individual's being in a situation.[14]

I use Piette's *minor mode* as a sensitizing concept that challenges the still dominant social anthropological tendency to scale up and away from individual dispositions too quickly. Piette's work does an excellent job, in my opinion, of radically opening the anthropologist's eyes to the existence of individuality outside of and apart from group formation, collectivity, and community. In its radicalism, however, his theory is not 'applicable' if one wants to retain an ethnography that focuses on interaction and forms of sociality and – as I do – even merge it with ethnomethodology. Following Piette entirely would mean substituting ethnography with what he calls 'phenomenography' or 'anthropography', not only focusing on individuals, but devoting all attention to

---

14. Although Piette does not draw the comparison, I find the similarity to Sigmund Freud's approach to psychoanalysis striking. In an anonymously submitted paper to the journal *Imago*, Freud analysed a marble statue of Moses by Michelangelo by drawing on the elaborations of a Russian art connoisseur who argued that one should pay attention to 'the significance of minor details' rather than to 'the general impression and main features'. Freud noted that such a method of enquiry was closely related to the technique of psychoanalysis (Freud 1914: 222).

continuously observing them, ideally throughout their entire life span from birth to death and by means of video documentation. His approach leaves virtually no space for studying higher-order categories such as 'community'. This is partly because he does not take into account the possibility that these categories might be our collaborators' own concepts; rather, he views them only as unnecessary analytical abstractions as they appear in the writings of Malinowski and other (structural-) functionalists, as well as in the work of the early sociologists for whom 'community' or 'society' were the objects of inquiry and individuals only units to be bypassed. While Piette's existential anthropology is clearly difficult to apply, especially if one does not want to completely give up on being an ethnographer and socio-cultural anthropologist with at least some hope of drawing conclusions that go beyond the idiosyncratic and particularistic, his well-founded criticism of anthropologists' (and other social scientists') tendency to brush over the non-strategic individual is worth taking on board. I am, therefore, trying to apply Piette's theory *and* retain my ethnography. I think this is doable since, as I have demonstrated, we can discern various groups coming into being in a situation, as well as the gradual shifting of we-formations, without having to either delve into people's mental or cognitive states or assume that they reflect at all times on their behaviour or are constantly conscious of all of their 'doings' (as ethnomethodology would have us do).

I now turn to the second part of this case study, which returns to the carts outside the Śrī Kāmāchi temple and involves following my interlocutors and others out of the temple and into the streets of downtown Yangon for a procession. Here again, different group formations can be observed, this time partly orchestrated and designed in advance by the temple trustees with the help of their staff and other members of the Viswakarma community, but not, as I will argue, entirely to their liking. They are different from the we-formation we encountered inside the temple, where it was linked to minimal integration behaviour and where it only lasted for a few seconds and then evaporated as soon as the people dispersed and the situation ended.

Possessing procession

After the three statues had been placed onto their respective decorated carts, which were being drawn by the six cows I had seen earlier (two to each cart), the three musicians playing the *tavils* and the oboe came out of the temple and positioned themselves at the very front of the procession. The first cart followed them slowly through the asphalt streets of Yangon, full of potholes and puddles of betel nut spit. The Buddha statue wobbled a bit on the first cart and needed to be fastened down in order to not topple over. 'In Myanmar, Buddha comes first', commented Amit Kumar when I asked him to elaborate on the arrangement of the carts. After Buddha came Ganesha, after Ganesha the old Śri Kāmāchi statue. All carts were lavishly decorated and a priest sat at the front of each, bearing a tray of utensils. I encountered a young boy whom I had seen earlier with his grandfather inside the temple, now riding high atop the first cart, overseeing the procession while remaining at a safe distance from the action that unfolded around the carts on the ground.

Wielding his knife, a helper to the priest on the first cart sliced in half a coconut that a family of worshippers had handed him on a tray along with other offerings. Having blessed the sweet water, the priest handed it back to the worshippers, together with their tray of now blessed offerings for further redistribution, making sure to remove the money that had been placed on the tray. Mothers then took it upon themselves to apply red *sindoor* powder to their family members' foreheads and distribute the food items, the coconut water, and the incense to their children. There was thus a sharing of ritual labour going on, with the priest performing the highest task of blessing the offerings; a helper handing him the trays, slicing open the coconuts, and sometimes performing additional acts such as noisily throwing the opened and emptied coconuts onto the ground in such a way that both animals and humans had to halt their progress for a second, slightly irritated, out of step, only to regain composure again and continue along the route; and worshippers sharing, applying, and consuming the blessed items. Moreover, shopkeepers offered free energy drinks in cans to those who passed by. Homeless families with their children roamed along with the procession, taking advantage of people's temporary generosity, and hawkers lined the streets, selling religious merchandise such as flower garlands and candles. Once bought, these items could be put to immediate use as the carts passed by, thus enabling spontaneous worship alongside those who had carefully planned their participation by buying trays directly outside the temple from the Śri Kāmāchi trustees or by assembling the necessary items at home. Going back and forth from one vantage point to another, I became immersed in this sensuous atmosphere. It was something that I had already experienced during regular *pujas* inside the temples, but it seemed heightened now that it had spilled over and saturated the city, with so many people moving through it and yet others leaning out of their balconies or peeking through open doors of tea shops, observing what was going on, and the temple trustees, who were ever-present, overseeing the procession and, somehow, like the children, central to the event, yet slightly distanced and less active, more observing.

All of the Hindu *pujas*, rituals, and processions I attended have stuck in my mind for their lavishness. To an outsider, the sheer variety of things that can be 'done' are overwhelming: the music, the lights, the sounds, the cutting of coconuts, the throwing of items onto the ground, the lighting of incense, the touch of the priest's finger on one's forehead. Following the procession throughout downtown, going from the first cart to the second, from the second to the third, and back, speeding up to join the marching musicians in front who, playing their instruments, continued to lead the way, it occurred to me that my feeling of 'being overwhelmed' might be an intentional side effect that was also experienced by the other participants I saw scurrying along, being busy with all their doings. It was striking to me how small children were made part and parcel of these practices, yet were also sheltered from being exposed too much: they were held up so that the priest could reach them more easily, they were gently touched and anointed and fed along with the adults only to be returned to the safety of their parents' arms. Gabriele Alex (2008: 526) has shown that, for Tamil Nadu, such 'tactile encounters' are considered especially important for children. Children are deliberately exposed to these sensory practices; their way of learning is through embodiment and through becoming entangled in the activities of others (see also Wenger 1998). They might remain passive, yet they occupy central positions in the way the events are orchestrated. They might not remember actively later on, but their bodies will know what to do; the smell of incense will be familiar, as will be the food and the energy drinks – a modern innovation that fits well with the general dynamics of such processions (see also Kapoor 2021). Their understanding will be more emotional and sensory than semiotic, developing in a pre-reflexive, pre-verbal way. Edgar Levenson (1998, 2018) has suggested that learning is always first bodily and only then cerebral; that children mimic and imitate before they 'understand' and are able to categorize their experiences. A procession such as the one I participated in 'emphasizes sensory and affective communication and the language of the emotions' (Tambiah 1990: 108). Moreover, according to Edith Turner (2012: 155), 'the sense of "the holy" is also the feeling of deepest respect for relation' – to the gods, one could argue, as well as to those around oneself who are engaging in similar behaviour. These are all embodied forms of engagement that allow for more than strategic interaction and practice and the display of 'community' to outsiders. In fact, the *Oxford English Dictionary* defines 'procession' as 'the action of *a body of people* going or marching along in orderly succession in a formal or ceremonial way' (emphasis added). I argue that, for the city dwellers participating in the procession, it is their immersion in the sensory experiences that is key to the event. Fredric Jameson has reiterated Sartre's admonition to beware of attributing 'communal' feelings to one's participation in, for example, a procession or a political rally. While this sense might be very real for the individual, what an individual experiences is of no consequence to those around him or her; it is ultimately an 'illusion of fraternity or communion' (Jameson [1971] 1974: 250, paraphrasing Sartre). Individual bodies, in other words, are not lost even when they come together and even when they become politicized, as is the case in Yangon, where the immersion of the worshippers' bodies in a spiritual experience has to be contained within strict requirements imposed by the state.

'Have they [the trustees] obtained a permit?' I overheard one person asking another along the way. This was one of the most common questions I heard community members asking each other at various events that were scheduled to take place outside their religious buildings. I hurried to catch up with Amit Kumar and quizzed him about whether he had he encountered any difficulties obtaining the necessary paperwork for the Śri Kāmāchi procession. 'Sometimes it's bad, but this time it was OK', he answered. Permits usually need to be obtained from the neighbourhood warden (*lu gyi*; lit. 'big man'), from the Yangon City Development Committee (YCDC), and from the neighbourhood police station. I continued to discuss with Amit Kumar the exact route the procession was scheduled and permitted to take. Pointing south

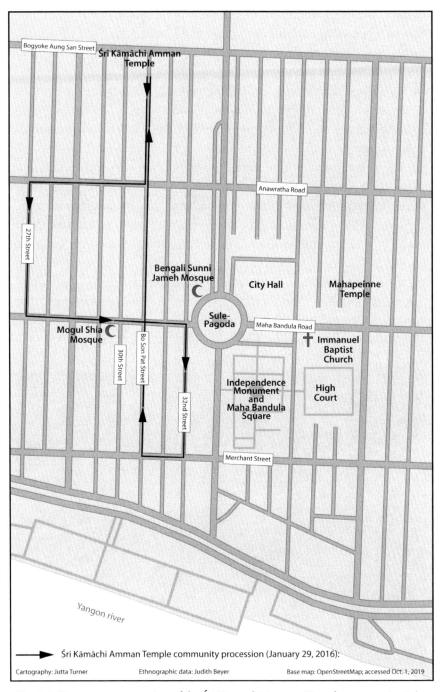

Śri Kāmāchi Amman Temple community procession (January 29, 2016):

Cartography: Jutta Turner   Ethnographic data: Judith Beyer   Base map: OpenStreetMap; accessed Oct. 1, 2019

Fig. 3.9: Downtown procession of the Śrī Kāmāchi Amman Temple community. 26 January 2016.

towards the Yangon River, he explained that it would 'go around Sule', but once we were on the street, we turned right into 32nd Street just before reaching the pagoda on Maha Bandula Road. There was thus no circumambulation of the major Buddhist landmark, but only a passing-by without coming into direct contact with it. Tracing our itinerary afterwards, I realized that we had stayed entirely within Pabedan township (see Fig. 0.5 and Fig. 3.12 below), for which the trustees had been given permission by the YCDC and the police.

The procession went on until 1:30 in the morning and ended back at the Sri Kāmāchi Temple from where it had set off. I went home to sleep and returned early the next morning to take in the aftermath: the sight of scattered flower petals from what had been a beautiful, large *mandala* that worshippers had laid out on the temple floor; the smell of cold incense; and a lingering feeling of fatigue and exhaustion. Some elderly men were sitting silently in a corner and nodded slightly upon my arrival, too tired to speak (Fig. 3.13). I sat down in a different corner and took out my notebook. I wanted to reflect on the reactions of some Yangonite Muslims I had encountered the previous night:

Fig. 3.10: Leftovers. The day after the procession. 27 January 2016.

Last night the city was still full of cars and the procession with the six animals, probably 1,000 people, all those lights, sounds and smells – in the middle of downtown – felt surreal to me. The way we passed by construction sites, tea shops and shiny new buildings… but so typical for Yangon at the same time! I found the reactions of some Muslims who were sitting in the tea shops along the roads or standing in front of their shops along Maha Bandula Road particularly interesting: They seemed to watch with what I sensed to be a mixture of interest and belittlement. Some were laughing a bit at the colourfully decorated animals and the people's ritualistic practices. When we passed by 30th Street, where the Shia mosque is located, I called up Akber Hussain [one of my key Shia interlocutors] and told him that I would be passing by his house in a couple of minutes. I think I sort of expected him to come out spontaneously and say 'Hello' or watch me walk by as I had done in Shia processions just weeks earlier under his watchful eyes. He said he was about to go to bed. When I told him that I am taking part in a Hindu procession, he made a condescending sound and hung up on me. The hanging up is nothing peculiar here – I have gotten used to being cut off on the phone. But the sound he made when he heard what I was doing was clearly negative. Once, when I was discussing Hindu ritualistic practices with Mukhtar Bhai [whom I introduced in Chapter 1] after we had been talking about Shia mourning rituals, he said, shaking his head in disbelief, 'How can they worship an animal?' (Field notes, 30 January 2016)

For my Muslim interlocutors as well as for those Muslims whom I saw observing from the sidelines, the procession was categorized through their own positionality: by means of religious differentiation whereby the worshipping of animals was the one major thing they did in fact *not* have in common, since Shia Muslims also carry out elaborate processions throughout downtown which involve the parading of lavishly decorated physical objects and sometimes even the presence of animals, for example a horse during Ashura. Thus, for bystanders, the event was clearly marked as 'Hindu', foregrounding religion and thus, as I elaborated in Chapter 1, ethnicity. I have already engaged in complicating how ethnicity gets related to 'community' through the example of Aadita Auntie and her sister Veena Auntie, who frequent the temple but do not consider themselves member of the Śrī Kāmāchi community, as their ethnic background is Gujarati, not Tamil. In the following section, I intend to further complicate the predominant way of viewing public processions through a religious lens that often highlights 'the potential for conflict' (see, for example, Kong 2005: 225; Singh 2011).

Maximal integration behaviour

The feeling of sensory overload in the temple and during the procession contrasted starkly with the way the procession was organized and the orderly fashion in which it made its way through the city night under the watchful eyes of the temple trustees. Csordas has argued that while spontaneity is 'a phenomenological criterion of the divine', a lack of control is 'a criterion of the demonic' (Csordas 2002: 34). In this procession, both dimensions needed to go hand in hand. That the procession was a public event was clearly indicated by the necessary official requirements that need to be in place before any religious practice, object, or person-nel can leave the designated area of a temple, a mosque, a church, or a shrine. Publicity was generated by the leadership of the Śrī Kāmāchi trustees, who used this opportunity to make the community visible to outsiders, to inscribe their belonging onto the cityscape, to turn – at least momentarily – part of Yangon into their own place.

One could argue that throughout my fieldwork I was conducting what Sherry Ortner has called 'interface ethnography' – her term for 'doing ethnography in relatively enclosed and secretive communities … attending events in which the closed institution presents itself to "the public"' (Ortner 2010: 211). But what people saw as they followed the procession either by marching along, waiting along the roadside, or watching from their balconies or out of bypassing cars depended very much on their own positionality and knowledge about religious life in Yangon. The street was thus less 'the dwelling place of the collective', as Walter Benjamin (1999: 423) proclaimed in a general manner in his *Arcades Project*, than it was a platform on which different kinds of classi-fication evolved alongside different ways of sense-making that could be experienced. To fellow Hindus, fellow Tamils, and fellow worshippers at the Śrī Kāmāchi Amman Temple, the procession was recognizable not only as a Hindu procession, but also as an identifiably Tamil event be-cause of the musicians who spearheaded the procession, and as an event orchestrated by the Śrī Kāmāchi Temple members because of the statue of Śri Kāmāchi and the presence of particular individuals, mostly the trustees and the priests, who – as public figures – are known to fellow Hindus, albeit often not by their names, as we saw in the case of Aadita Auntie. To non-Hindus, however, it was not immediately clear who was in charge of the procession beyond 'the Hindu community'. In any case, one could argue that there was more than one public.

In his work on (media) networks of Moroccan trance brotherhoods, Martin Zillinger speaks of the graduated creation of a public as a trans-portable practice (referencing Csordas 2007) and of the 'infrastructur-ing of trance', thus representing actors' practices as not only conscious and strategic, but also technical in the sense that they can be 'crafted' (Zillinger 2017: 48). His concept of 'graduated publics' challenges the binary division of public and private by emphasizing the actors' use of ritual 'boundary objects' (Star and Griesemer 1998; Star 2010). His approach allows for a more nuanced understanding of the way public events get mediated and categorized by diverse audiences. The question is always: Public for whom? or, Whose public? In my case, the event can be interpreted as a demonstration of how a particular procession is possessed by a particular group that claims authorship and ownership over its orchestration. But throughout the night, I encountered various other types of classifications that show that more was going on than the careful crafting of publics by a predominant group such as the temple trustees.

While it had been a matter of pride for Amit Kumar to parade the statue of Śri Kāmāchi throughout Yangon, showcase the beautifully decorated carts, and fill the air with music and incense, thereby alert-ing all bystanders and onlookers to the centrality of their temple in downtown Yangon, the procession also had to take state policies into account. The state was thus present throughout the event, even though the police station along the procession route was deserted, and no other official showed up during the entire time. However, this was not taken by the trustees as a sign of success or of having conquered public space. While John Berger has argued that public processions aim at 'captur-ing' parts of the city, thus 'transform[ing] the areas through which they march into a "temporary stage" on which they dramatize the power they still lack' (Berger 1968, cited in Kong 2005: 245), my impression with ethno-religious processions in Yangon is that they do not aim to 'take over' public space or use their public presence to revolutionize their position in the urban environment. With the regulations of the YCDC and the police, and their power to control every movement firmly in place, temple trustees were aware that they had to carefully mediate the state's demands and their own goal of performing their sheer existence. Rather than aiming to overthrow the order of things or taking a chance and altering the route in the absence of immediate police control, they were thankful to be able to partake in public at all, to be able to use the urban space and – for the duration of this procession at least – to exist on an equal footing with, rather than in subjugation to, the Buddhist presence which permeates almost every aspect of public life in Yangon and elsewhere throughout the country. In contrast to the restrictions placed on the processions and events of ethno-religious minorities, vast spaces were usually granted to Buddhist monks giving *dhamma* talks in downtown Yangon, often over a total of three nights.[15] On one such occasion that I witnessed, the streets were closed off to all but foot traffic, carpets were laid out for practitioners to sit on, and a canopied and elevated platform was set up for the monks. In the evening, free food and drinks from nearby restaurants were distributed, sponsored by the entire neighbourhood – including some of the Muslim and Christian families and business owners.

In contradistinction to Piette's *minimal integration behaviour,* I suggest labelling performances such as the Śri Kāmāchi procession – that is, those that remain within the geographical and political limits of allotted urban space and that have been orchestrated by the trustees in a way that appeases state officials and the police by enacting a well-known trope of 'community' by outsider minority groups – as *maximal integration behaviour.* By doing exactly as they have been told, the trustees remained firmly in the subaltern position that had been assigned to them as members of an ethno-religious minority since colonial times. The kind of 'integration' that was being pursued here is in line with the shallow definition of the term we so often encounter in our own societies, where it means that those smaller in number are either expected

---

15. In both the Hindu and Buddhist traditions, these teachings or instructional talks are often referred to as *dhamma* talks. *Dhamma* is a Pali word, derived from the Sanskrit *dharma;* the wide range of meanings of this principle covers 'the natural order of things' and 'righteous behaviour', as well as 'duty' and 'law'.

to fit in and adapt or are given the 'savage slot' by means of separate legislation and exclusionary rules, with 'religion' being the element of identification most likely to justify differential treatment. In a way, they were 'accommodating themselves to the facts', as Nietzsche put it, by which he meant that people had learned 'to bend one's back and bow one's head before the power of history ... and thus to move one's limbs to the precise rhythm at which any power whatever pulls the strings' (Nietzsche [1874] 1997: 105). In another way, however, some managed to rhetorically keep the upper hand, countering the boundaries that they encountered in terms of their own free movement and in the way the material setup of their procession had to be arranged by appropriating certain Buddhist practices and recategorizing them as Hindu practices, as the following section shows.

Buddha as a Hindu god

The procession did not cater exclusively to the members of the Śrī Kāmāchi Temple nor only to Tamils nor even only to Hindus more generally; it had to be more inclusive. A Buddha statue had to be displayed at the head of the procession, thus indicating that Buddhists, too, could participate. In this case, as in many other cases, people had to follow the dictum that Hindu locations and Hindu events need to incorporate Buddha statues on their premises and in their processions. And indeed, I observed that not only Hindus, but also Buddhists lined the streets of Pabedan township, waiting for the carts to pass by, with offerings in their hand and requesting that the priests stop along the route to help them perform a mobile form of *puja*. I also took note of the fact that they placed their money directly at the feet of the Buddha statue, and that while most Buddhists gave to Buddha and only some to Ganesha, almost all Hindus gave to Śrī Kāmāchi. One possible reaction to this arrangement of prioritizing the Buddha, which I encountered during various Hindu processions throughout my fieldwork, would have been to complain or to criticize the organizers for turning a Hindu event into a Buddhist one. But I encountered a rather different way of handling the maxim, 'In Myanmar, Buddha comes first', which Amit Kumar had cited by way of explanation when I inquired about the order of the three carts.

Aadita Auntie, with whom I had walked alongside the carts for some of the procession, explained to me, 'They [the Buddhists] give to Hindus as well', using the Myanma adjective *Hin-du* without a noun so that it sounded like she meant 'Hindu people', although her statement could also be interpreted as referring to Hindu gods (*hpe-ya*). Thus, in her view, by donating to Buddha in the frame of this procession, Buddhists were bestowing their good wishes and good intentions, and their material wealth, onto the Hindus via this particular Buddha statue that belonged to the Śri Kāmāchi Temple. By physically engaging with this Buddha statue, Buddhists became Hindu without even knowing about their temporary membership. Jon Mitchell has argued that artefacts such as religious statues may become physical media for storing memory and thus come to 'embody the very thing which they are trying to represent' (1997: 90). Maurice Merleau-Ponty reminds us that an object is real in that 'it is given as the infinite sum of an indefinite series of perspectival views in each of which the object is given but in none of which it is given exhaustively' (Merleau-Ponty 2007: 92). Both points of view allow for the incorporation of the observer's thoughts about the practices of others and recognize that while the objects may be accessible to all, they may mean entirely different things to different people. In other words, shared religious practice does not rely on shared assumptions about these practices or shared meaning. To the contrary, in what could be interpreted as an outright denial of a reciprocity of perspectives, Aadita Auntie had transformed Buddhists' ritual practice into one that profited Hindus. In doing so, she had turned Buddha into a Hindu god. Aadita Auntie's rhetorical shift was not, however, a 'reaching out across cultural differences through dialogue, aesthetic enjoyment, and respect; of living together with difference' (Werbner 2008: 2); rather, it was more a self-assertion of her own classificatory hierarchy. I had heard repeatedly on other occasions from my Hindu interlocutors that in fact 'Buddha was a Hindu'[16] and that 'Buddhism is part of Hinduism'. In Myanmar, this is part of Hindu lay practitioners' religious knowledge and understanding, but it is also backed by Hindu intellectuals, as the following example illustrates.

During my fieldwork, I frequently visited U Tun Aung, a well-known and publicly outspoken individual, an academic, lawyer, and former trustee of the Myanmar Hindu Association, to learn about his views on the history of Hindu religious life in Myanmar, on his role in the interfaith movement and, more generally, on 'Hinduism'. He laid out the

---

16. In Myanmar, this is a dangerous thing to say out loud.

pragmatics of being Hindu in Myanmar over the course of what turned out to be a series of private talks in the tradition of a teacher–student relationship:

> *U Tun Aung: To tell you the truth, Hinduism is not at all a religion. It is the civilization of mankind, NOT of the Hindus. It is the upbringing of the human race as it is written in the* Vedas. *Veda means knowledge; the Burmese* Bay-da *is a mispronunciation of* Veda. *It concerns knowledge – not of physical matter, not of chemical matter, not of biological or botanical matter – it is nothing but knowledge. And where does that knowledge come from, I ask you?*

> *J:* [I look at him silently and continue listening.]

> *U Tun Aung: You gain it by working on it. That's what Hinduism says. Hinduism never said that there is a god who created everything. The Hindus, they knew it from the very beginning, and they are well aware that there is no such thing as a powerful god. That is in reality nature, the energy of nature. This is where we start. Hinduism is energy of nature. Energy in Sanskrit is* bram. Bram *is energy. So, we worship* bram *and for the common man, we turn it into* Bramma, *a person called* Bram. *But energy has no form. But we form it into something, attribute some form to* Bram *and call it* Bramma. *There comes in God. Who is God, I ask you?*

> *J:* [I remain quiet.]

> *U Tun Aung: Nothing but eternal energy –* bram. *And to be very clear:* bram *has no attribute. But for the common man, he wants to feel God, so we say* Bramma. *We give human attributes to God which God does not have. … Hinduism is not a separate religion. It is the way of being a good human being. To put it in Sanskrit terms:* mhanap dharam. *So why did it become a religion, I ask you?*

> *J: Because man needs something to cling onto?*

> *U Tun Aung* [ignoring my suggestion]: *We are not Hindus. We are* amana dharamis, *karmic people, lovers of nature, of truth. That is what we call ourselves until today. Hinduism is a term that was brought in by the British. Hindu-ISM is something like social-ISM, commun-ISM or some other -ISM: an ideology of worship. Why did they make it so?*

> *J:* [I remain quiet, understanding that he does not want me to answer his questions.]

> *U Tun Aung: There is influence of one matter, one solid matter on another – which Newton tells us is the law of force, the attraction of matter. There is*

a vibrational influence from one body to the other. So, to tame that vibration, to bring it into harmony, you have got to do certain things. That is what is meant by prayer. We put our will into that, we put ourselves into that. You tame yourself and in Hindi we say manmandala:[17] *You build a temple in your heart* (a-lone-tar-mhar-pha-yar-tae). *There is one Muslim friend of mine and I was arguing with him on Facebook. He said, 'The Islamists are helping mankind; they do good for humankind'. And I said, 'Build a temple in your heart. Don't paint the pagoda that you build in your heart!'*

J [nodding]: Hmmm …

U Tun Aung: 'Don't put colours on it. Make it a temple of purity!' I said. But people often don't think too deep. So, you've got to tell them: 'Ok, ok. You want to worship a big stone? And you think this is helping you? It may be a BIIIIG banyan tree, too. Or maybe a big rock or some other symbol. He may say: 'This is helping me!' LET HIM GO AND PRAY TO IT. Don't say no to him! If it gives him confidence and due to that confidence, he is gaining internal strength…

J: Can you tell me whether the same principle goes for the Hindu gods and goddesses in the temples?

U Tun Aung: The SAME thing! The same thing! These ROCKS – they are NOTHING but rocks!

(Excerpt from transcribed recording, 11 April 2016)

At least three points in U Tun Aung's monologue are worth mentioning in relation to the Śrī Kāmāchi procession. The first point concerns his invocation that it was 'the British' who brought in the term Hinduism, a thought he did not explicitly elaborate on, but did so by emphasizing what he considered important instead, namely humans' will-power and how that will-power relates to the law of the attraction of matter. By implication it follows that Hinduism, as an ideology, as he put it, was 'brought in' as a way of controlling and governing colonial subjects. By aligning it with socialism and communism, he compared it to political forms of governance that both aim at communalizing 'the people' while maintaining a strict hierarchical difference between 'the

---

17. Combination of Hindi *man*, from Sanskrit *manas*: 'mind', 'heart' and Hindi / Sanskrit *mandala*: 'circle', but also 'group', 'association'.

people' and those in power.[18] He is clearly critical of such a stratification of 'the people', whom he terms 'common men', and of the loss of their individual will-power that he associates with it. He does not attend festivities, for example, but goes to temples when the buildings have fallen quiet, arguing that the spectacles surrounding them distract him from his inner work. The second point concerns his metaphor of 'building a temple in your own heart' which, as I interpret it, shows on the one hand how strongly metaphors of religious practice are interlinked with sacred property, that is, the locations where the worshipping of 'stones' takes place, which he deems necessary for 'the common man running in the streets'. On the other hand, it shows how important individual improvement is to him. If one is capable of building a temple in one's own heart, one can be considered an advanced human being. Crucially, this seems to be independent of a person's specific religious beliefs. The third point is related to the second point: in his monologue, U Tun Aung recalled a conversation with a Muslim friend whom he deemed equally capable of truly understanding the principle of *manmandala* or of being *mhanap dharam*, a good human being, irrespective of his personal religious identification.

We know that 'religion' is a modern category and an invention of western secular Christian modernity (Casanova 1994). Both Hinduism and Islam have been turned into 'world religions' in the course of colonial engineering.[19] U Tun Aung is so keenly aware of this dynamic that he uses classical quotes from British colonial scholars when speaking at interfaith events in Myanmar, which often take place under the auspices of foreign NGOs 'doing good' (Fisher 1997) and the Myanmar state, and involve the active participation of local key representatives of the various 'world religions'. These events are widely broadcast by state media, and are usually attended by the same people – priests, pastors,

---

18. I consider it important to take seriously his point of treating religion that has become an '–ism' as a colonial invention of 'the British'. While Turner (2014: 114) has argued and shown in her book that '[i]t would be reductive ... to assert that colonialism invented Buddhism as a religion or imposed religion where no such idea existed' (see also van der Veer 1993 for a similar argument regarding Hindu–Muslim communalism in India), this is precisely U Tun Aung's view when it comes to 'Hinduism'.

19. On the construction of the idea of Hindu(ism) as the product of a complex colonial encounter see, for example, von Stietencron (2005) and Pennington (2005).

monks, imams and, when possible, a representative from 'the Jewish community'[20] – who appear side by side and speak about the need to get along with each other in times of crisis and conflict. All this happens in a very stereotypifying manner in which the main tenets of each religion are always presented to those in attendance. The focus lies not on knowledge dissemination but on spreading 'harmony ideology' (Nader 1990; Beyer and Girke 2015). It is noteworthy that the number of Buddhist monks present is always greater than the representatives of all the other denominations combined, while the Muslims are usually only represented by one or two Sunni imams.

In his presentations at these events, U Tun Aung, who likes to see himself as an intellectual rebel, uses the famous quote from a memorandum on 'Indian Education' by Thomas Macaulay (1835), a British historian who introduced compulsory English-language education throughout colonial India: 'We must at present do our best to form a class who may be interpreters between us and the millions whom we govern; [a class of persons] Indian in blood and colour, but English in taste, in opinions, in morals and in intellect' (Thomas Babington Macaulay, as cited on U Tun Aung's PowerPoint presentation). The colonial powers wanted 'a reformed, recognizable Other, as *a subject of a difference that is almost the same, but not quite*' (Bhabha 1984: 126, emphasis i.o.), and it is clear that U Tun Aung – despite being critical of British colonialism – not only identified with that class of anglicized intellectuals, but also saw his own role as an interfaith advocate as a direct continuation of Macaulay's policies. I quote from another 'lecture' he gave me in which he explained that one of the concepts that had done serious harm in his society was that of tolerance:

---

20. 'The Jewish community' in Yangon is so small that in order to unroll the *Torah* scroll (for which a quorum of ten adult – often male – members, called *minyan*, is required), they need to rely on foreign visitors to take part in the ritual. In fact, the Yangon community consists of one family only. By setting up a tourist enterprise that caters predominantly to American Jewish tourists, the family's only son not only realized a business for himself, but made sure that the 'community' was able to perform its key rituals at all – at least every time tourists are visiting. The family takes care of the beautifully renovated synagogue in downtown Yangon, which is featured regularly in foreign media. Ruth Fredman Cernea has written a fascinating ethnohistory of the Jews in Burma, entitled *Almost Englishmen: Baghdadi Jews in British Burma* (2006; for a review, see Beyer and Johnen 2014).

Fig. 3.11: 'FOR THE PRESERVATION OF COLONIAL-ISM': U Tun Aung shows me a quote from Thomas Macaulay, the British colonial historian, that U Tun Aung uses in his presentations at interfaith events. 11 April 2016.

U Tun Aung: Hinduism has given you the DEMOCRATIC freedom of thought, FREEDOM of worship, and FREEDOM of everything from the very beginning. This person, he might consult the lunar tables, he might go to the temple daily in the morning. There are thousands and millions of formulas and everyone will do it in his own way. What will the outcome be? There will be thousands [of formulas]. Hinduism is the only religion in the world that always keeps on changing with the times. Even Gandhi-ji . . . some people keep him as an idol of worship.

J: Hmmm . . .

U Tun Aung: They say, 'He is our lord.' Let them say it! Do not stop them! He does not have the capacity to understand. If another needs nats *['spirits'], he will have his mythology just as you will have psychology, philosophy, and the real knowledge of things.*

J: Hmmm . . . So, you are saying that Hinduism cultivates an attitude of tolerance towards cultural specificities?

U Tun Aung: I am EXACTLY telling you it is nothing but tolerance. But you know, tolerance is a term you use when you are not very happy with something, but you still let it go. In Hinduism, tolerance is not such a term. You have GOT to be understanding. When I go around the country for interfaith dialogue events, people ask me different types of questions and I always make them feel happy by answering them. We should never hurt anybody, but I still give my answer that must never go far from the real truth. But within the limits ... with a little ... sugarcoating...

J: [Laughs.]

U Tun Aung: ... to please a guy. Because we are going around the country to make people understand. Having tolerance is understanding. Unless you have an understanding of each other, feel sympathy for one another ... [he interrupts himself]. *But nowadays, people do not want to say the word 'sympathy' – they say 'empathy' – but what difference does it make?*

J: Hmmm...

U Tun Aung: Tolerance starts in reality with a negative attitude, but now they have brought it down to a neutral attitude.

J: Who is 'they'?

U Tun Aung: The users of the language.

J: In English, you mean? [meaning the language] ... or ...

U Tun Aung: In English. Whereas in Islam they are very angry when you say 'tolerance' because they take it in a negative way.

J: Like 'having to endure something'?

U Tun Aung: To endure something that you are not very happy with.

J: Hmmm...

U Tun Aung: In reality, it is that. But here [in Myanmar] *we use 'tolerance' usually NOT in a negative sense.*

J: What is the Burmese word you use?

U Tun Aung: Thi:hkan-chin. Thi:hkan-chin is neutral. When your children hurt you, you say thi:hkan-de. You tolerate. It is not negative. They are not doing anything bad. So, tolerance in reality is neither negative nor positive. It can be a neutral word.

J: So, looking at the rituals in the temples: What would be the right attitude for you when you observe what people are doing?

U Tun Aung: Well, open-minded. You should be open-minded, understanding ...

J: [Repeats] Understanding.

U Tun Aung: ... You should tell yourself that if this is what they enjoy doing, let them have peace and joy.

What I find interesting in his reflection on the word tolerance is the way he looked at it from the various perspectives of different language users: 'in Hinduism', by which he meant Hindi and Sanskrit languages, the word has a negative connotation for him, and he agreed when I asked whether one can associate it with 'enduring'. He then talked about English, but spoke of 'the users of the language', to whom he attributed the power to 'bring it down to a neutral attitude'. In his next sentence he then aligned 'Islam' with a more negative attitude towards the term, then specified that he was talking about people ('they are very angry'). Again, it is not along the lines of religious markers of identification that such concepts are understood from an emic perspective, but rather along divisions of class and (colonial) power.

The very next line of Macaulay's speech on 'Indian education' reads as follows: 'To that class we may leave it to refine the vernacular dialects of the country, to enrich those dialects with terms of science borrowed from the Western nomenclature, and to render them by degrees fit vehicles for conveying knowledge to the great mass of the population', which is U Tun Aung's 'going around the country'. He applied 'a little sugarcoating' – which I read as his way of saying 'code-switching' – to get his message across, thereby allowing 'tolerance' to 'become neutral' in these contexts. His example of the term being used in Myanma (even switching to Myanma while explaining this to me) is also telling: he used the analogy of 'being tolerant towards one's children', who might hurt you but not mean to – they just do not know better.

What U Tun Aung is doing here, I argue, is establishing the foundation for various types of *wes*, namely of those who classify alike, be it in terms of philosophy, knowledge, and psychology (he and I), or regarding the capacity to act as a mindful human (he and his Muslim friend), or regarding those who understand 'tolerance' to be a relatively negative term (Hindus and Muslims), or those who understand it in a more positive light (Burmese Buddhists and 'the users of English'). In all our talks, I found that he created common ground much more on the basis of individual overlaps in terms of interest, worldview, and experience than in terms of ethnicity or religion. He also aligned his own position much more closely with those of Muslim interlocutors and friends than with his fellow Hindus who, to him, were 'common men' who worshipped stones, or with Buddhists and 'English', whom he associated with 'the state' – the contemporary one as much as the colonial one. This is why he labelled his PowerPoint presentation 'For the Preservation of Colonial-ism', as this is how he viewed the politics of contemporary Myanmar as well as of external Western NGOs: their aim, in his eyes, is governance in the name of 'interfaith dialogue' and 'tolerance'. While thus continuing to carry out the task Macaulay envisioned for anglicized Indians such as himself, U Tun Aung at the same time despised the way British colonial engineers had worked their way into the minds and bodies of the subjects they governed.[21] But in line with my argument on the perpetuation of the subaltern positionality that my interlocutors assumed for themselves, his aim is not to revolutionize the order of things; he does not call for an end to 'colonial-ism', but merely diagnoses its 'preservation'. He even actively contributes to it by identifying himself as a member of 'the anglicized Indian class', but sees his job as subtly critiquing this very policy at the events where ethno-religious othering in the name of harmony ideology takes place.

Like Amit Kumar, the trustee of the Śri Kāmāchi Temple who had to make sure that the procession stayed within the permitted limits of Pabedan township, who had to order the sequencing of the statues so as to appease the authorities, and who was able to talk of his difficulties with me only in private, U Tun Aung could tear down the established demarcations along ethno-religious lines only in his talks to me. He then was able to form new groups that might convince himself (and me), but that would certainly not convince the 'common men running in the street' nor those watching from the sidelines. When he is himself 'going around the country' to spread the message of 'tolerance' together with representatives of the other 'world religions', he is fully aware of the colonial legacy he is thereby re-enacting, and he is highly reflexive about the very concepts with which he is expected to do so.[22]

---

21. Another PowerPoint slide of his featured a picture of Karl Marx and one of his quotes: 'Indian culture is semi-barbaric and is responsible for degrading humans to worship cows and monkeys as Gods'. U Tun Aung entitled the slide 'Bastard Insult of Indian Culture', which clearly shows where, ultimately, his loyalties lie.

22. U Tun Aung's understanding of the concept of 'tolerance' is remarkably similar to that of the anthropologist Glenn Bowman, who argued that tolerance is 'the benign version of the will to exclusion, and is prone – when the space of autonomous identity appears threatened by the presence of another – to rapidly transform itself into xenophobia' (Bowman 1997: 41).

Conclusion

In the first case I have presented in this chapter, a *we* more or less inadvertently emerged through an individual becoming possessed within a temple; in the second case, a procession of worshippers and statues outside the temple allowed for various *wes* to become apparent in public; in the third case, *wes* were formed by an intellectual's reasoning about what constitutes an individual's humanity and how to accommodate the fact that many people need material objects in which to ground their religious beliefs. While remaining at and within religious buildings, the very sites that have traditionally been used and understood as locations where ethno-religious othering takes place, and with the very actors who have conventionally been deemed to be the experts when it comes to the authentication of these practices, I have begun to explore practices of *we-formation* that occur in these very places alongside *the work of community*.

Individuals struggle with the tension between the sensory and the communal, a struggle that can be discerned in their practices and that has little chance of ever being resolved. I argue that in order to observe these troubled practices and to listen to differing interpretations of what the uniting and dividing lines between individuals might be, we do not have to leave their temples, their streets, and their stories – the *loci classici* of 'community studies'. To apprehend the subtler forms of we-formation, we just need to relearn how to use and trust our own senses when carrying out anthropological fieldwork and resist our impulse to interpret and to construct meaning. In the following chapter I will be turning to the courts where, rather than challenging 'the state' directly, my interlocutors (and their ancestors) have cultivated a subaltern position whereby they fight 'it' with its own weapons. While subalternity is always to be understood as an already social category ('subaltern groups', in Gramsci's terms), I will also continue to pay attention to how individuals realize their own existence by setting themselves up as the key engineers of their community.

CHAPTER 4

The making of a community in court

Most of the individuals I am concerned with in this chapter are members of the so-called Kalai community, a term familiar especially to older residents of Kyauktada township in downtown Yangon. But I set out by introducing the community's lawyer, U Maung Ba, who has fought one of the more recent battles for the Kalai, to which he himself does not belong. From exploring his individual point of view as a Buddhist engaged in what appear at first sight to be Hindu matters, I turn to the religious building around which most disputes have revolved: the Mahapeinne (Ganesha) Temple at the central intersection of Pansodan Street and Maha Bandula Road. The movement of the priests through the compound subtly mirrors the general politico-religious hierarchy prevalent in present-day Myanmar, as already encountered in the previous chapter. The material arrangement of the statues and other objects in the temple, as well as the way the temple staff has been put together, reveals the temple trustees' efforts to maintain the temple as a multi-confessional place of worship that explicitly invites non-Hindu practitioners into their compound. I then turn to the court cases that members of the Kalai community have fought over the course of the twentieth century. The entanglement of colonial-era jurisdiction and lawsuits and their present-day repercussions are highly revealing regarding how communities have been and continue to be made in Myanmar, usually – as demonstrated by this case – through their concrete relationships to physical places of worship.[1] When writ-

---

1. In addition to participant observation in the temple and extended conversations with members of the Kalai community, the lawyer, priests, and religious experts, my principal sources for this chapter are documents – some dating back to the early twentieth century – that had been rather haphazardly stored in a set of old cardboard boxes stacked on top of one another in a shed in a corner of the temple compound. They were in very poor condition when I first saw them, and it took me and my assistant, Seng Myaw, an entire month to go through the boxes,

ing about their own community, the Kalai use several Myanma terms interchangeably, the most common of which are *kalai-tain-yin-dha:* and *kalai lu-myo:*. Whereas the first emphasizes their indigeneity as Kalai, the second is more neutral and could be translated as 'the Kalai people'.

The chapter extends existing historical scholarship on the case of the famous Rangoon merchant U Ohn Ghine, who bequeathed his estate – including the Mahapeinne Temple – to his wife, Ma Yait, and their daughter Daw Nu, as a charitable trust. Trusts in general exist mainly in common-law jurisdictions and are established when there is property that does not belong or should no longer belong to a private individual. This sort of property needs to be administered by trustees. In Myanmar, trusts in general are legally regulated by the Trusts Act of 1882. In a tangled series of civil lawsuits within this family that were first heard by the Chief Court of Lower Burma in Rangoon in 1913 and then, in 1921, even reached the Privy Council in London, the judges had to decide whether U Ohn Ghine had, in fact, been a Hindu or a Buddhist. While Buddhist law would grant a large share of a deceased person's estate to a surviving widow and would treat the eldest male and female children to relatively equal shares, with smaller shares going to younger male and female children, Hindu law would in most cases exclude the widow and daughters from inheriting shares of the estate. As it turned out, the judges not only decided who was to be responsible for U Ohn Ghine's temple and compound, but also ended up enshrining a new type of community that was neither entirely Hindu nor entirely Buddhist. While this historical case has been analysed by Aye Kyaw (1994), Ikeya (2013, 2017), and Turner (2019) and is mentioned in other publications as one of the first cases in which religious identity became mutable, my analysis is the first to contribute current ethnographic data to the debate, showing how this long-standing historical dispute continues to influence relations between Hindus, Buddhists, Kalai, and the state to the present day.[2] In this case, 'community' is being put to work even by those who are not counted

---

dry the documents, winnow out those of interest from others, and put them in chronological and thematic order. I then returned the sorted originals, along with a table of contents, to my key interlocutors as a way of thanking them for the time and help they had given me on this case.

2. I wish to thank Alicia Turner for discussing the case with me and for giving me an opportunity to compare our materials.

among its ethno-religious members, such as the temple's Buddhist lawyer U Maung Ba. Moreover, the very arrangement and organization of the Mahapeinne Temple allows for practices of *we-formation* to be realized, irrespective of ethno-religious belonging.

Realizing a Buddhist self in an 'unorthodox Hindu temple'

When I visited U Maung Ba in his downtown office for the first time in 2015, he began to introduce himself even before I had a chance to say who I was and what I wanted. So I listened while he listed an impressive array of occupations, specializations, offices, and tasks, including running his own law firm, writing screenplays for films, working as a counsellor for ASEAN, and lecturing university students on intellectual property rights. He ended his presentation with the following words: 'But I am not proud of any of these things. I am only proud of the fact that I am the founder and builder of the Mahapeinne Pagoda.'[3] When I asked why, he elaborated:

> All the other tasks are lower in rank, but I am a Buddhist and Yangon is at the heart of our country, and Pansodan Street [where the temple is located] is at the heart of Yangon. Before, there was no pagoda there, but I built one in 2001. I became friends with U Sanny [one of the Mahapeinne Temple trustees at the time], who was a film director, and since I respect Hinduism and I enjoy the vegetarian food that they offer on banana leaves, I spent time with him at the temple. Later, when I began to shoot documentaries of the major pagodas in Yangon – Shwedagon, Sule, and Botataung – I found a small booklet which mentioned the Mahapeinne Temple – and it turned out that some of Gautama Buddha's hair was brought there on its way to the Botataung Pagoda! So I wanted to build a pagoda in the temple [compound] and U Sanny agreed.

When I inquired further about how he built the golden-coloured stupa with a square foundation (see Fig. 4.1), U Maung Ba described that in the 1980s there were four people responsible for the temple affairs: he himself, U Sanny, a woman who saw to the statue of the Chinese Buddhist Bodhisattva Guanyin, which is also housed in the temple compound, and another person who led a group devoted to the

---

3. The structure to which he is referring would more accurately be called a stupa, but U Maung Ba consistenly spoke of it as a pagoda, thereby likening it to other famous Buddhist monuments in the city.

Fig. 4.1: The Mahapeinne Pagoda, which U Maung Ba realized, and a temporary lean-to where monks from the nearby monastery recited mantras. The blue bottles of water had been brought to the temple grounds by surrounding businesses and were later picked up once the water had been sanctified. 19 November 2013.

Indian guru Sai Ba Ba that gathered every week around the guru's statue inside the prayer hall.[4] The four individuals donated one lakh each to build the foundation of the pagoda. In a letter of 23 February 1984 to the chairman of the Kyauktada Township Civil Council, they make a clear distinction between themselves and 'pure' Hindus (*hin-du-si-si*), referring to themselves as *bo'da-ba-dha hin-du-ka-bya:* (lit. 'Buddhist-Hindu half-caste/half-breed'). In another letter from the chairman of the temple to their own lawyer U Maung Ba, the Hindus are described as *tamil-lu-myo:-hin-du-ba-dha-win* (lit. 'Tamil people of Hindu religion').

Prior to building the foundation, U Maung Ba had soil collected from nine famous pagodas throughout the country in which some hair of the Buddha is kept as a relic (so-called *shwe sandaw*) and buried the

---

4. Sai Ba Ba (1926–2011) lived in India and was a self-proclaimed guru who drew hundreds of thousands of devotees from all castes to his ashrams. Among other things, he preached love and harmony between Muslims and Hindus. In the Mahapeinne Temple documents that I was working with, I found a poster with his portrait and the slogan, 'Religions are different but the goal is the same: even cows can be different in colour, but the milk is the same.' Sai Ba Ba also had critics who accused him of being a charlatan and of sexually abusing young men (Brooke 1982).

soil samples at the base of the new foundation.[5] 'This is how we turned the place into "the land of victory" [*aung myay*]', he explained. The four then invited a monk whom he had gotten to know through his literary endeavours to preside over the inauguration ceremony:

> *We did not apply for permission from the Ministry of Religion because they might have disturbed our plans. We built the pagoda ourselves – we only needed two powerful men: a monk and someone in the township administration [laughing]. Both supported us and once we were finished, we made an official announcement.*

When I asked how the ministry had reacted, he laughed again and said, 'They were very angry, but nobody sued us. It was during the time of General Khin Nyunt, and I knew him personally.' After I had visited U Maung Ba in his office several times and we had gotten to know one another better, he shared a more personal story with me to explain why he had been so invested in the 'Buddhification' of the temple:

> *In the early 1980s, the four of us first discussed an idea of mine to bring Bodhi-tree saplings from Bodh Gaya in India to Yangon.[6] Pilgrims went [to Bodh Gaya] and brought many seeds back. We germinated some of them and planted the strongest one in the temple compound. I was already working as an advocate during the 1988 revolution and had been a member of the lawyers' association during the [student] uprising, and I went on a hunger strike with the others. Then the military took over and I stopped practising law altogether. Instead, I wrote more screenplays, as I had always been interested in film. But I experienced problems and difficulties, I lost my house. It was a very difficult time for me. So I began meditating under the tree at the Mahapeinne Temple – there I was: homeless and poor. That was when I became more interested in Buddhism. Then I shared my plan of building a pagoda at the temple site.*

As a professional writer, U Maung Ba has written extensively on the history of the Mahapeinne Temple in various journals and newspaper articles.[7] In these texts, he emphasizes the temple's cosmological Buddhist connection, its strategic location, the similarity to a temple in

---

5.   He did not remember all of the places, but mentioned Pyi Shwe Sandaw, Bago Shwe Sandaw, Bagan Shwe Sandaw, Botataung, Sule, and Shwe Dagon.

6.   Bodh Gaya is the place in northern India where the Buddha is said to have achieved enlightenment.

7.   I am not at liberty to cite the specific articles by title, as U Maung Ba is a pseudonym and specifying the articles would reveal his identity.

Bagan which has been mentioned in the chronicles as the 'Mahapeinne Temple' (see Cooler 2002: ch. 3), and how the pagoda came into existence. But in our talks he also acknowledged that in the early 2000s he had lost his influence over temple affairs for a while, as new family members of the Kalai community entered the temple administration and older family members, such as U Sanny, vacated their seats. He had never had an official position and, while he praised one of the new trustees, who is a key interlocutor of mine and who had arranged my meeting with U Maung Ba, as a thoughtful and well-educated man, he still argued that this trustee was 'new' and did not know the temple's true history. He had even argued with one of the other family members and, in his own words, only regained a central role in temple affairs once a challenge from the Hindu Association became imminent during the time of my fieldwork in 2015 (see below).

From U Maung Ba's personal story, we can see how an individual's own religious identification as a Buddhist can be inextricably bound up with a place that is publicly recognized as Hindu. His characterization of the three friends with whom he administered the temple in the 1980s furthermore reveals that those in charge of the temple at the time seemed to have had quite divergent individual motivations that kept them invested and investing in temple affairs: for U Sanny, the temple administration was a family matter; the woman who took care of the Buddhist statue was said to have catered predominantly to the 'Chinese goddess'; and the third man was a devotee of the Indian guru Sai Ba Ba. As it turned out, their divergent interests and motivations were paradigmatic of the kinds of people who frequent the Mahapeinne Temple. Visitors not only come for very different reasons to the temple – some to attend a *puja*, others to ask the priest for *arccanai* (see below), yet others simply to escape the hectic downtown buzz for a few moments and pray in silence – they also address very different spiritual entities, ranging from Buddha statues, Bodhi trees, and the pagoda to Indian gurus, Chinese goddesses, Burmese spirits (*nats*) and, of course, Hindu gods and goddesses such as Shiva, Kali, and the elephant god Ganesha, after whom the temple is named: Mahapeinne is derived from the Sanskrit *maha vinayaka* and means Ganesha in Myanma.

According to U Maung Ba, the Mahapeinne Temple is publicly known as 'the temple of the five religions': Buddhists, Hindus, followers of Sai

Ba Ba, individuals who come to see the *nat* Aba Boe Min Khaung, and those who pray primarily to Guanyin. Traditionally, this set-up would be characterized as syncretism, understood as 'the manifestation in one site of practices or beliefs identified with more than one religion' (Hayden 2002: 219). However, at the Mahapeinne Temple, relations between the different groups frequenting the temple do not really become manifest, as there is little, if any, direct interaction. There is, therefore, not much to motivate competition or conflict, which are important aspects of syncretic religious practices that often tend to be forgotten (van der Veer 1994). Robert Hayden (2002) has shown for India how processes of competition between Hindus and Muslims may manifest as syncretism, with religious festivals being carried out jointly, clerics from different religious denominations being present and officiating at the same time, and saints even having 'double identities'.[8] But rather than syncretic harmony (or at least convergence), Hayden emphasizes the aspect of ongoing competition and the inclination towards conflict whenever religious groups interact. He put forward the concept of 'antagonistic tolerance' as characteristic of plural religious landscapes, drawing on examples such as Yugoslavia for comparison. He argues that there are always two possible explanations for why religious space has come to be shared in India: one emphasizes (the state's) approach to equality for all its citizens, which allows a Muslim shrine to exist in a predominantly Hindu society; the other views Muslim religious presence as proof of the ongoing dominance of Muslims over Hindus. In Hayden's case study, Muslim symbols are ultimately excluded through the actions of the Hindu nationalist Shiv Sena party. He reminds us that '[u]nder religious nationalism, minority religions themselves are seen as illegitimate, and therefore symbols of their very presence may not be tolerated' (2002: 217). We are currently witnessing the continuing manifestation of such politics in contemporary India.[9]

---

8. See also Richard Temple's (1925: 9) work on shrines built in memory of the northern Indian Sufi saint Pir Badr al-Din Auliya: 'To the Buddhists he is a *nat*; to the Hindus he is a *deva* or inferior god; to the Muhammadans a saint; to the Chinese a spirit'. See also Kumar (2022).

9. So-called 'cow-related violence' (also known as 'bovine politics') is on the rise in India (Basu 1994; Abraham and Rao 2017; Sathyamala 2018; Staples 2018; Adcock and Govindrajan 2019). Recently, Shiv Sena has toned down their 'communal rhetoric' against Muslims in public discourse (Poojari 2021).

But what we have in the Mahapeinne Temple case is very different, as there is no direct competition between religious groups for control over shared space. What has been fought over for a century now, however, is control of the trusteeship, as it is through access to this office that claims to the entire estate can be made. In addition, the individuals opposing each other in this arena are not the same as those who frequent the temple. In fact, the way the temple has evolved (and continues to be modified since I began fieldwork in 2013) reflects efforts of the acting trustees to counter the danger of an outside takeover from either Hindus or Buddhists (or both). Their approach has been to allow a specific version of syncretism to emerge in the temple – namely, one where there is no actual sharing, no reciprocity, and no direct interaction, but rather an ostentatious co-presence of religious objects, religious practitioners, and religious practice.

Making the rounds: hierarchy and co-presence in the temple

When I followed the temple priests on the rounds of *puja*s that they carried out every morning and evening, usually without an external audience, I noticed that they always took the same route: starting from the Bodhi tree, they would begin by lighting candles in front of the large sitting Buddha statue underneath the tree. They would then turn towards the pagoda, circle it once, and proceed into the prayer hall, where an array of Buddha statues is quite centrally located. They would perform prayers there, again light candles and incense, and only then go back outside to pray in front of the statues of Shiva, Kali, Krishna, Ganesha, and others. Finally, they would return to the prayer hall and pass by the displays and statues of the *nats*, of Guanyin, and of Sai Ba Ba.

When I asked why they do the *puja* in this particular manner, their answer was almost identical to the one I had received in other places such as the Śrī Kāmāchi Amman Temple (see Chapter 3): 'We are in Myanmar, so we start from the Buddha.'

Three priests work in the Mahapeinne Temple at all times. From my first visits in 2013 until my last in 2020, two of them had remained the same, whereas the third had returned to his home country, Nepal, and was replaced by another one from that country.[10] Of the remaining two,

---

10. Both of these Nepalese priests were introduced to me as 'Gurkha', a name used for Nepali soldiers who fought in the Nepalese, British and Indian Army (and who

Fig. 4.2: Two of the temple priests begin the morning *puja* by lighting candles in front of the Buddha under the Bodhi tree. 2 November 2013.

one was also Nepalese, but born in northern Myanmar; the other had Tamil ancestors. All three were Brahmin, which was clear from the thin white robe they wore around their upper body. In addition to the priests, the trustees also employed a manager who was a Buddhist. During my fieldwork, this position was re-staffed twice – each time with a self-identifying Buddhist. The manager's task was to properly explain the temple to all (Myanma-speaking) visitors, to facilitate contacts with the nearby monastery, and to deal with all necessary paperwork with the city administration, the warden of the township, the police, and other state institutions whenever necessary.

There also were two cooks, a security person, and several helpers, all of whom lived in the adjacent hall on the compound, where each of them had a little room for themselves. Only one of the priests returned to his family in downtown Yangon every night; the others stayed at the

were not of Brahmin origin). The fact that the trustees used the name 'Gurkha' was in line with their acknowledgment that they knew little about Hinduism and the difference between Brahmin and non-Brahmin. Since Gurkha soldiers helped the Burmese fight against the Japanese in the Second World War, they are very positively received in Myanmar, which might be why the trustees chose to present them to me as such.

Fig. 4.3: One of the priests playfully teases an employee. She was folding donated sarees in the shelter on the edge of the compound. Temple staff store their belongings and sleep in the back of the shelter. 19 November 2013.

temple. All helpers identified themselves as Buddhist with the exception of the cooks, who were Hindus, and the family that took care of people's shoes outside at the entrance of the temple, who were Sunni Muslim. The atmosphere among the personnel was friendly and cheerful. They all received monthly salaries, free food, and accommodation, and enjoyed working in the temple.

But what kind of temple is the Mahapeinne Temple after all? For an institution to qualify as a temple, Arjun Appadurai (1981: 18–19) has posited the following requirements: as a sacred space it needs to provide a royal abode for the deity enshrined in it; as a process, it has a redistributive role where transactions between worshippers and deities are continuously enacted; and as a system of symbols 'it provides an arena in which social relations in the broader societal context can be tested, contested, and refined'. The Mahapeinne Temple fulfils all of these criteria, so its 'templeness' is not questionable from an analytical point of view, nor is it questioned locally. What is at stake, however, is its 'Hinduness'. Appadurai has also alerted us to the fact that a temple deity acts like a sovereign ruler, the rituals and processions carried out in its name resemble those for royalty, and the parts of the temple architecture 'are considered to be parts of the … divine body' (Appadurai 1981: 22). The Mahapeinne Temple, however, hosts not only a variety of Hindu gods and goddesses, but also non-Hindu statues and material objects, particularly Buddhist ones. Appadurai's model emphasizes the principle of one sovereign deity whose 'body' is the temple, albeit with the possibility that several 'subshrines' for 'subordinate deities' be present (1981: 23, 26). In the case of the Mahapeinne Temple, however, it is not clear from the way it is set up who that sovereign deity is, despite the reference to Ganesha in the temple's name. In the various historical documents I have gathered over my years of fieldwork, the temple is also referred to as the 'Vishnu Temple', the 'Śri Vishnu Bari-Temple', and the 'Kalai (unorthodox Hindu) Temple'. Nowadays, it is usually called by the English name 'Ganesha Temple'. The American art historian Don Stadtner describes it as 'one of only a few where many local Buddhists participate in Hindu rituals' (Stadtner 2011: 130). But why is Ganesha not more clearly the dominant deity, and why is it so important for Buddhists like U Maung Ba?

This question is best answered by listening to members of the Kalai community themselves, under whose trusteeship the temple has been since 1856, when a man called Cumara Pillay (his Burmese name was U Shwe Moung) applied for a so-called free land grant from the East India Company. The East India Company was an English (later British) trading company that was founded in 1600 and operated in India and then Burma from the mid-eighteenth century onwards. These land grants were given after the British brought large numbers of personnel from India to Rangoon (starting in 1840) to help them in the process of colonizing Burma. Cumara Pillay was granted the land and began to build a temple.[11] We do not know much about him, but judging from his

---

11. As I laid out in Chapter 2, religious land had been exempt from taxation. However, I came across tax receipts from 1941 showing that the temple was subject to 'municipal taxes' (which included a general tax, a tax for conservancy, and taxes on lighting and water). Moreover, on a copy of a map of the temple compound dating from 1952–1953, the property is marked as 'freehold land' (in contrast to other maps I have seen where religious land is referred to as 'sacred property' or so-called 'green land', after the colour that was used to highlight the respective part of the property that was to remain unaltered; on freehold land see also Rhoads 2018). I also found one receipt, dated 1950, for payment of rent on the land to the Rangoon Development Trust. Since all of these documents had been relegated to

last name, he was most likely a Tamil from Madras (today's Chennai). His son, U Ohn Ghine, however, is a famous figure in the history of Rangoon. Crucial parts of his life story are summarized in various court documents, and some aspects are publicly displayed on the very premises of the temple. The most noteworthy aspects of his life – and those especially cherished by my interlocutors – include having been presented with 'The Company of the Indian Empire' award by Queen Victoria and having attended the coronation of King Edward in London in 1902 as the only Burmese person invited. He invested in hospitals, the sports stadium, and other infrastructural projects in Rangoon, and also supported Buddhist reforms and Buddhist institutions in both Burma and India. When he died, his ashes were sent to India, where they were sprinkled in the Ganges River in accordance with Hindu rituals. After his father's death, U Ohn Ghine bought two more adjacent plots of land and, after his death in 1911, his daughter, Daw Nu, continued to take care of the property. The temple was completely destroyed in World War II by Japanese bombers, but Daw Nu rebuilt the foundation in 1952 and finished the renovations in 1955 with a Buddhist water-pouring ceremony in the presence of monks from the *sangha*. Every year the temple celebrates Shiva's birthday (*Shivaratri*), thereby joining all other downtown temples in a festival at which practitioners wander from one temple to the next until late at night. It was on Shivaratri 2013 when I first met U Thin Thain Moung,[12] the grandson of U Ohn Ghine.

Celebrating Shiva's birthday

On 10 March 2013, I spent the evening at the Mahapeinne Temple to attend the annual birthday party in honour of Shiva. People were arriving in small groups, with the women particularly well-dressed in colourful *sarees* and adorned with sparkling jewellery. Inside the temple compound I noticed that visitors did not really mingle, but rather remained

---

the old boxes in the shed while other documents (such as court decisions) had been carefully preserved, they must have been deemed of little value by the former trustees. Proof that the temple is theirs thus did not seem to rely on these kinds kind of documents or, perhaps because they give a conflicting account, they might have been deliberately set aside.

12. I deviate from the usual transliteration when I write 'Moung' instead of 'Maung', as this is how U Thin Thain Moung wanted it to be written.

Fig. 4.4: Entering the temple for Shivaratri. 10 March 2013. Colour version on page 287.

in their initial groups of a few individuals. There was no noticeable meet and greet, no 'Hello, how are you?' Everyone seemed to be going about their own business, which was to perform the *arccanai*, a form of private worship for which practitioners enter into contact with one or several of the deities through a temple priest who is asked to make an offering on their behalf. Similar to the procession I described in Chapter 3, offerings consisted of trays of fruit, candles, and powder that could be bought at the counter in the prayer hall for 2,000 kyat each. Since the demand was particularly high on Shivaratri, the trustees had invited additional priests from the outskirts of Yangon to help them, which made it possible for one priest to be 'stationed' at every statue. In the following, I delve deeper into what I call *the work of community* by way of a brief detour through the nexus of economic and religious anthropology.

Appadurai (1981), drawing on Marshall Sahlins's distinction (1972), has characterized *arccanai* as 'a *between* relation, the action and reaction of two parties' (Sahlins 1972: 188, emphasis in original), whereas *puja* worship is characterized as a redistributive process, understood as a '*within* relation, the collective action of a group' (Appadurai 1981: 33, emphasis in original). When the priests do their daily rounds in the morning and evening, they perform them in solitude, yet 'within', on behalf of an imagined community of worshippers who are non-present.[13] When practitioners hand them offerings, the priests are mediators 'between' these individuals and the gods. This differentiation holds true not only in the case of Hindu practitioners, but also for Buddhists who enter the Mahapeinne Temple with the aim of receiving a service for which they are remunerating the priests.[14] If one takes into account recent anthropological scholarship on the 'Buddhist gift' (Brac de la Perrière 2015; Coderey 2015; Sihlé 2015) that challenges claims about the universality of the gift as originally posited by Mauss ([1902] 1990) for the Buddhist context, it becomes evident that, with the exception of the morning and evening *puja*, all offerings fall into the category of 'a *between* relation', as they serve the same particular purpose: the provision of a service by the priests in their role as religious specialists and their remuneration through the practitioners. In other words, none of these offerings is a gift, not even the donations that are dropped in one of the many donation boxes that have been placed throughout the property.[15] Thus, no binding obligation between human beings is created, and no reciprocal exchange is initiated. In short, the elaborate *arccanai* do not help the creation or maintenance of community. And while the nature of *puja* is different, the de facto non-presence of community members (whoever they might be) while the practice is being carried out by the priests lets us equally question how this religious practice might enable the coming about or the strengthening of community in the temple.

---

13. Appadurai built a model of a 'three-way transactional system' in which temples, kings, and sectarian leaders were connected through what was transacted between them – honours, material resources, or both – thus 'uniting Brahmins and non-Brahmins in a single community organized by service to a single sovereign deity' (1981: 46). The 'day-to-day management of the temple was not a simple matter of a hierarchical pyramid of authority but rather involves the orchestration of a complicated set of "honorable" shares in the divine polity of the deity' (1981: 61).

14. I have some anecdotal evidence from conversations I overheard at the temple that Buddhist practitioners often come to the priests to ask them to ward off the evil eye. However, I did not interact with many Buddhist practitioners on a regular basis, and while one of the priests whom I asked affirmed this, I do not have more systematic data on what exactly brings Buddhist practitioners into Hindu temples, even unorthodox ones such as the Mahapeinne Temple.

15. The exception being donations by foreign tourists, who sometimes throw in a dollar bill after having visited the temple without buying a tray filled with offerings for a religious service.

Fig. 4.5: Receiving and passing baskets filled with flower petals from right to left. In the background on the right, a member of the staff (in a white shirt) places fresh flowers into the baskets. 10 March 2013. Colour version on page 288.

Even during Shivaratri, which I attended in 2013 and 2016, the practitioners were interacting with one another only through the mediation of material objects, such as the ritualistic passing along of baskets of flower petals while sitting in a large circle on the floor of the temple hall, and by repeating the prayers of the religious experts. Before and after this coordinated practice, I observed no interaction between them apart from conversations among those who had arrived together and obviously knew one another. Going from temple to temple during Shivaratri in both years, I found this pattern repeated. Whereas the procession of the Śrī Kāmāchi Amman Temple as discussed in the previous chapter had been organized by one temple and was joined by practitioners from the neighbourhood (both Hindu and Buddhist), Shivaratri is an annual gathering where all temples enter into a joint celebration with all statues remaining inside their respective places of worship. In this case, it is the practitioners who join in a procession through the entire downtown area, thereby connecting the temples through their movements. For this occasion, many Hindu families from the outskirts of Yangon, who usually do not frequent any of these locations, travel downtown. While the individuals who engage in various interactions described above remain strangers to one another, for the duration of the actual practice I would suggest that a *we* is nevertheless situationally being formed. For this experience, however, the individuals' religious denomination – whether Buddhist or Hindu – or any sort of knowledge about one another is irrelevant.

I have come to understand Shivaratri as a family-centred event as well as an opportunity for young people to cruise through the downtown area, going from temple to temple, spending a full night out with their friends. 'We are celebrating Shiva', said a young girl laughingly when I inquired where she and her friends, who were all sitting in an open pickup truck in front of the temple, were going to next. There was a lot of recorded music being played inside the temples in addition to the already raucous soundscape that the bells and gongs and drums produced, and the music blasting from the loudspeakers of every car full of young people only added to the cacophony. A few days earlier I had noted large posters in the vicinity of the various temples, on which the All Myanmar Hindu Central Council, an association formed by the Ministry of Religious Affairs and under its direct command, had warned of exactly such 'illegal' behaviour:

> The Hindu Maha Shivaratri … coincides with the matriculation exam period. Although this festival has a tradition of being celebrated in temples, sometimes pilgrims parade around town in their cars. While they are parading around town, they are engaging in illegal activities, such as carrying loudspeakers in their car and playing loud music which annoys the neighbours. The Hindu Central Council has been directed to ban these practices. We thus urge to all [members of] Hindu temples not to parade too noisily, and we will strongly monitor all such behaviour. (Poster signed by the chairman of the All Myanmar Hindu Central Council, 22 January 2016)

This message only produced laughter when I discussed it with my research assistants, for we were all accustomed to Buddhist sermons, both played from CDs and live on stage in the streets, which are commonly amplified by loudspeakers permanently installed throughout Yangon. These sermons would sometimes go on for several days non-stop and interrupted our sleep patterns. I found it to be an expression of wilful defiance that the young people continued to play music that one night of Shivaratri.[16]

---

16. One of the priests told me that similar written announcements had been distributed the previous year, but that enforcement was expected to be stricter this year. However, I did not see anybody stepping in.

The way people gathered during Shivaratri was thus very much along the lines of family and friends rather than along the lines of how community is usually understood in both the academic literature and the local discourse in Myanmar. While I walked around with the aim of closely observing the different *arccanai* performances that were being carried out in front of the various statues and the passing on of flower baskets inside the prayer hall, I was suddenly approached by an elderly man in his sixties who had been standing next to the pagoda, likewise observing the crowds. 'This is the place where Buddhists and Hindu worship together', he said in English. 'Anyone can come; you are also welcome here. We allow everyone to come and pray to whomever they want to pray to.' As it turns out, the person who initiated the conversation was the chairman of the temple and the nephew of Daw Nu, the daughter of U Ohn Ghine. The temple had always been in his family's possession, he explained. It had been founded by his great-grandfather, Cumara Pillay.[17]

'Every race and religion has the chance to worship freely'

While U Thin Thain Moung told me his family history in his own words over the following months, the trustees also made sure that all locals who entered the temple would be informed about it without even being required to speak to him or anybody else: the history of the temple is inscribed in stone near the Bodhi tree, that of the pagoda on a separate inscription nearby. Over the course of my fieldwork, several other objects appeared in the compound, among them a huge genealogical chart that the trustees put up in 2015 listing all family members of the Kalai community who had held administrative positions in the temple (see Fig. 4.6 below). The chart begins with the original founder U Shwe

---

17. Our talk in 2013 during Shivaratri was the beginning of a long-term engagement with his family's history and the temple. He introduced me to his family members, paved the way for me to access all documents that were in his possession, allowed me to contact other relevant figures, and let me film and photograph on the temple premises whenever I wanted to. Communicating in impeccable English with me, he would sometimes remark that if I had been a man, he would have enjoyed drinking whiskey with me while talking about his family history, but tea or coffee worked just fine for both of us. I owe him a great deal and thank him here for his openness and trust. Sadly, he died at the end of 2019 and thus did not live to see this book.

Fig. 4.6: Genealogy chart installed inside the prayer hall showing the Kalai family members with their respective office titles. On the right side of the chart hangs a portrait of Daw Nu, the daughter of U Ohn Ghine. 11 November 2015. Colour version on page 288.

Moung (Cumara Pillay) and his wife Daw Mayma, who was, according to the family, the first Burmese Buddhist woman to marry a Hindu. Their offspring, among them U Ohn Ghine, are thus listed as the first members of the Kalai community.

According to the chart, U Ohn Ghine married Daw Daw Yait (Ma Yait), and three children are listed: Daw Nu, U Aye Moung, and U Thain Moung, each with their spouses. Chit Maung, who initiated a notorious lawsuit against his mother and sister upon his father's death (see below), is not mentioned. U Thin Thain Moung is mentioned on the chart as the chairman. In another chart exhibited in the hall, the direct genealogy shows that he occupied the central position in the 'maintenance team', which is the term U Thin Thain Moung used to refer to the group of people in charge. The line of succession of leaders of this team starts with Cumara Pillay and moves on to U Ohn Ghine, Daw Nu, U Sanny and, finally, to U Thin Thain Moung.

Moreover, from 2015 onwards, several new documents were posted right at the entrance to the prayer hall for everyone to read, including a short history of the temple that focused on its founders and all the

Fig. 4.7: The late U Sanny (left) and the late U Thin Thain Moung (right) flanking the portrait of U Ohn Ghine in U Sanny's living room. Uncle and nephew are framed by Buddhist and Hindu altars. 15 November 2015. Colour version on page 289.

people who had donated statues or given money for renovations. The document also reiterates several times that the temple had been built for 'all races and religions'. Why were these texts made public and so prominently displayed inside the temple? And why was it deemed necessary to hang a genealogy of the 'maintenance team' inside the prayer hall? What are the connections between the 'maintenance team', the trustees to the family of U Ohn Ghine, and the Kalai community? To answer these questions, I now turn to a long series of disputes involving the family of U Ohn Ghine that centre on the issue of who has the right to the trusteeship of the Mahapeinne Temple. As we shall see, this question is entangled with the very identity of the Kalai community, and whether U Ohn Ghine was a Hindu, a Buddhist, or something else entirely. I tackle the copious data that I gathered on this extended case and its long trail of court documents by focusing on the role (colonial) state courts played in the making of a community, in order to formulate an argument about how individuals have fought 'the state' with its own weapons. This requires rethinking the conventional wisdom on the relationship between (colonial) state courts and the general population, particularly members of ethno-religious communities.

'To err is human, to forgive is divine'

In 1899, Burmese and Indian men ransacked shops in the coastal town of Moulmein (today's Mawlamyine) in their haste to buy socks. A local European judge had demanded that nobody should appear before him without 'proper attire' anymore. This angered the chief commissioner of British Burma, Albert Fytche, who argued that 'the mere wearing of a pair of shoes and stockings would enable any Burman to claim the right of walking into our Courts in a fashion dissimilar from anything he does attempt in any other place' (Fytche 1878, cited in Turner 2014: 111). Burmese should be allowed to enter courts without socks – not out of respect for their culture, but to ensure that they 'remained on a lower rung', Fytche said (ibid.). While Alicia Turner has analysed this episode in regard to the civilizing mission the British sought to undertake in Burma, I invoke it here as an early example that proves that 'Burmese and Indian men' seemed to have taken to colonial courts with enthusiasm. If nowadays scholars argue that '[t]he last place a person in Myanmar would go to resolve a dispute or assert their rights is a court of law' (Aguirre 2018), and that ethnic minorities in particular prefer alternative legal fora for dispute resolution (Harrisson 2018; Kyed 2018; Than Pale 2018), then we need to understand what has changed over the course of the last century or, perhaps, pay closer attention to who exactly no longer turns to the courts and who, in fact, continues to do so – and for what reasons. In the case of my interlocutors, interaction with the courts – colonial as well as present-day – has consistently been frequent. In all of my case studies I found historically important and even ongoing court disputes that centred in one way or another on the issue of trusteeship, that is, on who has access to religious property and the right to decide over it. Moreover, all of the groups I have been working with had their own lawyers, and in every case, it turned out that more than their religious building was at stake.

In Burma as well as in contemporary Myanmar, nobody expects the courts to be neutral. Maung Maung Kyi, a former Rangoon judge during colonial times and a devout Buddhist, put it as follows: 'There is no denying the fact that ideal justice has to give way sometimes to practical convenience' (1987: 94). While this might sound more threatening than anything, one of his examples is that when the Burma Socialist Party took over the government in 1948, it issued an amnesty order granting freedom to everyone imprisoned at the time in order to start with a 'clean slate'. Maung Maung Kyi justified this decision with the time-honoured maxim, 'To err is human, to forgive is divine' (1987: 103). Recently, Nick Cheesman has investigated Myanmar's colonial and current state courts as sites of political activity and interaction. While in his book he focuses on how 'the state' has mobilized the court system whenever it wants to invoke 'law and order', understood as instances where 'rulers make use of law for their own ends' (2015: 23), my focus rests on how my interlocutors and their ancestors have likewise approached state courts to do the same. In other words, state courts are not only sites of political activity and interaction where the 'haves come out ahead', to cite a classic notion from legal anthropology coined by Marc Galanter (1974) to describe how legal systems shield those already in power; state courts are also sites to which the 'have-nots' turn once they have found a hook with which to latch onto and enter 'the system'. I argue that in my case the 'hook' with which my interlocutors 'captured' a string of positive judgments from British colonial-era and later postcolonial courts in Burma was to invoke the category of the ethno-religious community.

The Code of Civil Procedure from 1908 regulates the affairs of ethno-religious communities in Myanmar to the present day. The code, along with many other laws, came into force when Lower Burma became part of India. In contrast to many other laws and codes, mostly those concerning the interests of potential foreign investors, this code has been amended only minimally in the time since Burma gained independence in 1948. It is the basis for all kinds of civil disputes, with the unaltered Article 92 of this code being particularly relevant to my case, as it concerns 'public charities' in general and 'trusts of a religious nature' in particular:[18]

> In the case of any alleged breach of any express or constructive trust created for public purposes of a charitable or religious nature, or where the direction of the Court is deemed necessary for the administration of any such trust, the Attorney-General, or two or more persons having an interest in the trust and having obtained the consent in writing of the Attorney-General, may institute a suit, …, to obtain a decree –
>
> a) removing any trustee;

---

18. See The Code of Civil Procedure [India Act 1908], Part V, Art. 92.

b) appointing a new trustee;

c) vesting any property in a trustee;

d) directing accounts and inquiries;

e) declaring what proportion of the trust property or of the interest therein shall be allocated to any particular object of the trust;

f) authorizing the whole or any part of the trust-property to be let, sold, mortgaged or exchanged;

g) settling a scheme; or

h) granting such further or other relief as the nature of the case may require.

I am particularly concerned with who may bring a lawsuit against 'a trust', under what conditions and in regard to what points. This law covers administrative issues, meaning how a trust should be dealt with; issues of personnel – that is, who should be entitled to administer the trust and who should not; and also decisions regarding what should happen with trust property and the issue of 'settling a scheme', meaning the charter or constitution of a religious trust. For my interlocutors, the boundaries between the trust, the property that the trustees should take care of, the community, and their family are fluid.

The coming into being of 'the Kalai community'

In Yangon, the court that has been and continues to be addressed in these cases is the Yangon High Court – it used to be called the Chief Court of Lower Burma – and it was the highest court institution in the country up until recently, when the government instituted a Supreme Court in the new capital Naypyidaw. But for Yangon, the High Court remains the central judicial institution. After we had gotten to know each other better, U Thin Thain Moung gave me some documents that he intended to submit to the Yangon City Development Committee (YCDC) in support of a request for a land ownership certificate stating that the temple indeed belongs to his family. The original land grant from the mid-nineteenth century had been lost, he claimed. According to him, the land was granted as private land. This seems to be likely, as a 1953 judgment by the High Court of Judicature in Rangoon, which was among his collection, stated the following:

... the Temple site in suit was acquired nearly a century ago for the purpose of building a Hindu Temple and the ancestors of the present defendants did erect one and manage the same. The original Trustees appear to have been 1. Jugeen Doss China Tumbe, 2. Coomarapa [sic] and 3. Yanappah who were later succeeded by 1. U Ohn Ghine, 2. Maung Mo and 3. Maung Po ... after whose demise the 1st defendant, the eldest daughter of U Ohn Ghine, and other members of U Ohn Ghine's family succeeded to these offices.[19]

Later, the judges reiterated that 'the management of the Temple affairs has been a family affair of the defendants who have imposed upon themselves the rather heavy burden of reconstructing the Temple' (§8). This judgment is particularly interesting as the disputing parties were fighting over a temple that – at the time of the lawsuit – did not exist, having been completely destroyed by Japanese bombers during the war. Immediately after the destruction, members of the Hindu Association (distinct from the Myanmar Hindu Central Board) began to make claims on the temple. The Hindu plaintiffs brought two charges against Daw Nu: misconduct and mismanagement. The misconduct concerned the personal failure of Daw Nu and her family to take care of the temple compound and its objects. The plaintiffs claimed that the temple's religious statues had been defiled and desecrated during the bombing and were not stored properly afterwards. Because of this misconduct, the property was no longer a temple, they claimed, and the statues were no longer sacred objects. Moreover, there had been no daily *puja* rituals performed in front of the statues. Witnesses testified that '[O]nce the images were removed from the places where they were permanently affixed in the Temple they had lost their sanctity and since the Temple had been descreated [sic] by the bombing, a sacramental ceremony is also required to be carried out.'[20]

Daw Nu argued against this claim, saying that the *puja* had been performed in front of the broken statues, which were housed in a temporary shed, and also that the annual festivals continued to be celebrated despite the destruction. The court supported her on this point, noting that she had already begun to restore large parts of the temple compound

---

19. *Shiwadhari Shukla vs. Daw Daw Nu*; Judgment of the High Court of Judicature at Rangoon, 9 June 1953, §3.
20. Witness Ar Mugan, witness J.G. Joshi.

in 1952. The judge spoke of 'a work of merit of the principal members of the U Ohn Ghine family' (§6). The judge also dismissed most other issues brought forward by the Hindu plaintiffs, such as their claim that the family had sold bricks from the temple buildings or erected stalls to sell products on the temple compound. In a leaflet that I found among the documents in the cardboard boxes in the shed on the temple compound, the Hindu Association, which claimed to speak on behalf of all Hindus, referred to the family's behaviour as an 'antireligious act' and urged the 'larger body of Hindu worshippers' to occupy the temple compound every Sunday for religious events. It is clear that their aim was to eventually take over the temple and its administration. However, the court rejected the charge that the removal of bricks was in breach of the trust scheme, concluding that it constituted an 'ordinary incident' after the war had left the temple in ruins and 'would not have merited the attention of the police authorities' (§8). The respective judgment not only ruled that Daw Nu had acted in accordance with the scheme in terms of the renovation of the premises, but also affirmed that she, as the daughter of U Ohn Ghine, along with other members of the family, had rightfully occupied the trustee positions.

Finally, the judges dealt with Daw Nu's request to alter several parts of the trust scheme of the temple in order to avoid future lawsuits. In the scheme, which itself was settled only after a lawsuit in 1935,[21] the trust was designated as the 'Kalai Temple Trust', and both temple and trust were 'required to be maintained for the use and benefit of Kalais and Hindus' (§3, 1953). As early as 1913, and subsequently in 1921 and in 1950, the court had decided on issues relating to the family of U Ohn Ghine. While these early cases have already been analysed in the literature in terms of the issues of intermarriage, inheritance, and personal status law (Aye Kyaw 1994; Ikeya 2013, 2017), for the purposes of my analysis the central question is how the Kalai community came into being, which is directly related to the ongoing disputes between members of U Ohn Ghine's family and the Hindu Association.

---

21. Rangoon High Court, Civil Regular No. 311 of 8 April 1935. The judgment comes out of the High Court of Judicature at Rangoon and is the outcome of a dispute between three Hindus acting as plaintiffs (Mr Bose, a plumber and contractor; Mr Nair, a doctor; and Mr Joshi, a merchant) and a Hindu temple priest and Daw Nu as defendants. The judge ordered the defendants to write a temple constitution (a scheme) regulating all administrative issues in order to prevent future disputes.

The second issue the judges tackled in their 1953 judgment was that of potential mismanagement. This concerned the trusteeship in particular. The Hindu plaintiffs argued that, according to the 1935 Temple Constitution, the board of trustees should be composed of '4 members of the family and one member of the so-called "Madrassi-Hindu community"'. This was not the case in 1953 because – as other documents show – the one Hindu trustee, an attorney at law, had resigned before the war and his post had not been filled. The family claimed that there had been no suitable candidates. Why, one can ask, this strange ratio of 4 to 1? Are the members of the U Ohn Ghine family not also 'Madrassi-Hindus'? After all, their ancestor, the founder of the temple, was a Tamil. And who, then, is the 'larger body of Hindu worshippers'?[22] The court again drew on the older 1935 judgment to settle the issue of mismanagement. In that judgment it was argued that the original temple 'was constructed by Kalais on land granted to them for the purpose, and that they since maintained and managed it for their own peculiar form of worship. Consequently, the temple is clearly the "Kalai Temple"'.[23] But we still do not know who the Kalai are. The court specified as follows:

> The defendants in this case belong to the community known in the past as Kalais who, under clause 2 of the Trust scheme, are described as children of Madrassi-Hindu males by Burmese Buddhist wives and descendants in the male line of such persons. The alleged Hindu status of members of this community had been in question before the courts of this country.[24]

Here, the court referred to two contrasting earlier judgments in 1913 and 1915, both from the Chief Court of Lower Burma, one in favour of Chit Maung, the other in favour of Ma Yait, his mother. The consolidated appeals were brought before the Privy Council in London, the highest court of the British empire, which came to a final decision on 1 August 1921, 'after a study of the life and habits of the members of this community'. The judgment centred on the following passage:

---

22. Today, Madrassi is a derogatory term for people from Chennai and is often used to refer generally to anyone coming from South India.

23. Civil Regular Suit No. 311 of 1933, High Court Rangoon (see n 20), cited in Judgment of the High Court of Judicature at Rangoon, 9 June 1953, §9.

24. Judgment of the High Court of Judicature at Rangoon, 9 June 1953, § 3.

> The combined operation of migration, intermarriage with people of another race and religion, and new occupations, may produce from the descendants of Hindus a community, with its peculiar religion and usages, which is outside Hinduism in the proper meaning of the word. The Kalais form such a community and are not Hindus within the meaning of section 13 of the Burma Laws Act.[25]

U Ohn Ghine had always supported Buddhist and Hindu institutions; he had sent his sons to Buddhist monasteries, but swore that he was a Hindu in order to claim that his daughter Daw Nu, who had been abducted by a Buddhist, had not 'eloped'. The 1906 judgment says that she was 'seized by a *kula* and a Burman'.[26] It turned out that as an individual, U Ohn Ghine was impossible to place within the rigid established categories the empire had come up with and with which colonial institutions were operating. The judges could only conclude that he and his family had acquired a 'non-Hindu status'. Thus, his identity was defined *ex negativo*. The more crucial and difficult part for the judges was to decide on the status of the Kalais as an ethno-religious group:

> [T]his raises the question of much more difficulty than that which arises in the case of a single individual to whom considerable latitude of action is extended before he is deemed to have deprived himself of the religion which gave him his law by anything that does not amount to clear renunciation of that religion. In the instance of a community the question must always be whether there has been continuity of character.[27]

The Privy Council subtitled the case 'Criteria for determining status of new castes or sects evolved from Hinduism', drawing on yet another earlier judgment that had determined that 'the formation of new castes is a process which is constantly taking place'.[28] What is particularly interesting in this case is that while the court identified migration, intermarriage and immersion in the new host society as the defining criteria for the

---

25. *Ma Yait vs. Maung Chit Maung and Maung Chit Maung vs. Ma Yait and Another*, Privy Council, 1 August 1921, p.155.

26. *King-Emperor vs. E. Maung and Six Others*, 3 Lower Burma Rulings 131 (1906: 135).

27. *Ma Yait vs. Maung Chit Maung and Maung Chit Maung vs. Ma Yait and Another*, Privy Council, 1 August 1921, p.160.

28. *Muthusami Mudaliar vs. Masilamani*, 1909.

coming-into-being of a new 'caste' (read: 'ethno-religious group', a.k.a. 'community') that allowed for or led to a separation from Hinduism 'in the proper meaning of the word', no experts or third parties were involved in this decision. When one goes back to the original lawsuit of 1913, however, where the term 'Kalai' was introduced for the very first time (at least judging from all documents that I have seen on the case), the phrasing we encounter there reads as follows:

> Maung Ohn Ghine is described *by Ma Yait* as being a member of the community of mixed Hindu and Burmese descent known as Kales [sic] professing the Hindu religion. *She described* Kales as the descendants of Hindu settlers by Burmese women *and says that* U Ohn Ghine and all the members of the community also worshipped at the pagoda, fed the [monks] and observed Buddhist fasts and festivals. I think it must be definitely decided as to which Act is applicable.[29]

From this wording we know that Ma Yait *herself* defined who a Kalai ('Kale') is, and nobody else. In 1905, she had been 'examined on oath on the Burmese Bible' and at that time still 'sworn [in] as a Burmese Buddhist'.[30] In the 1921 Privy Council suit, however, the reference to her decisive role is already lost when the judges stated that:

> It is clear that he was a Kalai, which means that he was the descendant of a Hindu who had married a Burmese woman. His parents also were Kalais, and he himself married a Kalai. His paternal grandfather was apparently a Hindu who had migrated from Madras to Burma and had married a Burmese. His son was therefore a Kalai and the latter married a Kalai. Maung Ohn Ghine was therefore a Kalai, and he lived in Burma all his life.[31]

Both Aye Kyaw (1994) and Chie Ikeya (2013, 2017), who have written extensively on this case, have omitted the entire question of how 'the Kalai' came about, focusing instead on the question of inheritance and intermarriage according to either Burmese Buddhist or Hindu law. But the whole case hinges on the creation of a new type of community that seems to have been based entirely on Ma Yait's account from 1913; prior

29. *Chit Maung vs. Ma Yait and Ma Noo*, Appeal No. 26, 22 August 1913, p. 363 (emphasis added).

30. *King-Emperor vs. E Maung and Six Others*, 9 February 1906, p. 140.

31. *Ma Yait vs. Maung Chit Maung and Maung Chit Maung vs. Ma Yait and Another*, Privy Council, 1 August 1921, p. 157 (emphasis added).

to that, the term 'Kalai' does not appear in court records. Why, one might ask, were the judges inclined to pursue this approach which, in turn, led to the eventual application of the India Succession Act and not either Burmese Buddhist or Hindu law? My hypothesis is that it was precisely the creation of a novel community that allowed the judges to *not* decide on the ethno-religious identity of U Ohn Ghine, as he was an individual to whom the existing system of colonial classification simply could not be applied. The Kalai constitute a case of what Ikeya has called 'neglected and erased intimacies of empire' (Ikeya 2017: 121), as the British did not account for the offspring of non-Muslim Indian men and local Burmese women. In other words, while there was a legal category for the offspring of Muslim men and Burmese Buddhist women (*Zerbadee*, a Farsi compound meaning 'below the wind'; see Chapter 5), there was none for the offspring of Hindu men who entered into marriage with local Buddhist women beyond the more general *kabya* ('half-caste', 'half-breed').[32] By declaring the Kalai to be a community, the judges might have simply followed the 'invitation' of Ma Yait, thereby engaging in a process similar to the one observed by Arjun Appadurai in his study in Madras, when he showed how a new meaning for the term 'Tenkalai' was generated on the basis of it becoming a local socio-political category. To repeat his finding (see also Chapter 1): '[t]his tacit reference to his Tenkalai affiliations is the first explicit and self-conscious invitation to the British to formalize the sectarian ideas as a principle for local temple control' (Appadurai 1981: 155). And as in his case, I consider it very likely that Ma Yait and later her daughter Daw Nu had begun to use state courts to protect and enshrine their right to the temple.

My argument is further bolstered when we continue analysing what else Daw Nu began to demand in 1953. First, she wanted to have the word 'unorthodox' added to the name of the temple, thus turning it into 'The Kalai (unorthodox Hindu) Temple'. The judges dismissed this demand, arguing that '[t]here is really no need to introduce this restrictive

---

32. The offspring of unions between Muslim men and Burmese women are locally and in the colonial literature referred to as 'Zerbadee' (from Persian *zir bad*, a term also describing a particular kind of ship, the 'Zerbadia'); see Bhattacharya (2007: 53), Yegar (1972: 33), Yule and Burnell (1903), cited in Thant Myint-U (2001: 51). According to Ikeya (2017: 121), the term was introduced into the census in British Burma in 1891, when only twenty-four individuals were recorded. Among my Muslim interlocutors, *Zerbadee* is not used as an endonym.

distinction. The unorthodox character of the Temple being an accepted fact, it must be left to the wish and inclination of individual Hindus to decide as to whether or not they would worship in it'.[33] They did grant her request to omit the words 'in the Tamil and English language' in several clauses of the temple scheme, where it had been specified that official notices should be published in three languages and official announcements had to be made public in Tamil and English newspapers, in addition to Myanma-language ones. They also granted her request to replace the word 'person' in clause 27, which specified who might be eligible to stand in a trustee election, with 'citizen of the Union of Burma residing in Rangoon'.[34] All these granted changes were initiated, I suggest, with the aim of easing the transferral of control from family members to family members, thereby making it more difficult for outsiders to acquire any position in the temple administration. The most important request of Daw Nu's, however, was the following:

> The defendants want to have the words 'in the male line' in clause 2 (a) omitted in order to include descendants in the female line as well. The *natural* tendency of the community towards further affinity and unity with the Burmese Buddhists of Burma in their social and religious beliefs and customs must receive due recognition and the omission of the restriction asked for should have the desirable effect of enlarging the membership of the Kalai community from among whom Trustees are to be chosen. The words 'in the male line' will accordingly be deleted from clause 2(a) of the Scheme.[35]

Daw Nu thus managed to alter the Constitution scheme in order to bypass the patriline. The enlargement of the 'membership of the Kalai community' is deemed a desirable effect by the court, which assumed the 'natural' tendency towards 'unity with the Burmese Buddhists of Burma'. The community of the Kalai, which were mentioned first in the 1913 decision, has thus become naturalized by the court and appears as

---

33. Judgment of the High Court of Judicature at Rangoon, §10. The judges were inconsistent, as they had already spoken of 'the office of Trustees of the Kalai (unorthodox Hindu) Temple' in their own judgment. The same phrasing is used in the trust scheme of 1935.

34. Judgment of the High Court of Judicature at Rangoon, §11.

35. Judgment of the High Court of Judicature at Rangoon, 9 June 1953, §10 (emphasis added).

a new legal entity separable and distinct from the 'Hindu community'. One could argue that the judges had ethnic harmonization in mind when they ruled in favour of Daw Nu in this case. This would make sense in the context of a time marked by violent conflict, civil war, and a regime that preached law and order. Nick Cheesman has characterized this time period as one where 'courts were … inconsistent in their stated guardianship role' (2015: 71). Moreover, during and after the Second World War, many Burmese Indians fled to India, and thus Yangon turned from an 'Indian city' into an increasingly Buddhist one with the majority lowland population – the Bama – moving in. Another sequence from the court judgment, referencing the 1913 judgment, further supports my hypothesis of ethnic harmonization:

> [T]he Kalai community could appear to have undergone a further change in their cultural and social outlook and it is but natural that with the change of political circumstance, they should tend more to identify themselves with the people of this country.[36]

In this case, the court's legal reasoning is concerned with the political circumstances the country finds itself in, namely its recent independence. Arguing that in these circumstances it would be 'natural' for the members of the Kalai community to identify themselves with 'the people of this country' is primordialist social engineering as its finest – especially as all family members of the U Ohn Ghine family at this point had been born in Burma and were Burmese citizens already. Acknowledging a new ethnic-religious group in 1953 in the Rangoon High Court of then-independent Burma was thus very much in line with the official colonial vocabulary and legal reasoning whereby race and religion were the terms through which identity was defined, difference was expressed, and adjustments could be made.

While the court thus helped to bring about an ethno-religious community by separating it from the Hindu community, the Kalai in fact comprise only the family of the original owner, U Ohn Ghine, even today. From the beginning the family's tactic has been to emphasize their intermarriage with Burmese Buddhist women, a claim that only makes much genealogical sense if a patriline is assumed after all. Another interesting aspect is that at no time did the courts inquire into

---

36. Ibid., §8.

the origins of the term Kalai. My hypothesis regarding the origin of the ethnonym is as follows: I assume that there must have been a direct connection to Madras, the present-day Chennai. The last name of the temple founder, Cumara Pillay, was also the last name of the founder of the so-called Tenkalai, the 'southern school' of Śri Vaisnavism – a Hindu tradition that worships Śri (another name for Lakshmi, the Goddess of Wealth) and her husband Vishnu. 'Kalai' is a Tamil word that means school, language, or culture (depending on the context). The Tenkalai, the southern school, branched off from the northern school in the eighteenth century as a result of long-standing conflicts over whether Tamil or Sanskrit sources should be considered authoritative for their religious practice. I am quite confident that 'my' Kalai in Yangon must have had connections to Appadurai's Tenkalai who were also – as a group – formed through interaction with the colonial judiciary, much as the Kalai were formed in Rangoon several decades later (see Appadurai 1981).[37] But neither the Kalai themselves nor the Rangoon court appear to have known about what was going on across the Bay of Bengal. There is, thus, a direct transfer of legal documentation in terms of laws and codes during late colonialism, but no interaction with judicial decision-making processes across the two countries, even though Burma was directly administered from Calcutta until 1937. We could talk about a *courte durée* in contrast to a *longue durée* in terms of the decision-making processes, which seem to be oriented towards particular events and concrete court cases only. But the effects and side effects of establishing communities in court were long-term: while the intention might have been to unite people, the outcome was rather ongoing disputes along newly created ethno-political lines. In Rangoon, the term Kalai had come into being by stressing intermarriage with Burmese Buddhist women, thereby cutting all pan-regional and theological ties to India as a country of origin and to the Hindu religion 'in its proper meaning', as the court had phrased it. In their interaction with me as well, members of the family downplayed their Hindu 'roots' in terms of their ethnicity.

---

37. Arjun Appadurai told me that he had not come across any documents that would show the direct migration of individuals from the temple he was studying in Tamil Nadu to Burma, but he considered it possible. He admitted that he never thought about the meaning of the term Kalai in itself, without the prefixed Ten- or Vata- (personal communication, August 2018).

While U Thin Thain Moung acknowledged that 'Buddha comes from India' and 'Buddhism and Hinduism are like the left and right hand of my body', he also told me to look at him attentively: 'Do I look like an Indian to you?' I tilted my head a little and asked myself whether he was referring to his skin colour, his facial characteristics, or his clothing. The family's primary association in terms of ethnic identification was clearly through their maternal line, hence Buddhism, and they emphasized that the real danger of a takeover would come from the Hindu Association and Hindu individuals, not from Buddhists.

But getting too close to Buddhism is dangerous, too. Art historian Don Stadtner (2011) mentioned how around the time of World War II Buddhists tried to take over the Mahapeinne Temple compound, as a hair relic from the Buddha had temporarily rested there before it reached the Shwedagon Pagoda. There appears to have been a lawsuit around this issue as well, but I have not found any documentation of it. What I did see, however, was how in 2013, on the occasion of a street ceremony devoted to giving donations to the monks of the nearby monastery, the small Buddha statue from the temple was paraded around parts of downtown by the temple manager, followed by ninety Buddhist monks,

Fig. 4.8: The (former) Buddhist temple manager leads the procession with the temple's own Buddha statue while staff distribute envelopes with money to the monks who pass by the temple on Pansodan Street. 19 November 2013.

who first were given cash donations by the temple crew and then stayed over several nights at the temple and received accommodation and food. One needs to know that many Buddhist monks in Myanmar expect meat to be served, while for Hindu priests this is strictly forbidden. The temple cook and the helpers nevertheless prepared meat dishes for the monks and served them. On other occasions, loudspeakers were installed on the property and monks were allowed to give *dhamma* talks for the neighbourhood from the temple compound. Finally, during the parliamentary elections in November 2015, parts of the compound were claimed by the city administration, which installed a polling station there. All this happened in a very matter-of-fact manner, without the family (or the trustees) being asked. Whenever I inquired from U Thin Thain Moung what he thought about these practices, he was outspoken, saying things like, 'When there are holidays, such as *kathein*,[38] usually the township announces when monks are coming [to our temple]. Then we have to bear all the costs. They announce, we do the work, and they take the credit. I could say, "I am not going to do it", but why should I? It's Buddhism and we might as well donate. We have extra money, so we do it.'

While Stadtner, writing about the different Buddhist symbols that one can find in the Mahapeinne Temple, said that 'this Hindu temple has sought to weave itself into Burmese Buddhist traditions' (2011: 131), we now know that this is only half of the story – or one part of the family's tactic to retain their autonomous status as the Kalai community. The *laissez-faire* attitude of U Thin Thain Moung regarding state institutions pushing Buddhism into the temple did not prevail when it came to the Hindu Association's efforts to claim the trusteeship. How fragile the family's status continued to be was revealed to me in 2015, when the issue of the rightful trustees of the Mahapeinne Temple resurfaced in a bout of public announcements for trustee elections in newspapers and on the blackboards of other Hindu temples in the downtown area. None of the family members had been involved; in fact, they did not even know about it. This was the occasion for the lawyer U Maung Ba, whom we met at the beginning of the chapter, to reappear and prevent another attempt to take over the temple.

---

38. An occasion for making meritorious offerings to monks and nuns that happens immediately following Buddhist lent.

Fighting off another takeover attempt

In 2015, while I was carrying out fieldwork, the Hindu Association announced an election for Mahapeinne Temple trustees through public notices posted in another downtown temple and by publishing the announcement in the *Myanmar Alin* newspaper on various dates between March and May 2015, without consulting the acting trustees of the Mahapeinne Temple at all. The first announcement in March 2015 called for elections 'in accordance with the court ruling of 1953, appeal No. 85', thus indicating that the writers knew about the 4:1 ratio for the composition of the board of trustees, with one trustee having to be a (Madrassi) Hindu. U Maung Ba, who had been informed by the family of U Ohn Ghine, and another lawyer reacted to this letter with a detailed writ of their own, in English, that they sent to the Hindu Association and also to the township warden of Kyauktada. In this letter, they defined the Mahapeinne Temple as a 'Kalai Temple' and 'of a separate religion and race with a different worship style and belief', and reiterated the by now familiar short version of the history of U Ohn Ghine. They also confirmed the 4:1 ratio, but held that 'the Hindu Association should not lead in forming a new board of trustees. ... Kalai Buddhist members and also others strongly protest against this.' They then threatened that should the Association not withdraw the announcement concerning new elections, they would 'take action according to existing law'. In response to this letter, the Hindu Association, again in the newspaper *Myanmar Alin*, declared that the claims of the lawyers were incorrect, that 'there are no people called Kalai', and that they would 'go ahead with the selection of temple trustee members on 10 May 2015 as planned'. In their subsequent response, U Maung Ba and the other lawyer then went back to the exact wording of the 1953 court case defining who the Kalai are, arguing in addition that the unauthorized announcement hurt the Kalai's 'dignity' and that such accusations are intended to 'delude people' and 'make the Kalai disappear completely'. Eventually, the takeover attempt petered out and no elections were held.

As of 2019, the composition of the board had not changed and still did not include a self-confessed Hindu trustee. But a generational change had taken place after U Thin Thain Moung retreated from his active engagement in the temple administration. When we met at the temple upon my return to Yangon in spring 2016, he had not even met the current Buddhist manager of the temple, and I was witness to their first talk. During this conversation, U Thin Thain Moung brushed off the lingering dispute with the Hindu Association, saying, 'There is nothing to be afraid of – the land is already bought and the house is already built. Let them do the painting, washing, and cooking, but we don't need no master'. This was his way of saying that, in his opinion, those in charge at the Hindu Association were the servants of a house that did not belong to them. Later in this conversation he used a similar metaphor to justify his own withdrawal from temple affairs and his nephew's stepping in to take over as de facto chairman: 'It is good that I am no longer in charge – if there are two masters in the house, both of them will get a headache.' A couple of days later, I again attended Shivaratri, where I met his nephew for the first time. He did not know who I was when he approached me – just as his uncle had three years earlier – with almost the same line of introduction: 'This is a temple where everyone is welcome – Hindus and Buddhists pray together here!' In contrast to the management of the temple, it seems, when it comes to practising religion, the two 'masters' are not only able to coexist in harmony without one of them having to stand on a lower rung than the other, but their co-equal co-presence is even necessary if the temple management is to remain in control of the religious building.

Conclusion

The current struggle between the Kalai family and the Hindu Association that I witnessed throughout my fieldwork puts into perspective the lack of interaction (or integration) between the various groups of visitors that I had observed during even the highest religious holidays. The orthodox Hindus – especially those of high caste and with connections to the Hindu Association – had no reason to mingle with the other visitors, let alone the Kalai family. Those interested in praying to Sai Ba Ba were uninterested in paying tribute to Guanyin. Those coming to have a curse of the evil eye lifted were interested not in the deities, but in the brokering capacities of the priests, to whom they left it to decide how to do their work. The multi-religious staff of the temple and the more regular visitors seemed to be practising amiable relationships, and a sense of belonging was offered by the temple through the continuity of the proprietors' involvement: everybody was welcome to worship whomever they pleased, but the family of U Ohn Ghine continued to steer a narrow course between Buddhist absorption and orthodox Hindu takeover. It is plausible, I suggest, to speak of tactical behaviour on their part. The women of the family in particular – Ma Yait and Daw Nu – struck me as having been especially well equipped to 'read' the colonial predicaments, to position their family in a favourable way, and to ensure that their husband's and father's property remained within the family, that is, on their maternal side.

While I have criticized what I see as an overemphasis on strategic behaviour in interactionist studies, in this case I think that some individuals at least have very deliberately put the category of community to work in their name. However, not all events and not all alterations to the temple compound have been initiated by the family. I can, for example, trace the presence of the Chinese goddess Guanyin, prominently displayed within the prayer hall, to an ethnic Chinese Buddhist township warden who had realized his personal wish by having the statue placed inside the temple, and the presence of Sai Ba Ba goes back to the private initiative of two people, neither of whom is Kalai or part of the family. We also know of U Maung Ba's life story and what led him to pursue the construction of the pagoda within the Mahapeinne Temple grounds in accordance with his own personal path towards enlightenment. While none of these happenings was planned or even foreseen by the family members, over the last century they have cultivated a *laissez-faire* attitude when it comes to how quite diverse individuals seek to realize their sense of self through donations of money and objects, as well as through new construction, renovations, and the organization of religious worship. I have shown how we can, even in this unique case, detect various practices of *we-formation* where individuals interact with one another during religious events. None of these practices, however, depended upon or even intended to invoke community. Community, in a paradoxical turn of events, began to matter once colonial era courts wanted to categorize the widow and children of U Ohn Ghine as Hindu and apply the respective personal status laws to them. In the name of community – this time the Kalai – Ma Yait and her offspring, among them U Thin Thain Moung, managed to keep both the Hindu Association and the state at bay. By challenging colonial categories, they helped entrench them. Their position, I suggest, continues to be subaltern: they escaped one ethno-religious community, but only by having the courts create a new one. This one, however, they are not willing to share with anyone else.

CHAPTER 5

Marrying 'up': self-objects, race, and class

S itting cross-legged on his living room floor in an upstairs downtown apartment, Mukhtar Bhai informed me that he is a 'Hindustani', a *kalar*, a black man. His skin being dark, he never tired of pointing out to me that mine was 'white like that of a princess'. The existence of race was undisputed for him and he related it to the colour of skin: the darker one's skin, the lower one's status. In Myanmar, discourses of 'racial purity' (*lu-myo: yei than sin hmu*) are not confined to those in power, be it 'the state' and its personnel, or even the Bama Buddhist majority, but are so pervasive that some of my Muslim and Hindu interlocutors not only self-identify as *kalar*, but also reproduce and perpetuate the associated characteristics that come with this derogatory term. Skin colour is not only ranked according to standards of beauty, but also to issues of class and intelligence.

I got to know Mukhtar Bhai and his family over the course of five years. Our families became close friends as our son, who was four years old in 2015, was the same age as his youngest child. Mukhtar Bhai approached me during one of the mourning processions and introduced himself as a Shia businessman trading in gemstones. He wore many other hats in addition to this job: he worked for a large bakery owned by a Sunni Muslim; he was a manager of a small company that arranged work visas to other Southeast Asian countries, Australia, and Saudi Arabia; and he earned some money as a broker of properties, making use of his vast network of business contacts. He had travelled widely, lived in Thailand and the Middle East, had been to the United States, and spoke several languages; we communicated with each other in a mix of English and Myanma, depending on who else was present at a given moment.

In this chapter I explore how Mukhtar Bhai tried to reconcile his ideology of racial purity with his own 'mixed' genealogy and complicated family history and the fact that he himself had married across communal

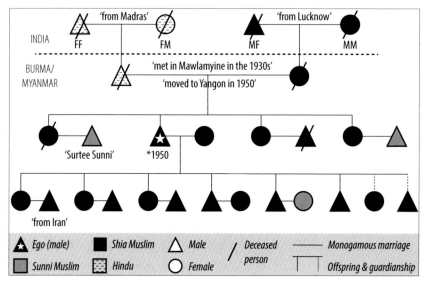

Fig. 5.1: Family tree of Mukhtar Bhai (ego). Data gathered in Yangon, 2016.

divides.[1] His family history thus reflects not only the history of the Shia community at large, but also demonstrates the long-term structural effects of colonial-era personal status laws and their recent repercussion in the so-called Race and Religion Laws of 2015.

Entangled family histories

Mukhtar Bhai was the only son of a man who had come to Burma in the 1930s from the coastal Indian town of Madras (today's Chennai) and a woman who had migrated to lower Burma with her parents from Lucknow in landlocked northern India. His father was a Hindu, and his grandfather (whom he never met) was 'a doctor and a vegetarian', said Mukhtar Bhai. While vegetarianism is not to be automatically understood as Brahminical, as several Brahmin subcastes do eat meat (Singh 2011: 440), this allusion suggests that his father was a high-caste Brahmin. His maternal grandparents, however, and therefore also his mother, were Shia. According to Mukhtar Bhai, when his parents got married in the coastal city of Moulmein (today's Mawlamyine), where his father lived when he was not working on one of the big ships that criss-crossed the bay between India and Burma, his father's Hinduness

---

1. Intermarriage here refers to unions within rather than across the larger religious denominations.

'had not been an issue' for his mother's parents. Moulmein at that time was a bustling seaport and home to a significant number of Shia. A large Shia mosque located in the downtown area today stands deserted for most of the week, but is still frequented by Shias for Friday prayers. Mukhtar Bhai did not know whether the marriage of his parents had, in fact, ever been officially registered, but he said it had not been necessary for his father to convert to Shia Islam.

Mukhtar Bhai's parents moved to Yangon in 1950 so his father could take on permanent employment with his family close by, which had not been possible when he worked on ships. His father bought a flat in Bo Sun Pat Street, in the downtown area, where Mukhtar Bhai was born that same year. As the building was old and crumbling, a couple of years later his parents moved the family to Thaketa in the eastern part of the city, where they bought a large parcel of land (see Fig. 0.4). After his parents' death, Mukhtar Bhai, as the only son in the family, inherited the land. He paid his three sisters their share according to *sharia*,[2] and subsequently sold the land when he got married in 1974. He bought a one-floor apartment on 54th Street, where he stayed with his wife until 2002. They then moved to 48th Street, where they first bought one and then another floor in a six-storey building for his expanding family. In 2007, he bought the two-floor apartment in 37th Street, where he lived with his wife, his oldest son, his daughter-in-law, and their baby, as well as with a young boy and girl of whom he is the guardian.[3] This flat is right in the centre of downtown – which has become one of the most expensive areas in the city. He was planning to move even closer to the Mogul Shia mosque on 30th Street when I last visited him in 2020. Sadly, he died later that year.

---

2.   Inheritance within Muslim families in Myanmar is regulated by Islamic law. In case of a family dispute over inheritance among Muslims that is brought before a state civil court, the case will be decided by drawing on Muslim personal law (to be found in Burma Act 13 from 1889). This area of law is mostly decided by applying colonial-era case law that can be found in English-language handbooks and that has not been overruled (e.g. *Habiba vs. Swa Kyan*; High Court of Rangoon 1937; see also Crouch 2016; Rhoads 2020).

3.   I never asked Mukhtar Bhai about their stories. I sensed that this was a sensitive topic for him and his wife, and since he always made a point of indicating that, to him, these are his children (while at the same time often asking me if I thought they actually resembled him or his wife), I treat them as such.

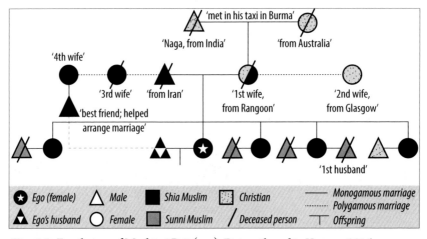

Fig. 5.2: Family tree of Mushtari Baji (ego). Data gathered in Yangon, 2016.

Mushtari Baji, Mukhtar Bhai's wife, told me how her maternal grand-parents had met in a taxi in Burma, and that her grandfather was 'a Christian Naga[4] from India' and her grandmother 'an Australian lady' who had come to Burma on a visit. Her mother, their only child, married a Shia man 'from Iran'. Besides her mother, who had been his first wife, her father also married another Christian 'from Glasgow', with whom he had two children. The second wife never lived in Burma, but stayed in Scotland with her children. While Mushtari Baji's mother converted to Islam, her father's second wife from Glasgow never did. A third wife was a Shia woman from Yangon. After Mushtari Baji's mother died, her father married yet another time. The son from this fourth marriage, Mushtari Baji's half brother whom she referred to as her 'brother', eventually became Mukhtar Bhai's closest friend, and it was he who introduced the two. Mushtari Baji's parents had five daughters. She was the second child and the only one to marry a Shia. Her other sisters all married non-Shia men: three of them Sunni (one remarried after her first husband died) and one Christian.

Marrying 'up'

While the two family trees reveal that intermarriage was not at all un-common, they still obscure the challenges inherent in each such decision such as, for example, the concerns of a woman who enters a polygamous

---

4. Naga is an ethnonym that refers to several ethnic groups residing in north-eastern India and northern Myanmar (Joshi 2012).

marriage or those of a son who no longer shares the religion of his father. 'Marrying 'up' within one's own religious denomination proved to be as challenging. One day in spring 2016, Mukhtar Bhai, Mushtari Baji, and I were deeply engaged in a discussion about two different factions within the Shia community. The existence of these factions had become clear to me after a couple of months of fieldwork; it was especially noticeable during processions, and had also come up in conversations with other Shia Muslims. During this discussion Mukhtar Bhai brought up the issue of intermarriage to demonstrate that, in fact, intra-Shia factionalism was not a problem. Relating factionalism to intermarriage, he explained how he met his wife and what marrying an 'Iranian Shia' meant for someone like him:

> *There is no separation. But in the mosque, they say, there is. Akber Hussain might say that the split is very deep, but it is not deep. If it was deep, how could I have married my wife? How could I have married an Iranian? It was her family's wish. At the time, my father-in-law was on a ship at sea. Nobody was taking care of her [his wife]. So, my best friend [Mushtari Baji's half brother] told me, 'You could take care of her and her family! Surely you can!' But I said, 'I have never even seen your sister! But I love you. I agree with you.' After two months, he showed me his sister – we met in the cinema [laughing]. And then he came to me – angry: 'Why didn't you come to my home yesterday?' But I had been scared ... [laughing]. But then I agreed and I took care of my father-in-law. He was very nice, like an American. Pure and white – like you. Very nice. He understood English and Urdu, but more English. His life took place mostly at sea. He was one of the ... everyone says this in our majority[5] ... one of the old shipmen, working under the SS Prome.[6]*

---

5. His choice of words was significant. His English was quite good and he certainly knew the difference between 'majority' and 'minority'. The fact that, in Myanmar, Shia are far smaller in numbers than Sunni is known to everyone; that even Hindus and especially Buddhists are numerically greater is equally obvious. I understood his reference to 'majority' to be an indication that, for him, 'being Shia' was preferential to any other ethno-religious denomination; the word demonstrated the strength of the 'community' while leaving unspoken who, then, the 'minority' must be. When I pressed him on his choice of words, he merely specified that he meant 'our community'.

6. Prome is the former name of the town Pyay. The 'SS Prome' was the name given to two steamer ships of the P. Henderson & Co./British & Burmese Steam Navigation Co., one acquired in 1893, the other in 1937. See http://www.theshipslist.com/ships/lines/burma.shtml (accessed 18 July 2022).

In both family histories, the parents had already intermarried: Hindu–Shia in Mukhtar Bhai's case, Shia–Christian in Mushtari Baji's case. As the system is patrilineal across the board, it had never been an issue for Mushtari Baji whether she was, in fact, 'pure Shia' or not. Her maternal side did simply not count. What counted, however, was that her father was 'from Iran', which serves as an emic marker of high class among Shia in Myanmar to the present day. It was particularly important to Mukhtar Bhai that his three elder daughters had all studied in Iran and that his oldest daughter was even married to an Iranian, now living in Iran with her family. He associated 'being Iranian' with 'purity' and 'white' skin. He attributed his readiness to marry Mushtari Baji to the pleading of his friend, which he gave in to, and to wanting to honour his father-in-law, who – like his own father – had been a sailor and was still well respected long after his death.

Mukhtar Bhai and Mushtari Baji began to tell me the story of how they met while we were discussing the division between 'Hindustani Shia' and 'Iranian Shia'. This division is known to have existed since the arrival of Shia Muslims in Myanmar: at the onset of colonialism in Burma, Iranian Shia were said to have occupied high positions in the Burmese Buddhist hierarchy (as ambassadors of their home countries, advisers to the king, legal experts, and wealthy businessmen[7]), whereas Hindustani Shia are often characterized as the prototype of the Indian dock worker or rice paddy farmer. They were among the hundreds of thousands of seasonal labourers, the ones ruining their health in the abysmal housing conditions in Rangoon, the ones trying to scrape together some money to bring back home to India, but oftentimes dying in Burma instead.

Depending on the context and the positionality of the individual I was conversing with, however, I received very different accounts whether this split between Iranian Shia and Hindustani Shia was still prevalent and of any relevance today. According to U Maung Maung Ta, the late

---

7. Members of the Iranian Shia (also known as Moguls) have sought to evade the particular stereotypization often attributed to the Indian minorities by considering themselves high-status outsiders. Consider the following quote, attributed to Major Arthur Phayre during his diplomatic mission to Ava in 1855: 'The feeling both of the Armenians and Moguls in Ava appears to have been always one of bitter jealousy and dislike to us. In our absence, they felt themselves the representatives of Western knowledge and civilization, but by our presence they are cast into the shade, and resent it' (Yule [Secretary of Major Arthur Phayre], cited in Yegar 1972: 17).

managing trustee of the Mogul Shia Mosque and author of a book titled *Myanmar and the Shiah Muslims in Myanmar* (Maung Maung Ta 2004[8]), in which he not only compiled his own family history but also that of the community, this division remains pertinent and permanent in Yangon:

> [I]n Yangon there have always been until today, Shia Muslims who are not descendants of the Iranians that migrated into Myanmar. These descendants of various Indians and Pakistanis have always been envious of the 'Moguls', as the descendants of the Iranians came to be called. The forefathers of the Moguls had built almost all the religious landmarks in Myanmar. (Maung Maung Ta 2004: 117)

In this quote, U Maung Maung Ta drew a direct connection between the 'religious landmarks' of the Shia and the envy of the non-Mogul Shia. Envy is a deeply self-centred emotion that is usually not shared or confessed to others, as it concerns a damaged perception of an individual's self-worth. But it is also inherently relational. As early as the late eighteenth century, Kant – in a view that is broadly accepted even today – said that 'the standard we use to see how well off we are is not the intrinsic worth of our own well-being but how it compares with that of others' (Kant [1797] 2003: 206). In the case of U Maung Maung Ta, it is he, an 'Iranian Shia', who attributed low self-esteem to 'the Hindustani Shia' as a group. My Hindustani Shia interlocutors might even agree with this description, and in fact often alluded to their 'inferiority' themselves. But I think it is more fruitful to understand these references as a way for U Maung Maung Ta to boost his own perception of himself *vis-à-vis* his immediate co-religious *others*. In the following sections, I explore in more detail how this self-image relates to the mosque and how, more generally, not only the issue of 'factionalism' but the very possibility of 'being' an individual can be related to religious buildings. I thus show how we can understand individual self-formation as anchored in Shia religious buildings such as mosques, *imambargah*s, and *astana*s.

Shia buildings

There are two Shia mosques in Yangon: the Mogul Shia Mosque on 30th Street, and the smaller Punja Mosque on 38th Street. While the first is famous and known as one of the hallmarks of colonial heritage,

---

8. Another source of information on the Shia community in Rangoon is Karmel Afsheen's *Under Five Flags: Life Like a Turbulent River Flows* (2011).

Fig. 5.3: The main hall of the Mogul Shia Mosque is used by men and women alternately. The screened-off women's section is to the left and is used when there are joint services. 2013.

the other is tucked away in a side street and not listed as a historical building. The two mosques are, as such, paradigmatic of the way the different factions are said to operate. The Mogul Shia Jamaay Masjid,[9] as it is officially called, was first erected as a simple wooden structure in 1854, administered by the Iranian Mazindarani family. A well was drilled in 1852 on the order of Arthur Phayre, who was the commissioner of the Pegu Division, and is still there today.[10] The wooden building was

---

9. From the Persian *masjed-e jame*, indicating that this mosque is the central congregational mosque in the city where the Friday prayers are held.

10. According to U Maung Maung Ta, the Mazindarani family members 'were more interested in the *Azadari* [the organization of practices related to mourning and commemoration] of the Shia Muslims and less in the trusteeship/administration of the *masjid*' – which he might have argued in order to demonstrate that his 'taking over' of the trusteeship several decades later did not conflict with the original and continuous right of the Mazindarani family, who had first managed the wooden mosque in 1854.

demolished in 1914 and replaced in 1917 by a large stone structure with steps made of marble imported from Italy. It underwent large-scale renovation in the 1960s and again in 1998, in both cases with money coming from wealthy Shia businessmen.

During the time of my fieldwork and after several years of negotiation with the Yangon City Development Committee (YCDC) as well as some internal disputes, another round of renovations commenced. It was high time, as the ceilings of the offices located underneath the main hall were in danger of collapsing, and water had already started seeping into the ground floor.

Adjacent to the mosque, the Mogul Hall was built in 1910. The ground floors were turned into eleven shops that were rented out to generate a steady income for the mosque, and the upper floor was used as a hall for weddings and other festivities and also provided living quarters for the head imam of the mosque. From 1912, for a couple of years at least, a *madrasa* was housed in one of the upper rooms, where children were taught Persian and learned how to read the Qur'an in Arabic. The school was opened in 1912 by the Young Men's Persian Association, which had been in existence since 1909 and whose name was later changed to The Persian Association, indicating not only the dominance of the 'Iranian

Fig. 5.4: Mogul Hall on Maha Bandula Road, with shops on the ground floor. The minaret of the adjacent Mogul Shia Mosque on 30th Street is visible in the background on the left side. 2013.

Shia' in all affairs related to communal life, but also the broadening of their interests and the expansion of their membership base to include women.[11]

When the Aga Khan[12] visited Burma in the 1920s, he was interested in visiting the hall, but 'the members of the association were in a dilemma as the set up at the association was unfurnished and not presentable and diplomatically declined the Aga Khan's visit, saying it would be a strain for the Aga Khan to climb to the third floor' (Maung Maung Ta 2004: 219). U Maung Maung Ta chose to phrase the situation in terms of a 'dilemma' that was solved 'diplomatically', depicting the members of the association in a position of control as they politely declined the Aga Khan's request, rather than as desperately cancelling the visit. When the association, by then under the name Iran Club, was closed down in 1978, however, he was not so diplomatic with his words. The situation did not involve an outsider, but a member, namely the last president of the club himself, and 'a collection of henchmen as members of the Club's Committee' (2004: 235), who had brought this sad state of affairs about. According to U Maung Maung Ta, the president had bribed the committee members and then one night moved his own family into the premises of the club inside Mogul Hall. Under the title 'The demise of a community asset', U Maung Maung Ta's final words on this issue were as follows:

> Shame on all who participated to help destroy communal property and pride. A list of those who collaborated with [full name mentioned here] and received payments long before it was put to sale, is in the files, but shall be omitted in print here, to help them live in regret and repentance and shame. (Maung Maung Ta 2004: 235)

In this quote, communal property is mentioned alongside pride. 'Pride' here refers to communal pride that is invested in the building and which reflects back on the community for having built it, for claiming usage rights to it, and for knowing that it is through this building that one can convey to others a certain image of Shia-ness. The antidote to (excessive) pride is shame or shaming, as U Maung Maung Ta is well aware. But in the anthropology of emotion, shame is usually classified as

---

11. In 1921, the name of the association was changed once more to Iran Club.
12. The Aga Khan is the highest living Islamic authority of the Ismailia, the second-largest branch within Shia.

affectual, felt in the individual body and at a time when one's own act of conduct has been pointed out as improper by others, thus after a transgression has already occurred (see Röttger-Rössler and Markowitsch 2009; Scheff 1988). The term evokes a situated negative emotional experience (Casimir 2009: 283), so we can understand U Maung Maung Ta's 'list' as serving to make sure that the misdeed will be remembered much longer than the actual emotion could possibly be. The litigation strategies we have encountered thus far, as in the case of the Mahapeinne Temple (Chapter 4), can be viewed in a similar light: property disputes about religious buildings do not solely aim at clarifying the question of who the rightful owner or trustee is, but are pushed by individuals who want to make use of legal or bureaucratic means to instil a sense of shame in others, to 'help them live in regret and repentance and shame' regarding their misconduct, in U Maung Maung Ta's words. In addition, such a manoeuvre takes the burden of loss or failure from oneself. Finally, law suits like the one described by U Maung Maung Ta are also aimed at an observing audience, which will now remember the shameful behaviour of others.[13] The building has been closed off for years now, as the Yangon City Development Committee (YCDC) determined that it is in danger of collapsing. As with many religious buildings of minorities, it is particularly hard to obtain official permits to renovate, so the Mogul Hall stood deserted still in 2020, with only the shops on the ground floor continuing to operate.

The second Shia mosque in Yangon is the Punja Masjid, which was built in 1877 on the site where a wooden structure had been built in 1855.[14] The building was constructed on a total of five plots of land that

---

13. It is important to note that law suits involving personal laws drew on the English model of a trust and neither entirely captured the subtleties of *sharia* nor the specificities of the (local) context. Muslim personal law in Myanmar has its roots in Section 13c of the Burma Laws Act of 1898. The Mussalman Wakf Validating Act, No 6 of 1913, The Mussalman Wakf Act No 42 of 1923, The Muslim Personal (Shariat) Application Act (1937), and The Dissolution of Muslim Marriages Act (1939) are the key references here.

14. The name 'Punja' does not refer to 'Punjabi', as one might think (given that 'Hindustani Shia' frequent it nowadays and form its board of trustees as well as the core staff of the administration), but stands for the 'Holy Five' (from Persian *panj*, meaning 'five'): the Prophet Muhammad (a.s.), his son-in-law Hazrat Ali (a.s.), his daughter Fatima (a.s.), and his two grandsons Imam Hassan (a.s.) and Imam Hussain (a.s.).

Fig. 5.5: A view of the street outside the Punja Masjid. 2016.

had been donated by four different Shia donors, who had acquired them from the British authorities as private land. Two brick buildings next to the mosque were donated by a widow in 1900. Up until 2002 the trustees had always been Iranian Shia, but then a successful take-over by 'revolutionaries', as U Maung Maung Ta called them, brought in 'new blood' (2004: 206). The reference to new blood can be interpreted in light of the fact that all but one of the new members were younger than the former trustees had been, but it can also point to the fact that all of the new trustees (with the exception of the one senior one) were now Hindustani Shia – of different 'blood'. U Maung Maung Ta was not fond of this change, emphasizing that all of them had 'overstayed their elected period of duty according to the scheme [constitution of the mosque] and [that] new elections are long overdue' (ibid.), thereby basing his complaint not on race, but on their misconduct in regard to bureaucratic procedures.

Relating buildings to a sense of self

Not only are the family histories of my interlocutors mapped onto the histories of these two religious buildings, but they also serve as 'self-objects' (Kohut 1971), that is, as sites for a pre-reflective self-as-subject to emerge.

Following Légrand (2007) and Sartre ([1943] 1992), I understand pre-reflective self-consciousness as a minimal form of self-consciousness, namely one where the self is not (yet) taken as an intentional object.[15] Légrand illustrates the concept with the following example:

> To consciously perceive a tree is already to be pre-reflectively self-conscious: it involves self-consciousness in the sense that the tree is perceptually given *to me*, there is a conscious first-person-perspective, a dimension of mineness. This self-consciousness is pre-reflective since the intentional object of the experience is the tree rather than oneself. (Légrand 2007)

According to Sartre, who was drawing on Husserl, this type of self-consciousness is 'the only mode of existence which is possible for a consciousness of something' (Sartre 1992: 14). How does that guide us in understanding Mukhtar Bhai's engagement with the mosque? While community is often understood in terms of joint or common ownership of property, and religious buildings are usually perceived to be places where community manifests itself, these buildings are never only communal places even if they appear (and are intended to appear) as such to the public. I hold that engaging with objects such as the buildings in which religious practice takes place shapes an individual's sense of self as well: it is through the engagement with matter, literally, that individuality and a sense of 'we' can be, but does not need to be, shared; it can be, but does not have to be, about community. When Husserl uttered his rallying cry, 'Back to the things themselves!' ([1928] 1980), which was picked up and amplified by Sartre and many others, he was not calling for a material turn in philosophy, but was, rather, interested in seeking a middle ground between two extreme views: one that took the world as existing 'out there' and another that focused predominantly on treating it as a construction of the mind. According to Husserl, 'things' – which can be any-things (e.g., even categories) – are always subject-related, but never completely subject dependent. The 'things' I choose to focus on are religious buildings, which I see as mediating objects that help us explore the relationship between individuality, intersubjectivity, and community. 'To understand what people are and what they might become, one must understand what goes on between people and things',

---

15. See also Miguens et al. (2016) for a recent discussion.

argued Csíkzentmihályi and Rochberg-Halton (1981: 1). In their book *The Meaning of Things: Domestic Symbols and the Self,* the authors focused on possession and consumption and their respective impact on the development of an individual's self and the way individuals are able to relate to others (see also Belk 1988).

In anthropology, we know that relationships between people are often mediated through the material world.[16] John and Jean Comaroff have argued that it is a 'growing Eurocultural truism that the (post)modern person is a subject made by means of objects', and that consumption 'determines definitions of value, the construction of identities, even the shape of the global ecumene' (2001: 4). But, of course, more is at stake than possession and consumption or symbolic representation when it comes to how individuals relate to objects. Christoph Antweiler (2004: 299–300) wants anthropology to pay more attention to the mutual references between 'actors in their bodiliness' and the built environment, particularly in cities. Gell (1998), Ingold (2007, 2011), Keane (2003, 2005), Ladwig (2012), Miller (2008), and Heidemann (2018) call for a broader understanding of objects and their agentic relationship to individuals, sometimes in terms of 'attachments' or 'atmosphere'. Rather than engaging with literature on the so-called 'ontological turn', which takes such a position to the extreme (see, e.g., Henare, Holbraad, and Wastell 2007; Holbraad and Pedersen 2017), I follow Obeyesekere in his dictum that public cultural symbols (such as religious buildings) do have unconscious motivational significance for an individual (1981: 13). These buildings are not only important sites for *the work of community,* but also for prior processes.

From a psychological-existentialist perspective, Heinz Kohut (1971) saw a self developing in relation to self-objects, by which he meant a child's caregivers. Taken in a more literal sense, however, the 'objects' can also be material objects such as the buildings I am concerned with here. In the cases discussed in this chapter, my interlocutors do not necessarily work consciously and strategically towards forging new senses of self or towards personal 'becoming' when they engage with religious matter(s) – at least, they never suggested to me that they do so. While we cannot know, to put it concretely, whether or not Mukhtar Bhai

---

16. See Brown (2001), Dant (2006), Buchli (2002), Tilley (1999, 2011), and Turkle (2011).

consciously worked towards becoming accepted as an 'Iranian Shia', it would be very limiting to assume that an individual is consumed with nothing but strategic action. Mukhtar Bhai's tactical mind was revealed to me during a commemoration ritual for which I had just purchased flowers outside the Mogul Shia mosque to help decorate a replica of a grave (*mafa*). Mukhtar Bhai, who had seen this, came up and told me I should make a wish when I place the flowers on top of the replica, but he instructed me to wait a bit before doing so: 'Only when the crowd has gathered will you hang them [the flower garlands]. Then people will be happy. If you hang them now, only these few ladies [who were already sitting in front of the *mafa*, praying] will see you. Later, there will be so many people – at that time, you will put it.' By aligning their practices with objects such as the religious buildings themselves or the objects hosted therein, I hold (in the idiom established earlier) that individuals experience a sense of 'we' which, in turn, impacts the very ways they can 'be' in the world. 'We think with the objects we love', argued Turkle (2011: 5), but we could also turn this sentence around: we can love (and sense other emotions such as envy, shame, or pride, as mentioned by U Maung Maung Ta) when we have objects to relate to. Or, in Daniel Miller's words, 'the closer our relationships are with objects, the closer our relationships are with people' (2008: 1). Sartre has likewise argued that we experience ourselves '*across* a material object ... . Materiality puts its seal on our solid community, and *we* appear to ourselves as an instrumental disposition and technique of means, each one having a particular place assigned by an end' (1992: 543, emphasis in original). In a recent article, Tine Gammeltoft (2018) has linked what she calls 'intersubjective belonging' (through the idiom of kinship; cf. Sahlins 2013) to 'territorial belonging', where the notion of ownership and place become a way to talk about family relations where '[p]laces exercise claims as much as persons' (Edwards and Strathern 2000: 152). She writes that '[r]ather than being extrinsic to the self, ownership relations render people part of one another' (Gammeltoft 2018: 88).

While the development of self, the practice of forming a *we*, and the invocation of communal divides are all enabled through the possession and consumption of objects, individuals first of all need to be able to access these objects. I have already shown in Chapter 3 that one does not need to be a 'card-carrying' member of the community to enter a Hindu temple and carry out rituals, whether alone or alongside others. I would argue that in the case of Muslim practice, too, when one enters a mosque, one does so always as an individual first and, on certain occasions, as a member of the community. Throughout my various fieldwork stays I have met several visiting Muslims at the Shia mosque who worked for telecommunications companies or other large-scale enterprises and were on business trips or temporarily based in Myanmar. They were always welcome to carry out their daily prayers at any time; a nod, a *salam*, a handshake, and sometimes an exchange of a few words would suffice.

Depending on the context, the individual aspect might be more pronounced, while at other times it could be more important to fulfil one's public function as a member of the religious community and to perform according to the expectations of others. In their 'theory of access', Ribot and Peluso have distinguished property from access, defining the former as the *right* to derive benefits from things and the latter as the *ability* to do so (2003: 153). If access is feasible, actors hold 'a bundle of powers' (ibid.) in contrast to 'a bundle of rights', as Maine (1861) had originally characterized property relations. *Controlling* and *maintaining* access, which Ribot and Peluso identify as complementary social positions (2003: 158–159), are indeed crucial, as access to property is not only fought over (see Chapters 4 and 6) but, more importantly, used as a mental and material node by means of which, as Légrand has put it, one can come to experience oneself from a first-person perspective. This, in turn, is part of the dialectical process of *we-formation* that takes place apart from and even despite community.

To illustrate: While Mukhtar Bhai's marrying 'up' was a one-time event that turned him into a member of a well-respected 'Iranian Shia' family, he was constantly cultivating his belonging through the work he did for the Mogul Shia Mosque. He would visit the premises daily and made sure to attend Friday prayers, when most of the mosque's members were present, but he was also engaged in the administration, particularly aiding the elderly and ailing managing trustee U Maung Maung Ta with paperwork and other organizational tasks. While having internalized racial hierarchies according to which he himself remained *kalar*, thus at the bottom of various categorizations, through these practices he made his own (new) 'Iranian Shia-ness' more apparent or real for himself. One could, with the terminology I have established in the introduction, argue that for him, too, *the work of community* acted transversally: while he was painfully aware that categorizations such as race would not go away, his way of relating himself to the 'Iranian Shia' through the mosque itself affected the very possibility of who he could 'be'. The fact that he was always seeking opportunities to move his family closer to the vicinity of the mosque, where many 'Iranian Shia' live, supports this argument.[17] Based on my exposition of these details, one could certainly interpret Mukhtar Bhai's actions as instrumental and opportunistic, but I do not have any proof that this was indeed the case. He never justified or theorized his doings, and I did not discuss them with him in these terms. However, instead of assuming that he was being purely strategic, I find it important to emphasize that, independent of his motivations, these practices certainly had an impact on how he related to himself. In other words, even acting strategically for an outside audience (here, 'the community') will have an impact how an individual begins to feel about him- or herself in the end. In the terminology of ethnomethodology, Mukhtar Bhai was becoming Iranian Shia by 'doing "being Iranian Shia"'.

Another example of where religious buildings take on the role of self-objects concerns the issue of charitable trusts. We have already seen in Chapter 4 how the application of colonial-era trust law has affected disputes, discourses, and practices in the context of the Mahapeinne Temple and how it helped to constitute the Kalai community. In addition to general colonial-era trust law, Islamic law recognizes the concept of *waqf*, that is, property an individual has donated to Allah and which is not to be given away, sold, or inherited (see also Rhoads 2018, 2020). Trustees are required to take care of such properties, whether they be buildings, shops, or parcels of land. In Yangon, *waqf* buildings either belong to families (*waqf-alal-aulad*), like some of the *imambargahs* and *astanas*, or to the community (*waqf khairi*), such as the two Shia mosques. Whereas personal status laws deal with immovable objects, personal law itself, unlike general laws, is not bound to national borders, but rather attaches to individuals: if an individual converts to another religion, not only does his or her religion change, but the personal law that will be applied also changes. This is particularly the case regarding family issues such as inheritance, marriage, divorce, child custody, and

---

17. This recalls Uncle Ghaffar's statement in Chapter 2, 'We want to be near our culture', by which he meant living in close proximity to their mosque.

guardianship. Personal laws, in other words, are personal because they move with the person from one 'community' into another. In the words of a British colonial officer, 'The community is divided into great classes, each of which is supposed to be governed by its own personal law. When they have no personal law, they have no law, except what we choose to invent for them' (Temple 1887: 335). Often, it was through the courts (and these laws) that an individual's religion was determined in the course of the court case. The fact that within a particular religion a range of very different legal (customary) procedures for marrying, divorcing, inheriting, or regulating child custody might have been in place has been consistently ignored (see Cohn [1965] for an early analysis). The result was state-orchestrated religious legal pluralism.

Mukhtar Bhai once gave me a document in which he had spelled out for the community why it should be considered *khianat* – Arabic for a breach of trust – to turn such trust property (the mosques and the objects therein as well as all money that is being handled in their name) into private property. The document had been signed by U Maung Maung Ta and was distributed to all the members one Friday after the *juma* prayer. The term *khianat* means betraying the trust of another and is usually used together with its Arabic opposite *amanat*, which is translated as 'trust' and, in the Islamic legal context, relates to *waqf*, something that has been entrusted. In Mukhtar Bhai's letter to all *Shia ba-dha-win*, literally 'members of the Shia religion', Mukhtar Bhai warned that converting *amanat* into *khianat* is a sin and would be punished both by Allah in one's afterlife and also by the strong law (*pyin:-htan-de u-pe-dei*) of this world (Arab. *ad-dunyā*). He clarified that 'if members cannot contain themselves, we need to ask the country [*naing-gan-do*] for help', by which he meant the state, specifically state courts. 'Our country is not a kingless country', he declared. He began to write this text after it had become obvious that some valuable objects from inside the mosque, such as antique chandeliers, had been sold. He had a particularly strong reaction to this news and was furious when he told me about it. Likewise, when the debate resurfaced about who actually owned the eleven shops that were built into the outer walls of both the Mogul Shia Mosque and the Mogul Hall, Mukhtar Bhai channelled his anger into a text. He cited from the Qur'an extensively, lamenting that all those who betrayed the trust (in both senses of the term) of the community were no better than

Yazid, who murdered Imam Hussain (a.s.) in the battle of Kerbala, the traumatic event that to this day undergirds Shia identity. In its second meaning, *khianat* can be related to the out-marrying of one's daughters. This, too, is understood as a breach of trust that diminishes the wealth of one's community. In this understanding, women are part of a body politic, and it is through them that issues of identity, belonging, power, and purity are made manifest. Mukhtar Bhai, according to these tenets, would certainly have tried to prevent the marrying-out of his daughters to Sunni men, but he had no problem with his second-youngest son marrying a Sunni woman.

Bridging the Shia–Sunni divide

For many of my Muslim interlocutors – particularly Shia – the division within Islam is held to be of further-reaching significance than that between Muslims and non-Muslims: the 'narcissism of minor differences' (Freud 1930) within one's own religious community usually not only trumps the differences that individuals cultivate with regard to religious *others*, but demands a rhetorical positioning easily as complex as that required for notionally wider religious divides. It might also end up being far more challenging for establishing a sense of self, as in the case of Mukhtar Bhai's family.

A word is in order here regarding my own positioning and my Shia and Sunni interlocutors' discussions of their relationships with each other. Sartre has argued that one way he handled the gaze of the third was to 'ally myself to the Third so as to look at the Other who is then transformed into *our* object' (Sartre 1992: 538). While in his work on ethnicity in Burma, F.K. Lehman (1967) has argued that ethnic categories are 'non-dichotomous' and have a 'reticulate structuring' as they are 'mediated by some third category' (see also Leach 1959), it seems that Mukhtar Bhai tried to draw me over to 'his' side by teaching me about Shia Islam and by focusing on the bad deeds of Yazid, the murderer of Imam Hussain (a.s.). It seemed that my very presence created an occasion to forge that sort of *we*, so that 'the Sunnis' would become more tangible as an *other*. Whenever we collect data based on conversation (regardless of whether it is free-flowing, semi-structured, or in a formal interview), we risk inadvertently encouraging our interlocutors to accommodate us by re-orienting themselves to figure us 'in'. I consider it likely that there is an overreporting of communal conflict precisely because most of the research that has been conducted with ethno-religious minorities in Myanmar has been interview-based, and conversations about strife with an observing, listening third substantially encourages people to express themselves in terms of ethno-religious communities locked in communal conflict, which in turn solidifies this impression in the mind of the listener (see also Moerman 1965). But when I observe who Mukhtar Bhai interacted with in his everyday life, I see a very different picture. For example, in April 2016 my family and I attended the birthday party of one of Mukhtar Bhai's grandchildren, his third daughter's youngest daughter. On the occasion, Mukhtar Bhai introduced us to his second son, who had come with his wife and their newborn baby. When he introduced his daughter-in-law, he noted without hesitation that she is Sunni. I had to try to contain my surprise, especially as I had long been aware of his opinion about intermarriage between Sunnis and Shias. While he accepted his grandchild as part of his family, he did not interact with his daughter-in-law – at least not that I could see. He had also boycotted his son's wedding, but had given them money to help start their own household.

Moreover, Mukhtar Bhai was working for a Sunni businessman who had hired him specifically because he was Shia. Mukhtar Bhai believed that the boss considered him more trustworthy than a Sunni because he would be a step removed from being a direct competitor who might try to hurt his boss and his large business, a worry the boss nurtured towards his more immediate circle of Sunni acquaintances and partners. Mukhtar Bhai also admitted that his two youngest children took part in the Islamic teachings at the Sunni *madrasa* right opposite his house. The imam had asked him to bring them over, Mukhtar Bhai explained to me, and for the sake of 'being a good neighbour', he complied. He also frequently hosted Sunni neighbours at his house for tea and *paratha* snacks. I knew they were Sunni only because when I entered his home and met them, he introduced them to me as such, as if to demonstrate that there are 'no problems' with Sunni and Shia interacting in the private realm of the household, and even sharing food with each other. Finally, he was a member of a mixed Sunni–Shia circle of businessmen who, on a rotational basis, would pool their money so that one of the members could purchase goods or invest in a project. In his everyday life, in other words, he interacted with as many Sunni as Shia. His discourse about *them* when none of them was present, however, often remained hostile: *they* were the ones who had killed the Prophet's (a.s.) grandson. There was no way he would ever be able to forgive that. I consider it important not to take these statements out of context, however, as it was most likely my presence and my non-alignment with either side that encouraged him to produce this strong stance in the first place. Nevertheless, during the two months of mourning that Shia practice every year (see Chapter 6), and on several other occasions as well as during all Friday prayers, the antagonism between Sunni and Shia is turned into the ritually displayed categorical difference that we know about from the extensive literature on 'the split' between Sunni and Shia.

Singh (2011) has explored what she calls 'the political theology of the neighbor' in the case of neighbouring castes and tribes in Rajastan, putting forward the concept of 'agonistic intimacy' in order to highlight a form of relatedness 'whose coordinates are not predisposed entirely toward either oppositional negation or communitarian affirmation' (Singh 2011: 431). Likewise, Veena Das (2010) has written about a

Fig. 5.6: Mukhtar Bhai holding his youngest grandchild. His Sunni daughter-in-law (far right) observes him with a smile. 2016.

Hindu–Muslim marriage in Delhi, also focusing, on the one hand, on the entwined family histories of the couple and their everyday lives and, on the other hand, on the overall political embeddedness of this intermarriage in potentially violent surroundings in which marrying across castes and religions is frowned upon. While studies such as these highlight inter-religious neighbourliness, relations between people of different denominations within the same religion still lack proper investigation, particularly in Myanmar. Conflict-oriented perspectives still dominate such studies, and in the case of both India and Myanmar, neighborhood is mostly thought of in communal terms, and communities are then assumed to be in latent conflict. Even Singh starts from the assumption that 'potentially hostile neighboring groups' exist (Singh 2011: 430).

In U Maung Maung Ta's book we find yet a different way of engaging with the relationship between Sunni and Shia in Myanmar. He offered the following explanation for the 'slightly inflated' number of Shia Muslims in the country's 1983 census, which lists a total of 20,000 Shias: 'Sunni Muslims … declared themselves as Shiites to escape from the harassment and restrictions of the Wahabi teachings of do's and don'ts in the Wahabi sect of Islam currently afloat in Myanmar' (Maung Maung Ta 2004: 31). While I have no way of assessing the validity of this statement, it was a common topic of conversation among my other Shia interlocutors as well. The statement demonstrates an effort, I argue, to present the Shia community as a category of refuge to which Sunni Muslims resorted to evade worrisome orthodox trends within their own sect. U Maung Maung Ta could have easily declared the large number of Shias in the 1983 census to have been correct and a demonstration of his sect's importance, yet he – and others – decided to acknowledge that the number was inflated, but through their explanation converted their de facto demographic inferiority into moral superiority: it was the Shia community that gave Sunni shelter by allowing them to hide – metaphorically and on paper – within.[18] I argue that the approach my

18. In 2014, the Ministry of Immigration and Population of Myanmar and the United Nations Population Fund (UNPFA) conducted a joint census that identified people's religious affiliations along seven categories (Buddhist, Christian, Muslim, Hindu, Animist, Other, and no religion). The publication of these data was significantly delayed, which spurred rumours among Myanmar's Muslim population of intentional underreporting of the percentage of Muslim citizens in the country.

Shia interlocutors take vis-à-vis their immediate Muslim *other* is also paradigmatic of the way both Shia and Sunni relate to Buddhists: they are completely aware of their numerical inferiority and would never think of directly challenging the majority. Their positionality – not unlike those of many Hindus (as I have laid out in Chapters 3 and 4) – is shaped by an attitude that counters the de facto dominance by first acknowledging their subaltern position, and then rhetorically turning it into an asset. What is achieved in doing so, I argue, goes beyond gaining the rhetorical upper hand in a particular situation; it informs how an individual comports him- or herself in everyday life beyond the fleeting moment in which such legitimizations would have to be uttered.

A final historical example of Sunni–Shia interaction that continues to have an impact how Sunni and Shia relate to each other in Myanmar is the story of U Abdul Razak and Ko Htwe, both of whom died martyrs' deaths on 19 July 1947. U Abdul Razak, a Sunni Muslim and the minister of education at the time, was in a cabinet meeting when renegade soldiers burst into the meeting and opened fire. Ko Htwe,[19] a young Shia and U Abdul Razak's bodyguard, tried to prevent the assassination. Both Muslims perished in the attack and were soon after buried in a Sunni cemetery in the Tamwe township of Yangon. According to U Maung Maung Ta, this joint burial was organized 'to show unity amongst Muslims in Myanmar' (2004: 66), but according to the family members of Ko Htwe, the British would only agree to hand over the two bodies for burial separate from the other (Buddhist) dead if they were buried together in one place. The two bodies were transferred to the Sunni graveyard at night. Ko Htwe, the youngest of those assassinated and in an inferior position as a mere bodyguard, and coming from far-away Mandalay to boot, as a Shia effectively had to 'follow' his boss to the latter's Sunni graveyard where they now lie side by side. Each year on Martyrs' Day, the families of the two men – Shia and Sunni – gather at their graves, which they recently renovated together, to pray for their dead relatives. Since about 2017, this formerly quite private event at the Tamwe cemetery has become heavily mediatized and also widely disseminated via social media by the families themselves.

In order to pray at the graveside of her uncle Ko Htwe, Ma Ma Gyi and all other women of her family have to enter a Sunni graveyard –

---

19. His Muslim name was Ali Asgar Mazindarani, indicating his Iranian origin.

Fig. 5.7: Ma Ma Gyi, a relative of the martyred Shia Muslim Ko Htwe, prays at his grave. He was buried in a Sunni cemetery alongside U Razak, the former minister of education, whose assassination Ko Htwe tried to prevent. 2015.

which is generally considered forbidden for women. She has no problem doing so, however, and when I went with her, she assured me that it would be fine for me, too. Sometimes it can be uncomplicated to align discordant ideology with practice. In individual cases, otherwise stark contradictions – in this case between Sunni and Shia and regarding gender relations – can be ignored.

When talking to relatives of Ko Htwe, they never exclusively portrayed him as a 'Shia martyr', but as someone who had sacrificed his life for the country. In other words, they did not use this dramatic family event to unite as Muslims vis-à-vis a non-Muslim *other*. And who could that *other* have been anyway? The person behind the assassination was hanged in 1948, the British colonial state no longer exists today, and the contemporary Myanmar state, which keeps on cementing the Muslims' marginal position across all areas of political life, did not exist at the time (see Girke forthcoming for more details on the martyrs of 1947; see also Walton 2015). There is, in other words, no common enemy that they can blame for their ongoing suffering.

The ethnographic material within which I centre individuals and their families also provides a necessary, complementary perspective regarding a set of widely debated new laws, the so-called Race and Religion Laws, that were said to have been put in place to protect Buddhist women, but in fact target ethno-religious minorities, particularly Muslim men, by making it more difficult for them to intermarry, to exercise the right to divorce, and to regulate inheritance.

The Race and Religion Laws

The so-called Race and Religion Laws were drafted by a group of monks in 2013 who formed an organization called *Ma-Ba-Tha* (Organization for the Protection of Race and Religion). The organization was banned by the government in May 2017 due to its preaching and instigation of hate against Muslims, particularly Rohingya. By then, these laws had already been approved by Parliament in 2015 and enacted by then-president U Thein Sein. These four laws are the Monogamy Law, the Buddhist Women's Special Marriage Law, the Population Control Act, and the Conversion Law. In the literature, these laws are said to have further exacerbated the divide between Buddhists, Hindus, and Muslims, and that they have raised strong opposition from local activists as well as international scholars.[20] The Monogamy Law is not addressed to a specific religion, but applies to all citizens of Myanmar. It criminalizes adultery, thereby making polygamy a crime and significantly alters the rights to property in cases of divorce that result from such a breach of marriage. In the case of an adultery conviction, the woman will be granted the right to all property from the marriage. This law, along with the Buddhist Women's Special Marriage Law, which builds on the earlier Buddhist Women Special Marriage and Succession Act from 1954 and on the Buddhist Special Marriage and Succession Bill from 1937 (Appendix I, 4; Appendix II Resolution No. 3), thus not only impacts the rights of ethno-religious minorities, but also alters so-called Burmese Buddhist law, with unintended side-effects. Myanmar is the only country in the world that maintains a body of family law specifically for Buddhists.[21] Crouch argued that the law 'has largely

---

20. See, for example, AWID (2014); Cherry Thein (2014); Thin Lei Win (2015); Crouch (2015); Walton, McKay, and Khin Mar Mar Gyi (2015); Frydenlund (2017a, b).

21. For more on the non-codified Burmese Buddhist law (locally referred to as 'Myanmar customary law'), see the work of the late Andrew Huxley (1990, 1998, 2006).

been defined by men and by its perceived opposites, Hinduism and Islam' (2016: 87). It also leads to a hierarchization, with Burmese Buddhist law trumping Islamic law (Crouch 2016: 91). Many Buddhist men in effect practise polygyny themselves – something the monks under whose initiative these laws were drafted had overlooked or chosen to ignore.[22] Since the laws have come into effect, it has given Buddhist women the means to sue their promiscuous Buddhist husbands for adultery.

While the supposedly 'high status' of Buddhist women in Burmese Buddhist law has been deconstructed in recent literature (Harriden 2012; Ikeya 2006, 2011, 2013; Than 2014; Turner 2019), the claim that Buddhist women are better off than Muslim or Hindu women is still prevalent among the local population. At the same time, however, narratives of Buddhist women needing special 'protection' from being lured into Muslim and Hindu marriages are also frequently peddled in public discourse. The Conversion Law specifies that in order to convert to another religion, one must apply to a registration board at the township level to obtain a certificate. Applicants will be questioned by at least four people to ascertain whether they truly believe in the new religion, and will be given a 'study period' of 90 to 180 days to familiarize themselves with its tenets. While the law states that conversion is a right and that once converted one may marry, inherit, and enjoy property rights in accordance with the (customary) laws of the new religion, the procedure is intimidating and invites extortion and bribery. It also gives the registration board the power to determine whether, in alignment with art. 21 §4 of the country's Constitution, the application has or has not been submitted with the intention 'to promote feelings of hatred, enmity or discord between racial or religious communities or sects' – which is an offence punishable by up to two years' imprisonment. The Ministry of Religious Affairs, which oversees the procedure and has been granted powers to issue further directives if deemed necessary, works 'for the purification, perpetuation, promotion and propagation of the Theravada Buddhist Sasana [teachings]' (Ministry of Religious Affairs n.d.). This Conversion Law has been justified on the grounds that it serves the interests of (vulnerable) women, but it does make inter-religious marriage

---

22. My first Myanma language teacher taught me the folk notion that a Burmese man is married 'where he hangs his *longyi* to dry', i.e., wherever a woman will wash his clothes for him.

dauntingly difficult, particularly if a Buddhist woman intends to marry a non-Buddhist man, for which – in the case of Islam – conversion is generally a requirement.

Finally, the Population Control Act is exactly about what the title implies: it introduces a so-called 'birth-spacing' period for women of three years between children, particularly in areas that are deemed 'prone' to high birth rates. While claiming to improve living standards and advance maternal and child health, the law in fact opens up the possibility of targeting Muslim women in particular, whose reproductive decisions are now scrutinized by a 'Township population control healthcare group' and who can be punished for having too many children.[23]

There is now ample literature on the description and assessment of the Race and Religion Laws and their putative targeting of and effects on Buddhist–Muslim partnerships, as well as on the long history of classifying intimate relations between Buddhist women and Muslim men as an assault on Burmese tradition and the nation.[24] Historical literature shows how current debates mirror the immigration debates of the 1920s and 1930s, which cultivated the stereotype of the 'avaricious Burmese woman' who marries the 'Indian immigrant' for his money, only to be abandoned by him when he returned to India (Mazumder 2014). Yet the phenomenon of intermarriage within religious faiths, such as between Sunni and Shia in Myanmar, who are bridging communities on their own terms, has been overlooked so far.

These laws are a classic example of an outcome of what Appadurai (2006) has termed the 'fear of small numbers'. Crouch has hypothesized that 'we are likely to continue to see the use of law to construct and contain religious communities – particularly non-Buddhist communities' (2015: 10). While this might have been the aim of those who drafted the four new laws, the reality looks far more complex if one starts focusing on individual life histories and tries to understand how 'Burmese Indians' have negotiated their sense of self within and across communal divides. Practices of

---

23. This law adds to discriminatory measures in Rakhine state which, since the early 1990s, has imposed a strict two-child policy on ethnic Rohingya Muslims on an on-and-off basis, renewed in 2013 and coupled with the predicament that a couple would only be allowed to register their marriage if they agreed. The policy is still enforced today.

24. Ikeya (2017); Nyi Nyi Kyaw (2018b); Schissler, Walton, and Phyu (2017).

we-formation partly align with and partly contradict *the work of community* as it is (made) visible in public. I have shown that among self-identifying members of these ethno-religious communities, conversion, divorce, exogamy, and polygamy have been practised, are considered normal, and are often openly discussed features of daily Muslim (and Buddhist) family life. They are, on the one hand, deeply personal practices that concern the life histories of individuals, but at the same time they are communal in that they immediately invoke the category of the ethno-religious *other* – especially in the case of intermarriage.

Conclusion

Let us return once again to Mukhtar Bhai, who cited, as his principal motivation for marrying Mushtari Baji, wanting to honour his father-in-law who, as a sailor like his own father, could not take care of his own daughter. In a corner of his flat in downtown Yangon, Mukhtar Bhai had arranged a small shrine, similar to those one can find in many Buddhist and Hindu households, which he turned into a 'Shia shrine', as he put it. In it, he placed an amulet of Imam Hussain ibn Ali (a.s.), a hand of Fatima made out of cardboard, an electric candle, and a small vase with a plastic rose. To the left of the shrine, he had a model of 'his father's ship', leaving it unclear whether the model had belonged to his father or if it was a replica of the ship his father had worked on. The walls surrounding the two sets of objects were decorated with large glossy photographs of Islamic religious buildings. I understood this installation in the shrine which is used by both Hindus and Buddhists in Myanmar as Mukhtar Bhai's creative way of dealing with or perhaps envisioning and realizing his own image of self. He had aligned for himself the ancestry of his paternal (Hindu) line with the Iranian Shia line of his father-in-law through the two men's joint profession as sailors. He also connected this with his own religious identity, which he brought into the picture with the majestic buildings of Islam.

In his first principle of existentialism, Sartre contended that man materializes in the world first, then encounters himself and only afterwards defines himself – 'man is nothing other than what he makes of himself' ([1946] 2007: 22). This principle is in line with both earlier existentialist thought as well as with ethnomethodology. Søren Kierkegaard said that 'life can only be understood backwards. But ... it must be lived forwards' (Kierkegaard 1997: 306), and Garfinkel held that actors usu-

Fig. 5.8: Mukhtar Bhai's 'Shia shrine' (centre), with his 'father's ship' to the left and photographs of Islamic religious buildings. 2018. Colour version on page 289.

ally present rationalizing accounts of their practices *ex post facto*. I have here predominantly discussed the 'new generation' of individuals alive during much of the twentieth century, whose parents were part of the 'Indian class' in colonial Burma, of which U Tun Aung (see Chapter 3) had already spoken and to which we can assign not only him, but Mukhtar Bhai and, to a degree, U Maung Maung Ta. They all had to come to terms with the significant transformation and the 'erosion of paternal authority' (see Butler 2008 on Sartre) in the aftermath of colonialism, authoritarian governance, and two decades of military dictatorship. In part they achieved this by cultivating what Modonesi (2014) has called a 'stagnated subaltern position' (see Introduction) vis-à-vis the former British imperial and the current Bama Buddhist regimes. Their own disposition in an authoritarian, at times dictatorial Burma has always been embedded in a situation of internal colonization that was only briefly lifted around the time of preparing for independence in 1947, when Muslims died alongside the national hero General Aung San, and that continued to define them as members of ethno-religious communities throughout.

To this day I am given bags of Lipton tea to take home to my family when I leave after spending a day at my interlocutors' houses because, as Mukhtar Bhai put it, 'English tea tastes better than ours'. My interlocutors continue to cultivate and uphold these cultural virtues long after the empire collapsed and Burma became an independent state. They also continue to refer to the streets of Yangon by their colonial names, even though all of them were renamed in 1998 when Rangoon turned into Yangon: they live on Phayre Street, not Pansodan Street, and on York Street, not Yaw Myint Gyi Street. That Mukhtar Bhai referred to the independence monument in Maha Bandula Square as 'our independence minaret' (see Chapter 2) is in line with this thinking: he spoke of the independence monument first of all in Muslim terms, acknowledging the postcolonial nation through the lens of the ethno-religious community because there is no space for them to partake equally in a national discourse as *citizens* only, even as they quietly might wish for just that. It is too early to tell whether this situation will change should the current attempted military coup be defeated and all people of Myanmar work towards establishing a federal democratic country based on true equality.

In this chapter I have demonstrated the continuation of 'racial politics' within even the smallest ethno-religious groups, where ideological repertoires of colonial and state control are replicated. My interlocutors' ability to envision their religious lives as members of communities and their public lives as citizens of Myanmar is impacted by the continuously felt presence of their forefathers. Mukhtar Bhai dealt with this 'thrownness' (*Geworfenheit*), as Heidegger has called such existential being in the world, by marrying 'up', thereby altering his communal belonging by becoming part of the high-class 'Iranian Shia'. He substantiated his personal efforts not only by sending all of his daughters off to Iran, even managing to marry one of them to an Iranian man, and by accommodating a Sunni woman in his family, but by devotedly working for the community. At no point, I argue, did Mukhtar Bhai intend to embrace his 'Hindustani' origin or celebrate his blackness as 'empowering'; he consistently viewed it as a reminder of his inferior race and the pervasive impurity that he was always trying so hard to overcome.

CHAPTER 6

Belonging, suffering, and the body of others

On 2 December 2015, I arrived at the Mogul Shia Mosque around 8 p.m. It was the night of Arba'een, forty days after Ashura, and I was joining some of the Shia women who had already begun to gather to perform *matam* (chest-beating) to commemorate the death of Imam Hussain (a.s.).[1] Many had brought their offspring, and I observed how children as young as one or two years old were incorporated in all activities right up through the early hours of the morning. At 9 p.m., the women moved out of the mosque and switched locations with the men, who had been performing *matam* in the Hazrat Abbas Astana on 32nd Street.

During the two-month mourning period, Shia the world over commemorate Imam Hussain (a.s.) and the other martyred imams of the *Ahl-ul-bayt* (People of the House) with a sequence of elaborate rituals and processions in and around mosques, commemoration halls (*imambargahs*), and places of worship called *astanas*. In Yangon, Shia men and women sing eulogies (*marsiya*) and lamentations (*noha*) during the time of mourning, participate in processions with battle standards (*alams*) and decorated replicas of the sepulchres (*zarees*) of the martyred imams,[2] and engage in chest-beating (*matam*). Men also engage in rituals of bodily self-mortification such as flagellation with blades, swords, and razors and running bare-footed over burning coals. Through these practices, they embody the suffering of the martyred imams and join millions of other Shia worldwide in their mourning. Ashura, which takes place on the tenth day of the first month of mourning, called

---

1. As in many other parts of the Islamic world, the fortieth day after a person's death is commemorated with – depending on the regional tradition – a gathering, reading the Qur'an, sharing food, erecting a tombstone or, as in the case of the commemoration of the Shia imams, with lamentations, chest-beating, and processions.

2. All replicas are decorated with either red or green pieces of cloth, indicating whether the imam had been poisoned (green) or beheaded (red).

Moharram, is the single most important day and commemorates the martyrdom of Imam Hussain (a.s.) and his extended family in the Battle of Kerbala (680 CE) in what is now Iraq. Arba'een, known to be the largest commemoration of peace across the world, takes place in the second month, Safar. Moharram starts with the sighting of the new moon and with taking down the red flags that fly atop all religious buildings all year around, and replacing them with black flags that, in most cases, bear an image of a white dagger. Once the new moon is visible again at the end of the second month, the mourning period ends. This is symbolically marked by taking the black flags down from all religious buildings. The mourners also change out of the black and white clothes they had been wearing for the last two months into more colourful ones, indicating the beginning of spring and a time to rejoice.

As with the other chapters in this book, I first foreground people's experiences, which in this case are made tangible through acts of embodiment and centre on the use of ritual objects during Moharram and Safar. The younger Shia members form the core of the labour force and shoulder the bulk of the work that is carried out throughout the mourning period in the various religious associations (Urdu: *anjuman*), whose members organize the mourning rituals and processions, birthday events, and other festivities related to the imams and their wives and children, provide security during these events, take care of offering food to the public, help construct the wooden frames for the *zaree*s, and help raise funds for all these events. Alicia Turner has noted that in the nineteenth century, 'associations were quite the fashion in Rangoon' among 'the cosmopolitan communities', among which she counts 'Hindus and Muslims' (Turner 2014: 75). She speaks of a 'sea change' that enabled laypeople to assume positions of leadership, leading to 'a small army of vice-presidents and honorary secretaries' (2014: 77) assuming (and fighting over) office. Turner, who focuses on Buddhism, then discusses this development in light of a 'Buddhist moral community' that emerged as much from people's reactions to a perceived decline of the state of *sāsana* (the teachings of the Buddha) as from 'the colonial condition' (2014: 107) in the country. Famous monks at that time blamed 'uncivilized' groups for spoiling the 'karmic fruits' (2014: 105): 'Ledi Sayadaw tied behaviour to concrete problems for the community: the presence of those perceived as uncivilized and mentally handicapped in their midst'

(2014: 106). She understands community as 'made manifest through the collective moral project to preserve the *sāsana* [that] created a new mode of ethical subjectivity for Buddhists in colonial Burma' (2014: 109). The *anjumans* I am concerned with here have followed suit and built on similar institutional developments in Muslim-dominated countries such as Iran, as well as in colonial India and later in Pakistan.

To foster an understanding of these mourning rituals as existential situations through which individuals come to experience themselves and others, in the first part of this chapter I draw on Jean-Paul Sartre's theory of the body (1992) and Tine Gammeltoft's framework of belonging (2014, 2018).[3] I relate the first two dimensions of Sartre's tripartite theory of the body, namely 'the body for itself' and 'the body for others', to two modes from Gammeltoft's framework: 'belonging as loss' and 'territorial belonging'. I leave Sartre's third dimension, which he refers to as 'the third ontological dimension of the body', as well as Gammeltoft's third mode of 'political belonging', for the second part of this chapter, where I work with an extended case study that I call 'the Flag'. I link Sartre's 'third ontological dimension of the body' and Gammeltoft's 'political belonging' to ethnomethodological and anthropological literature on gossip and rumour (Rosnow and Fine 1976; Haviland 1977; Bergmann [1987] 1993; Kapferer [1987] 1990; Fine et al. [2005] 2017) and legal anthropological theories on the transformation of disputes (Felstiner et al. 1980–1981; Nader 1990, [2001] 2004; Nader and Grande 2002). Through several stages I trace why the eventual and potentially threatening emerging opposition of 'Bama Buddhists' versus 'Shia Muslims' resulted not in an actual dispute, but in silence. Such silence, I suggest, is emblematic of the disposition of my interlocutors' stagnated subalternity as I have elaborated throughout this book.

---

3. Anthropological studies of the body, which foreground experience, the relationship between self and others, and the relationship between the body and the political, are – to a large degree – inspired by the early existentialist literature. For example, Steven Van Wolputte (2004), drawing on Merleau-Ponty (whose work partly concurs with and partly opposes Sartre's), conceptualizes the body as a 'precarious project of subjectivation' in which bodiliness means intercorporeality. What he calls a 'body self' is understood as always extending in space and place, in material culture and in the bodies of others. For Terence Turner (1994), too, the body is a 'material infrastructure' where selves are produced and belonging is negotiated.

Fig. 6.1: Women and children in front of the Hazrat Abbas Astana. On the right: a black Shia flag and eleven *alam*s (battle standards) on a wooden structure that will be carried during the procession later. Arba'een, 2 December 2015.

'Live like Ali, die like Hussain!'

The slogan 'Live like Ali, die like Hussain!' was written in English on a banner inside the ground floor hall of the Hazrat Abbas Astana. Ali, not to be confused with the child martyr Ali Asghar (see below), is said to have been the Prophet's (a.s.) first male follower. As he embraced Islam when he was still a child, he never took part in the pre-Islamic worship practices found in Mecca at the time, and thus represents a particular sense of purity of faith. My interlocutors explained that Ali (a.s.) lived his life as if he were the mirror of the Prophet (a.s.), and Hussain's (a.s.) death was the ultimate act of sacrifice and is considered by many even outside the Shia faith as an inspiring moment of resistance against oppression. The motto provides an outlook on everyday Shia life, and not only during the mourning period. It reinforces another saying that I was taught very early in my fieldwork: 'Every place is Kerbala, every day is Ashura!', indicating that no matter where and when, an existential part of 'being Shia' means that one carries within oneself a sense of suffering and pain, but that one also comports oneself with a sense of humility and pride in light of being able to bear such a heavy burden (see Dogra 2019).

Fig. 6.2: Two excited young boys performing *matam* by themselves, waiting for the *zaree* of Imam Hussain (a.s.) to be brought outside of the *astana*. Their t-shirts read, 'Laibak, ya Hussain!' (I am here, O Hussain!) Arba'een, 2 December 2015.

After performing *matam* in the *astana*, the women waited outside the building for the men from the mosque to arrive. Fizza Baji was eager to tell me how she and her husband Akber Hussain had already brought milk to the *astana* for 'baby Ali Asghar' earlier in the afternoon of Arba'een: 'We offered milk because he died thirsty. He was six months only; a six-month-old baby only drinks milk.' On Arba'een, it turned out, Shia in Yangon commemorate not only the martyrdom of Imam Hussain (a.s.) and the other ten imams of the *Ahl-ul-bayt* (People of the House), but also the death of the youngest person martyred in the Battle of Kerbala, Ali Asghar, the son of Imam Hussain ibn Ali (a.s.) and his wife Rubab.[4]

A wooden structure bearing the eleven *alam*s – one for each martyred imam – had already been placed in front of the *astana*'s main entrance. When the male participants arrived, some young men from the Hydery Anjuman who were responsible for the ensuing procession on behalf

---

4. Ali Asghar had been taken by his father to the camp of his enemy, Yazid, to negotiate for water for the women and children of his family, who had already been living under siege for several days at the time and were in danger of dying. But, as the story goes, Yazid had the baby killed on the spot, showing no mercy.

of the Hazrat Abbas Astana went upstairs to bring the *zaree* of Imam Hussain (a.s.) down, accompanied by loud wailing and shouting from those waiting outside.[5]

Once the *zaree* was on the street, an elaborate procession was set in motion. The men from the Hydery Anjuman carried the *zaree* from 32nd Street to the Shah Abbas Astana on 38th Street, followed by the wooden structure with the *alams*. Around the same time, the Abbasia Anjuman first brought eleven *alams* from the Punja Mosque to the Mogul Shia Mosque to accompany the black replica of Imam Hussain's grave (*mafa*), which had earlier been brought from the Abbasia Anjuman.[6] When members of the Hydery Anjuman, whom I followed along Maha Bandula Road past Sule Pagoda, City Hall, the Immanuel Baptist Church, and the Mahapeinne Temple, had reached the *astana* in 38th Street, the *zaree* came to a halt and the men entered the building to perform *matam* in front of the white *zaree* of Imam Raza (a.s.), the eighth imam, and the black *zaree* of Imam Hazrat Ali (a.s.), the first Shia imam. Some women were filming the event on their cell phones, others waited in the courtyard talking with other women, often lightly touching their chests with their right hand only, thereby mirroring the chest-beating of the men inside the building. In general, I noticed a wide range of emotional and energetic investment throughout the procession. Some of this investment became visible through the division of labour, with certain men taking leading roles in singing the lamentation songs (*noha*) and others beating their chests in a very pronounced and ostentatious manner, thereby supporting the leading singer as well as those men in the inner group with the rhythmic striking of their bodies. In other cases, it seemed to be more of an individual decision whether and how intensely to participate. Many people remained on the sidelines at all times, seemingly self-absorbed, while others chatted with each other or talked on their phones. Some people wandered away from the group, while others stepped in at a later stage. Once the lamentations inside the

5. The Hydery Anjuman was 'founded in the year 1947 at the Shah Abbas Astana. ... The first President was Hajee Agar Ahmed Bindahneem' (Maung Maung Ta 2004: 112). Since then, all acting members have been members of the 'Iranian Shia' faction.

6. The Abbasia Anjuman 'is one of the oldest Shia *anjumans* in Myanmar' (Maung Maung Ta 2004: 112) and is staffed by members who belong to the so-called Hindustani Shia (see below).

Shah Abbas Astana were over, milk tea was served outside the building. Only then did some women enter the hall to touch the *zarees* or simply to sit down inside for a minute and rest. This was when I saw the young mothers and their infants, dressed in green clothes with red headbands onto which 'Ali Asghar' had been written in Arabic.

'How would you feel...?'

As I came to learn in the coming months of fieldwork, it was younger women in particular who had become interested in altering some elements of how the commemoration of baby Ali Asghar was carried out. I learned that, starting a couple of years earlier, not only did they dress their infants in costumes, but they also decorated a cradle in honour of Ali Asghar. Moreover, it appears that Ali Asghar now also has his own *zaree*, which was stored in the Hazrat Abbas Astana. The initiative had come from young women for whom Rubab, the mother of Ali Asghar, was an important figure to emulate. It was through dressing their infants as Imam Hussain's (a.s.) son that they could envision themselves in the role of the mother of a martyr: 'He is so precious to me...', said Zara, a 23-year-old acquaintance of mine, about her little son after I had initiated a conversation with the words '*mash'Allah!*', indicating that I was congratulating her without explicitly referring to her son's outfit. 'Now

Fig. 6.3: Embodying Rubab, the mother of Ali Asghar, this young mother dressed her own child as the martyred six-month-old son of Imam Hussain (a.s.). Arba'een, 2 December 2015. Colour version on page 290.

imagine you lose your son the way Rubab did', she continued. 'How would you feel?' We had met each other at the mosque many times before and she therefore knew that I, too, was the mother of a young son, whom I had often brought along. While I am usually very open when it comes to the participatory part of participant observation, my first reaction was to push away the intruding thoughts and images that had immediately begun to enter my mind. I did not want to follow her any further down that path. I found it deeply disturbing, as if I were actively inviting despair. But it helped me understand that in her case, as well as in those of the other young mothers I engaged with that night and in the subsequent days, that was exactly what she was doing: deliberately conjuring up the scenario of Ali Asghar's murder by entertaining the thought that it could have been her own child.

It was through their infants' bodies that these young women tried to come as close as possible to an intense feeling of suffering and self-sacrifice that went beyond imagination. This stance, I suggest, provides us with a twist on the existentialist position held by Sartre, who argued that self-consciousness arises in the gaze of the other. In the case of Ali Asghar's martyrdom, the subjective experience of oneself as another is enabled by relating to the very body of one's child – not its gaze, and not fully others' gazes, either. It also alters Sartre's take on the corpse as 'that pure past of life' (1992: 456), that turns a completely external 'event' into an intersubjective, intercorporeal situation. Part of it surely is performative in the sense of a conscious enacting with an observing audience in mind, for example when mothers held their babies facing out towards others or lifted them upwards as if offering the (dead) body to Allah, a gesture I later also found frequently depicted in photographs from similar Shia events worldwide. But part of it is, I suggest, not aimed at impression management. When women dress their children as Imam Hussain's (a.s.) son, they have found for themselves a particular way of embodying Rubab and therefore of experiencing a form of existential suffering where they, to quote Sartre again, 'put the corpse at the origin of the living body' (1992: 452).

The display of emotions was, on the one hand, expected from them during the mourning period, when members needed to publicly demonstrate their pain collectively through shedding tears, wailing, and lamenting; on the other hand, such an 'existential exercise' allows one to explore one's sense of self, as it has the capacity to shatter any taken-for-granted-ness about the way we go about our everyday lives. It was by deliberately probing into the dark abyss of what a mother might feel if her child were to die – something Zara encouraged me to experience myself – that they pursued a specific understanding of who we are as individuals. At the same time, embodying Rubab allowed these mothers to express solidarity and feel communion with other mothers from their faith worldwide.[7]

Tine Gammeltoft has written about 'belonging as loss' in the context of selective reproduction in Vietnam, where women who had to have abortions or who experienced a stillbirth had to 'push this child-to-be out of the zones of memory within which deceased kin members are usually cared for with affection, love, and respect' (2014: 234). In my case, women actively pushed the 'child-that-is' *into* these zones of memory in order to conjure feelings of suffering and pain. And in Vietnam the danger of being haunted by a deceased child if one is even thinking about it – let alone commemorating it – stands in stark contrast to my case in Yangon, where women summoned the spectre of a child murdered centuries ago through the bodies of their own living infants. Gammeltoft argues that '[a]nthropologies of belonging are also anthropologies of lives *in potentia*: investigations into not-fully-realized identities and relational possibilities, into lives that could have unfolded but did not' (2014: 235). While her interlocutors oriented themselves towards the future, in my case women oriented themselves towards the past.

When I later reported to Akber Hussain that I had met several women with 'baby Ali Asghars' during the procession, he commented upon it in a rather neutral way: 'They saw it on TV. It is popular now.' It turned out that this 'tradition' had only recently emerged, starting in 2013 in Iran, where nowadays the 'Day of Ali Asghar' is being commemorated in mosques and even stadiums. In Iran, this particular innovation is only a piece in the puzzle of the state's long history of orchestrating the Battle of Kerbala as part of state ideology (Good and Good 1988; Khosronejad 2006, 2013). But in Yangon, the innovation was pushed by young moth-

---

7. When I watched interviews with women in Iran conducted on the 'Day of Ali Asghar', many emphasized that they were thinking of women in Syria who are currently experiencing a kind of suffering similar to Rubab's, which made them realize that Syria was not a safe place to raise one's children.

ers themselves. When they also arranged for a permanent *zaree* of Ali Asghar to be incorporated into the events during Moharram and Safar, they were backed by some elderly women from the Mogul Shia mosque for whom this presented a welcome occasion to perform in their roles as 'noha and *marsiya* khans' (Maung Maung Ta 2004: 91), that is, as eloquent lead performers of the lamentation songs who set the style, tone, and rhythm of the event. They oversaw how the cradle and the *zaree* were decorated, where food offerings needed to be placed, and how food was distributed among the women once the lamentations were over.

I took part in such an all-female event on 6 December 2015 at the Mogul Shia mosque and noticed how the younger women let the elderly ladies of the mosque take centre stage. But when I later spoke to the young women, they emphasized that it had been their idea and initiative from the beginning.[8] It turned out that while material alterations to *waqf* property are officially forbidden, there is significant leeway in granting individuals opportunities to alter the temporary arrangement of the religious objects housed in these buildings.[9]

---

8. Judith Schlehe and Evamaria Sandkühler (2014) show how it is often through new religious practices that women in particular claim space to express themselves and transcend established hierarchies.

9. Throughout fieldwork, I encountered several other cases of innovation that revolved around the mourning period. Ko Swe, for example, a young unmarried relative of the family in charge of the Shah Abbas Astana, a family *waqf* building, once told me how he had seen in his dream a replica of a sepulchre (*zaree*) of the fourth Shia imam Zayn-ul-Abidien (a.s.). Ko Swe then proudly showed me some pictures on his cell phone of the *zaree* that he himself had built according to his dream. The *zaree* was stored in the vicinity of the *astana* building, to be brought out on the 25th day of Moharram, when the martyrdom of the fourth imam is commemorated. This is worthy of mentioning because 'traditionally', this imam 'never' (according to other interlocutors) had a *zaree* – only a replica of a grave (*mafa*). Another interlocutor of mine said of Ko Swe's dream, 'He *said* he dreamt it!' thus indicating that he understood there to be a difference between dreaming and talking about a dream. Dreams are a frequent motif in Islam. In Afghanistan, for example, it is said that the shrine of Hazrat Ali, the first Shia imam, was built in the twelfth century after a local mullah had a dream; alternative versions speak of several hundreds of noblemen having had the same dream. The shrine was built on the spot where an investigation had detected a tomb that had been destroyed by the Mongols. For more on the role of dreams in Islam, see Edgar (2011), Felek and Kynsh (2012), and Mittermaier (2011); on the relation between dreams, omens, and magic, see Louw (2010). Ko Swe's innovation was tolerated.

Fig. 6.4: Women first decorated the cradle of Ali Asghar by placing shawls, pieces of cloth, and flower garlands onto the replica and the *alam*, then offered food and sat down to pray in front of these objects. Mogul Shia Mosque, 6 December 2015. Colour version on page 290.

Conspicuous suffering and the individual body

Once our group had left the Shah Abbas Astana on 38th Street where I had encountered the young mothers with their babies, we continued towards the Punja Mosque for another round of *matam* inside the build-ing and then proceeded along Merchant Street. It was already 2 a.m. when my companions and I, illuminated by the lights of the electrical rods and the distant glowing of the Sule Pagoda in the north, ran into the group from the Abbasia Anjuman at the broad intersection of Merchant Street and Sule Pagoda Road. They had proceeded from the Mogul Shia Mosque towards the Bindaneem Imambargah on 30th Street to come meet 'our' group.[10] The members of the two *anjuman*s, facing each other, continued performing *matam*. While they were definitely

10. Like all *imambargah*s in Yangon, the Bindaneem Imambargah is a so-called fam-ily *waqf* building, administered by members of the Bindaneem family still today. As in other cases of religious property, there is a trail of colonial-era court case documents to be found. For more on the family history, see Afsheen (2011). For an analysis of a personal law case concerning the intermarriage of a man from

215

competing in terms of style, rhythm, and sheer volume, they were also sharing the same space and oriented themselves towards each other. After this stand-off, which lasted for about ten minutes, the two groups switched sides so that 'our' *zaree* could proceed towards the Bindaneem Imambargah on 30th Street and 'their' *mafa* could carry on towards the Punja Mosque. They would later come full circle back to the Mogul Shia mosque, to which our group was eventually heading as well.

These two *anjumans* represented the two factions – the 'Hindustani Shia' and the 'Iranian Shia' – that we encountered in the previous chapter. U Maung Maung Ta, the deceased former managing trustee of the Mogul Shia Mosque, wrote of the 'Hindustani' Anjuman called Abbasia as follows:

> The *anjuman-e-Abbasia* (Abbasia) is one of the oldest Shia *anjumans* in Myanmar. The deserving and natural control of the Mogul Shia Jamaay Masjid by the Iranian Mogul community in Rangoon had raised eyebrows and become a bone of contention between the Mogul Shias and the rest of the other Shia in Rangoon, especially the Indian Shia immigrants or those born in Burma of Indian subcontinent origins. Hence the natural emergence of an *anjuman* uniting all non-Moguls in it *to contest, if necessary,* with the Mogul Shia. (Maung Maung Ta 2004: 112; emphasis added)

U Maung Maung Ta does not indicate the possible grounds on which the two factions might contest with one another, but the way he phrased it recalls classic anthropological texts on religious factionalism such as *Saints and Fireworks* (1965), in which Jeremy Boissevain described the processions of Catholic *festa partiti* on Malta, and James Watson's *Fighting with Operas* (1996) in Hong Kong. In both cases, the anthropologists analysed religious processions as a way of transposing their interlocutors' historically transmitted inclination towards antagonistic violence to the ritual sphere. As such, they provide a rather functionalist argument whereby religion fosters communal cohesion (in a Durkheimian sense), but at the same time religiously organized factions also oppose one another as a way of venting and reducing tensions, only to be integrated once again into the general community. But as I looked more closely into how the respective young people within the

the Bindaneem family and a Burmese Buddhist woman in the mid-nineteenth century that was argued before the Privy Council in London, see Ikeya (2017).

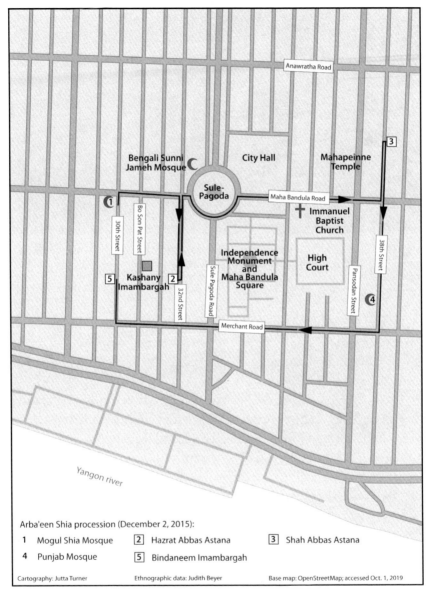

Fig. 6.5: Shia procession on Arba'een. 2 December 2015.

two *anjuman*s interacted with one another, I found that some people, even as they were integrated into the choreography of the faction to which they respectively belonged, stood out individually. Once we had reached the Bindaneem Imambargah, I positioned myself opposite the religious building at the entrance of a veranda facing the street and the

Fig. 6.6: Senior men (middle) performing *matam*, with the lead performer in the middle (circled, without shirt). A group of women (lower left) observe them while lightly beating their chests. Two other men (right) are engaged in a conversation. Arba'een, 2 December 2015.

members. For half an hour I remained at this spot, alternating between video-recording what was going on in front of me, taking photographs, and looking around, trying to observe as much as possible of what was happening on the sidelines.

Directly in front of me, several younger men began separating themselves off from the seniors to their left, who had formed a circle in front of the *zaree* of Imam Hussain (a.s.), and from the women on the sidelines. They carefully arranged their positions in two ways: first by forming two rows facing each other and second roughly by height (and age), with the shortest standing furthest to the right or, alternatively, between the two rows, as if being sheltered (see the green arrows in Fig. 6.7.). I had witnessed similar arrangements on other occasions where senior men would form circles around the children who were learning to perform *matam*. In the complex spatial set-up that emerged outside the *imambargah*, members were thus grouped not only according to division of labour, age, and gender, but also in regard to what I came to understand as *individual* inclinations to act out their suffering that were, nevertheless, still embedded in the formation of various we-groups. Some of the young men, for example, had decided to leave their shirts on (not pictured); all decorations on their clothing indicated loyalty to Imam Hussain (a.s.), by way of various colours,

Fig. 6.7: Despite Arba'een being a commemoration where flagellation is not expected, some youths decided to engage in self-mortification anyway. The green arrows show the two opposing lines of youths, the white circles those who are filming. Red arrows indicate onlookers' lines of sight. Arba'een, 2 December 2015.

styles, and motifs.[11] These young men engaged in conversation while only lightly beating their chests. They occasionally looked over to their fellow age-mates to the right who had decided to take their shirts off and had begun to self-flagellate with razors in both hands. This conspicuous part of the group was also keenly observed by several women, some of them their relatives, who were recording with their cell phones (white circles), and a few men who stood further in the street, forming a third parallel row (orange arrow). The youths were, however, completely ignored by the group of senior men on the left side as well as the Shia cameraman who was videotaping the whole time – his lens and attention rested firmly on the senior men throughout.

Towards the very end of *matam*, a very young boy was allowed to try out razors, too, while most of the older boys had already begun to gather their belongings, which they had put in front of themselves on the asphalt. This performance of *matam* can also be said to involve a coming-of-age element, as young men learn how to properly perform *matam* by themselves, but not so much by mimicking the elders, who

11. Slogans on the T-shirts included: 'Youth are a symbol of hope', 'Imam Hussain (a.s.) – Mankind's greatest martyr who exposed the true face of terrorism', 'Anjuman-e-Hizbul-mehdi since 2012', 'There is not another day like yours, O Hussain', and 'Labbak'a ya Hussain (a.s.).'

Fig. 6.8: Learning how to suffer: under the eyes of watchful female relatives, these young boys self-flagellate with razors in their hands. Arba'een, 2 December 2015.

were not engaging in any self-flagellation. Rather, their bodies were aligned with and juxtaposed to one another. Facing the person directly in front of them enabled them to mirror the gestures of the other, so that even as each was occupied with his own body and the pain that he inflicted on it, he simultaneously oriented himself outwards, towards the individual standing opposite. The surrounding age-group provided a less direct mirror, and, more distant yet, the senior men on the left side, the women and the other bystanders on the sidelines, and, last but not least, the religious building in front of them combined to form a material ensemble towards which their practices were addressed. Each one was, to use Sartre's concepts, alternating between first relating to his body as it appeared 'for itself' (*pour soi*) as a psychic object, experienced from within as it 'exists itself' (*le corps existé*), and second as it appeared 'for the other' (*pour autrui*) and is seen from their perspectives as an object in the world (*le corps-vu*).

When observing the self-flagellating youths closely, I noticed how many of them switched between these two states: first, regularly checking their blood-stained chests and touching their own blood with their hands, and second, looking up and around.[12] One boy turned around slowly in a full circle – as if wanting to see how many in the audience might have had their eyes on him, or, to quote Sartre, whether 'I am indeed that object which the other is looking at and judging' (1992: 350). While 'being-seen' (*être vu*) is a form of self-experience through the other, self-flagellation actively marks and questions the body's boundary. Bodies are opened up and made vulnerable; these are moments when 'the pure contingency of presence' is encountered; a situation for which Sartre uses – apt in the case of self-flagellation – the concept of 'flesh' (Fr.: *chair*).

To me, the boys' gestures and postures revealed the two ontological states (as Sartre called it) of experiencing the body: on the one hand, feeling self-conscious and objectified by others; on the other hand, proud and maybe even boastful, thus constituted as individuals as well as a part of a *we*.

Under the rubric of 'territorial belonging', Tine Gammeltoft is concerned with how individuals 'develop, practice, claim and nurture attachment to places' (Gammeltoft 2018: 86), while simultaneously becoming subjected to the claims that places exert on people (Strathern 2000: 152, cited in Gammeltoft 2018: 86). I suggest that we can understand this second type of belonging, for which she draws on anthropological literature on kinship and place (Edwards 1998; Lovell 1998; Stasch 2009), not only in relation to physical objects such as religious buildings, but also more generally to the world as such, which includes other individual bodies in movement.[13] The *wes* that came into being in front of the Bindaneem Imambargah that night were realized through individuals acting 'for themselves' as much as 'for others'.

---

12. For a discussion of touch and belonging in the context of discourses of (un-) touchability and an alternative theory of the body that draws on Scheper-Hughes and Lock's (1987) terminology, see Alex (2008).

13. Merleau-Ponty argued similarly when he wrote that 'my existence as subjectivity is merely one with my existence as a body and with the existence of the world, and because the subject that I am, when taken concretely, is inseparable from this body and this world' (Merleau-Ponty [1945] 1962: 408). Rupert Stasch (2009) aligned body and world when writing about his Korowai interlocutors' relation to land: 'Owning land is like having a body or a voice. A place is a kind of second body, a footing in the world by means of which a person acts expressively towards others or stays carefully separate from them' (cited in Gammeltoft 2018: 87).

While there seemed to be some sort of cultural script in place as to how one positions oneself during *matam* (since the spatial arrangement according to age-groups did not seem to have happened spontaneously), only half of the youths began to self-flagellate. In this context, it bears emphasizing that the self-flagellating youths were almost completely ignored by the senior men – those on the left and the many elders who stood on the sidelines – as well as by the cameraman who was document-ing the procession. When I later asked what the youths' motives might have been to transgress from the cultural script on Arba'een (which, to reiterate, usually does not call for self-flagellation), Akber Hussain, who had been present during the event himself and had turned his back to the self-flagellating youths the entire time, simply commented, 'Because they want to.' I understood his comment as acknowledgement that the other members granted the young men a lot of freedom and space to express themselves through these acts of creative self-realization. No account was demanded, and others' practices were barely policed. From these tolerated practices, which are of literally existential importance to the young men performing them in this context, I now turn to more outward-oriented action that led to the muting of the young people, the explicit enactment of community, and to what Tine Gammeltoft has called 'political belong-ing'. Or, in Sartre's terms, to 'the third ontological dimension of the body'.

'The Flag'

The Kashany Imambargah is located on Bo Sun Pat Street in Pabedan township in downtown Yangon (see Figures 0.5 and 6.5.). From the out-side, it looks like a regular house. Nothing indicates that on the second floor there is a prayer hall that has been in the hands of a Shia family since 1896. The original building has since then been demolished, but the Kashany family has retained the religious space. Initially, the *imam-bargah* had been managed by its founder, Mr. Kashany. After his death, his family took over: his wife Amina Begum, their eldest son Mirza Sadiq, their second son Ebrahim, and the two daughters Khairunnisa Begum and Fatima Sultan (Maung Maung Ta 2004: 212). The property is locally categorized as 'family *waqf*'. I am recounting the following story in a sequential order on the basis of what my interlocutors told me and what I subsequently found out through local media and by spend-ing time at the mosque and the *imambargah*.

It was the last day of Safar, 10 December 2015, when a black flag with a white sword and Arabic letters was raised outside the windows of the Kashany Imambargah. Once raised, it quickly caught the attention of Win Ko Ko Latt, a man well known in the public sphere as someone active in the Peace and Diversity Party, a marginal political group that strongly advocates a Buddhist state with Buddhism as the official state religion and does nothing to hide its anti-Muslim political stance. He posted a picture of the flag on his Facebook account at 1 p.m. on 10 December, accompanied by the following comment: 'I have informed the authorities about this flag. They will investigate it.' The same day, the local newspaper *Sandaw Chein* ('Standard Time') published an article entitled 'Spreading the news on social media about launching an ISIS flag'. In the article, the journalist stated that word of a flag that resembled the flag of the so-called Islamic State had been spreading on Facebook. A screenshot of Win Ko Ko Latt's Facebook post accompanied the article. The journalist noted that the press had found out that the Yangon regional police, particularly officers of Pabedan township, and neighbourhood administrators had gone to the building to demand that the flag be taken down.[14] The article also gave the statement of the Shia administrator of the building, who said that the flag had been raised in commemoration of the grandchild of the Prophet (a.s.) who was killed in Iraq 1,400 years ago. Four days later, the online English-language news portal *Coconuts Yangon* picked up the thread and wrote an article entitled 'Authorities ask Shi'ite Muslims in Yangon to take down "ISIS flag"'.[15] In this article, the journalist reported that the community had complied with the request to take down the flag, although they were 'not happy about it'.

Irrespective of what had happened that day, the commemorations on the occasion of the martyrdom of the 11th Imam Hassan (a.s.) proceeded on the night that the new moon rose, with another procession through the downtown area. When I walked along with the members of the Hydery Anjuman, I did not sense any fear or precaution among the members or those with whom I spoke during that night or in the following days. As usual, there were no police on the streets when we

---

14. In a photograph that someone from the mosque had taken of this contingent, I saw that in addition to the people mentioned in the article, a representative of the Peace and Diversity Party and two monks had gone to the mosque as well.

15. *Coconuts Yangon*, 14 December 2015.

marched across intersections and paused in the middle of streets for *matam*. The first I heard of the case was when several members mentioned it to me that night on their own initiative, asking, 'Have you heard about the flag?' 'Have you heard what has happened?' I was then immediately let in on gossip concerning who might have put up the flag: several young men from this *anjuman* told me that the trustees themselves had put up the flag in order to divert attention from their own mismanagement as well as from the matter of elections for the Mogul Shia Mosque. Several days earlier, the younger members of this *anjuman* had dared to invite the trustees to the Kashany Imambargah to discuss these matters, thereby challenging the trustees' authority and claiming a voice for themselves. That night, the men gossiped that it might have been the managing trustee himself who had put up the flag which – in contrast to other black Shia flags – not only depicted a white dagger, but also had a line of Arabic script on it – which was unusual in Yangon, but not necessarily problematic. The impending elections alluded to here had been a frequent topic of gossip throughout my fieldwork. After the managing trustee of the mosque, U Maung Maung Ta, died at the beginning of 2015, there had been no elections even though they were stipulated by the Constitution of the mosque. Instead, U Maung Maung Ta had appointed a successor just before his death: a junior relative of the old man who remained rather aloof from public affairs during the time of my fieldwork. In the following days, other members, who were not part of this youth group, told me that the flag incident had been due to 'the Sunnis' wanting to cause problems for 'the Shia', whom they disrespected and did not wish well. Yet again others held that it must have been 'monks', by which they meant members of that radical wing of the Buddhist *sangha* which had also overseen the drafting of the Race and Religion Laws that targeted Muslims in Myanmar. This particular version, however, was not as widespread as the other versions; it was only mentioned to me by two people, and only after they had first offered other explanations and then only eventually admitted that 'no one really knows'.

Two days after the mourning period had come to an end, the trustees and clergy of the Mogul Shia Mosque got together and issued an official letter that they addressed to the President of the Union of the Republic of Myanmar, the Senior General of the Armed Forces, Aung San Suu

Kyi in her role as head of the National League for Democracy, the Prime Minister, and several senior police officers of Yangon. The letter embedded the concrete case within the overall political 'transition' of the country and began by stating that in 2015, 'free and fair democratic elections were successfully held by the President U Thein Sein and the government'.[16] The signatories then accused Win Ko Ko Latt in his function as party chairman of 'breaking the law, causing conflict, spreading racism and violence'. They continued to explain the meaning of Moharram and Safar. They described at great length the purpose of the black flags and the commemoration period of the Shia and emphasized that they have held these commemorations in the townships of Pabedan and Kyauktada (see Fig. 0.5) for more than one hundred years with legal permission from the authorities. The letter then addressed the necessity of adhering to the country's Constitution when it comes to freedom of religious expression. They warned of dangerous developments in the country, particularly the interference of nationalist parties in the religious realm, which would contradict the country's 2008 Constitution. Finally, they described the behaviour of the party leader as an 'insult to the dignity of our President U Thein Sein' which might have 'a negative effect on the overall peace and development of our country'.

The letter is three pages long and was signed by 73 members, all of whom provided their Burmese names instead of their Muslim names, as well as their national identification card numbers, and included photographs of the day when the Party members and monks had visited the trustees in their office in the mosque to demand removal of the flag. Shia members without the pink ID card that marks them as full citizens (i.e., belonging to the country's officially acknowledged '135 races') and those completely without Burmese citizenship did not sign the letter. The others sent the document off – and never heard anything back. When I would ask for an update on the case over the following weeks, the answers I inevitably received were 'Nothing. It's over', and 'It's all quiet now'. Others had stories to tell about how certain important individuals had come to join their side and speak out for them. I was told, for example, that a well-known monk who was otherwise part and parcel of controversial portrayals in the local news due to his stance on

---

16. For an overview and a critique of the literature on 'transition' in Myanmar, see Girke and Beyer (2018).

Buddhism and nationalism had promised to defend 'the Shia community's century-old tradition' of commemorating Moharram and Safar.

Trying to make sense of this case, I wondered: Could it be that the managing trustee himself had deployed a symbol that would be associated with the wrong type of Islam, leading to a public outcry? Did he thus purposefully provoke the rumour that laid blame on the entire community only to then rise to the occasion and 'rescue' his fellow members from being associated with terrorists and the community from having their religious practice taken away by the state? Could it be that the threat of a full-fledged dispute between the Shia community and the Buddhist Bama majority offered an opportunity for the managing trustee to speak on behalf of his community, to unite its members, and to challenge the grievance publicly by addressing the highest officials in the country? This is a possible if convoluted interpretation that carried some weight with some of my interlocutors, but – in the end – I cannot know whether this was what was truly going on. When it comes to gossip and rumour, finding out 'what really happened' misses the point, because gossip and rumour are always about social relations, and not about discrete, disconnected items that could become 'known' in their own right. Instead, the case at hand demands attention to the communicative processes that were set in motion, as the interlinkage of gossip and rumour and the work to counter them has implications that go far beyond 'the Flag' incident.

In need of explanation: gossip, rumour, and dispute avoidance

In their famous article 'The Emergence and Transformation of Disputes: Naming, Blaming, Claiming', Felstiner et al. (1980–1981) investigated disputes from what they called a 'transformation perspective', placing individual actors at the centre of their analysis. Their contribution drew more attention to what was going on before a dispute case evolved, that is, it de-emphasized the analysis of formal legal procedures in dispute studies. Paying 'attention to individuals as the creators of opportunities for law and legal activity' (1980–1981: 633), they delineated three stages: first, realizing that a particular experience has been injurious (*naming*); second, attributing this particular experience to the fault of another individual (*blaming*); and third, making the attribution public by voicing a grievance and demanding remedy (*claiming*). The authors argued that only when a claim is rejected in whole or in part by the accused other (who is still at this point merely informally accused) does a case become a dispute proper.[17] In the following, I will equate gossip with naming, rumour with blaming, and the actions of the trustees and other senior men in the name of community as a form of claiming.

Gossip usually happens in face-to-face situations and it is orally transmitted (or, in these times of social media, between individuals in private chats) and consists of talking about others rather than addressing them directly regarding their somehow problematic behaviour. It is at least partly clandestine and thus always deniable. In classic anthropological studies on gossip that emerged from the 1960s onwards, gossip was understood in terms of its normative function, as being a socially integrative tool that facilitated exchange of information and monitoring of fellow members' actions for evaluation and eventual correction (Gluckman 1963). It has traditionally been studied in the context of acephalous societies, in villages and later also in urban neighbourhoods. In subsequent studies, the disintegrative potential of gossip, its capacity to exclude others from discourse, its relation to power, and its potential for individual self-realization, as well as its gendered dimension, were acknowledged (Paine 1967; Coates [2004] 2013). A mediating position was taken by interactionists such as John Haviland (1977), for whom gossip is a meta-cultural resource that helps one make sense of the world. It is also 'most obviously instrumental in furthering *factional* ends' (1977: 8). Gossip and community become conjoined in this particular approach not because gossip works on the basis of a certain level of intimacy and familiarity, but because it is through gossip that such levels of intimacy get

---

17. Their approach was one of the first to decentre legal anthropological attention, which had often been limited to observing trials in courts or other legal forums, from the formal disputing stage. See also John Holleman (1973), who made an even earlier plea for including what he called 'trouble-less cases' of everyday life as an integral part of legal anthropological analysis, and Keebet von Benda-Beckmann (1984) for a systematic overview of the pre-trial, trial, and post-trial stages of disputes. See also Sally Falk Moore (2005: 350) for a particularly poignant critique of 'local dispute watching' as 'the principal form of social voyeurism in legal anthropology' and Beyer and Girke (2015) for a take on the importance of studying disputes and alternative dispute resolution in the formation of an anthropology of the state.

negotiated in the first place. For F.G. Bailey, for example, gossip groups are 'moral communities' who are 'prepared to make moral judgments about one another' (Bailey 1971: 7). It is often the case that through gossip boundaries are drawn, uniting some individuals while alienating others, no matter how small a thus constituted particular we-group might be. Whether gossip acts in a binding or constraining capacity and whether we treat it as providing us with a commentary on the world around us or as a way to find meaning in situations of ambiguity are empirical questions and issues related to one's theoretical inclination.

One critique of anthropological approaches to gossip has been put forward by the ethnomethodologist Jörg Bergmann, who, in his monograph *Discreet Indiscretion: The Social Organization of Gossip* (1993), has argued that the dilemma with gossip is that if we approach it as a specific object of scientific inquiry, it loses its main characteristic, namely its mundane obviousness. Bergmann problematized what was to that point the standard anthropological approach of treating gossip as a form of social control (as Malinowski did) or as a mechanism for creating and maintaining the coherence of social groups (as Gluckman did), both of which are functionalist approaches. When we understand gossip in that way, according to Bergmann, we are no longer scrutinizing gossip as such, but control or coherence, thereby dismissing gossip and investigating community. He then goes on to review literature that interprets gossip as informal information management, particularly in light of Goffman's concept of 'impression management'. Bergmann concludes that this approach, in which gossip is viewed as a mere 'technique' that is put to use in an individual's interest, is just as functionalist as the earlier approaches were. He also dismisses the position often held in legal anthropology that gossip is only the first informal step of adjudication that then progresses, eventually, to involving the police and official legal institutions. Ethnographic studies are usually about the supposed effects of gossip, he argues, but without the actual gossip being reproduced. But Haviland, at least, does pay attention to what he calls the 'native theory of gossip', particularly the way public information gets separated from private information, the question of truth versus hearsay, and the general ethics of telling tales on people (Haviland 1977: 39).

It seems to me that the reason we have more stories about gossip than actual gossip also has to do with the very structure of gossip itself:

gossip requires a direct *other* to whom information can be passed and an absent *other* about whom people talk. In many cases, anthropologists only hear about gossip when somebody makes the effort to tell them directly. Only when gossip is overheard is this not the case, but often gossip is told in a way that is aimed at explicitly excluding a potentially overhearing third party: individuals lower their voices, speak softly with a hand over their mouth or directly into another's ear. All this makes gossip, in contrast to other types of talk, much more difficult to overhear. During my fieldwork, I encountered gossip predominantly in my role as its direct recipient. Hence, I cannot easily generalize from the material I gathered regarding the wider function of 'the story' that was being spread. Instead, my focus needs to lie on the telling of it as such: what was being told and how was it evaluated or framed by the speaker?

First, in line with Felstiner et al., I understand gossip as a form of naming. I had first heard about the internal gossip while walking with members of the Hydery Anjuman during the procession for Imam Hassan (a.s.). The individuals I spoke to emphasized that this 'news' was shared with me because I knew enough about the *anjuman's* internal affairs. As it was mostly young people and people in their late thirties sharing the 'news', the we-group that formed at this stage was not only based on *anjuman* membership as such, but also on age. Gossip reached me only *after* the rumour about the flag being an 'ISIS flag' had already begun to spread via the media – of which I had been unaware at that point.

Looking back, I now consider it highly likely that my interlocutors' gossip about the possibility of the mosque's managing trustee having planted the 'wrong' type of flag had a very concrete purpose: the rumour had at that time already been 'out' for a while and required a counter-narrative. I know from my fieldwork in Kyrgyzstan (Beyer 2016: 147) that it can be crucial for individuals who suspect that they might become subjects of gossip or rumour to actively and pre-emptively spread news about themselves before others get a chance to. While no longer able to alter the course of events, this way an individual can at least try to direct the interpretation of the rumour or gossip so as to present themselves in a better light. The young people who shared the news with me that night might have wanted to make sure that I heard it from them first, and not from others or from the media. While not being 'one of them', I was certainly positioned to be on 'their side' once other *others* entered the picture. I suggest that in any case my interlocutors had to come up with a plausible version of gossip to account for this rumour – even if they knew full well what had happened themselves. It was striking to me that the version most frequently peddled that night was that of an internal manoeuvre, staged by the Shia elders against the younger people of the *anjuman* who had this time transgressed from 'the way things are done here' (that is, a cultural script) in a way that could no longer be tolerated or ignored as discrete individuals' 'creative' outlets, such as when young mothers dressed their infants as Ali Asghar or when a group of youngsters decided to flagellate themselves during Arba'een. 'They do not like us for asking them to come to the *imambargah*', said one. 'They do not want to hold elections', said another. 'Don't trust the trustees!' said a third, which poignantly summarized their stance vis-à-vis the elders. In this case I thus suggest viewing gossip not as an instrument of sanction or coherence, but as something that legitimated a course of events that had already begun and that demanded an explanation by an individual or a group.

Second, we can understand rumour as a form of *blaming* in the sense of Felstiner et al. In contrast to gossip, rumour is aimed at a wider external audience. It lays blame on a specific actor or group of actors by identifying them and holding them accountable while still withholding a direct accusation at this stage. Rumours are, in contrast to gossip, 'collectively constructed explanations for circumstances or events that may be, for various reasons, difficult to explain' (Kroeger 2003: 244). They are said to circulate most actively in times of uncertainty, and often relate 'to collective hopes and fears that reach beyond the moral behaviour of individuals' (Coast and Fox 2015: 223). Rosnow (1991) has identified four factors that must be present for rumours to be transmitted: a) they must be outcome-relevant for the audience; b) they must increase personal anxiety; c) they must have a generalized uncertainty at their core; and d) they must be credible at least to a certain extent. While the first two factors take into account the effects of rumours in regard to an individual's experience, the latter two factors are more group oriented, so that spreading rumours becomes a form of collective 'problem solving' (see also Shibutani 1996: 17). As in the case of gossip, these approaches border on the functionalist, where the focus lies on meaning-making or on resolving a situation that is deemed to be extraordinary. In Myanmar, rumour has also been mentioned in the literature as 'a barometer of people's hopes and fears' (Larkin 2007). James Scott has argued that rumours are part of a 'hidden transcript' that allows subordinate people to express views that differ markedly from those of their superiors (Scott 1990). While these views are in line with those of other anthropologists who understand rumour as a weapon of the weak that helps them overcome power imbalances (Scheper-Hughes 1992; Masquelier 2000; Kirsch 2002), what seems to have escaped Myanmar scholars is that the rumours with the most dramatic consequences are circulated by members of the demographic and religious Buddhist majority and feed on an abstract, generalized fear of Muslims.[18] Muslims, however, are clearly not only a minority in the country, but are also in a position of subalternity, as I have argued throughout this book. Moreover, while Kroeger maintains that 'all rumours' tend to die down once people turn to more immediate matters such as elections (Kroeger 2003: 252), in this extended case it was because of an impending election that the youths saw it fit to react to the rumour with gossip. Rather than constituting separate forms of 'hearsay' (Rosnow and Fine 1976), I consider it likely that the gossip was a direct reaction to the rumour in that it required the potentially affected individuals to come up with an account that made sense of something that was beyond their control and at least partly returned control to them. While rumour can indeed be understood by means of Rosnow's four factors, I suggest that rumour itself can lead to the production of gossip along these same lines. The difference would be that now the audience is an internal one and the anxiety is felt by the targets of the rumour, not by the intended outside receivers. In the case of the flag, gossip developed because of a 'generalized uncertainty', as Rosnow put it, and apparently there was also enough 'credibility' to the rumour to lead the young people of the Hydery *Anjuman* to gossip rather than deny or ignore the rumour. Thus, in this extended case, gossip is not small talk and rumour that which develops out of it; it is, rather, the other way around.

Third and finally, we arrive at the *claiming*, or disputing, stage of Felstiner et al.'s schema, which does not occur until there is direct inter-

---

18. Harrisson (2018) has encountered various anti-Muslim rumours during her fieldwork in Mawlamyine, mostly related to food consumption and variations on the master narrative of a Muslim 'takeover' of the country, thus, to issues of 'purity and danger', as Mary Douglas (1966) put it.

action between potentially opposing parties. In the case at hand, I relate this to three different situations: first, to the younger members' earlier effort to schedule a meeting in the Kashany *Imambargah*; second, to the party members', monks', and police officials' visit to the mosque to meet with the trustees and demand the removal of the flags from all religious buildings; and third, to the trustees' and other members' letter to 'the state' in which they set the record straight in terms of their history and directly accused the Peace and Diversity Party member of sowing discord in the country on the basis of religion. In all three cases we have direct accusations against a different party – one directed at elders by younger members within the 'Iranian Shia' faction, a second levelled by different office holders at one another, and the third by senior Shia members who were acting on behalf of the community targeting everyone else who had accused them. The third claim, however, is different from the first two in that there was no face-to-face interaction. When writing to U Thein Sein, the President of Myanmar, and several other key office holders, including Aung San Suu Kyi, the trustees and senior members decided to use a tactic that I have also encountered with my Hindu interlocutors in the case of the Mahapeinne Temple: directly complaining in written form to 'the state', be it via litigation in the courts or through letters, produces a trail of documents that can later be pointed to as evidence. It is also a demonstration of actively realizing one's right as a citizen, a move that had been as crucial for the Kalai community in the case of the Mahapeinne Temple as it was for the senior Shia men in this case.

In the first case of claiming, the 'invitation' to meet at the Kashany *Imambargah* to discuss elections was orally extended by the younger members to their elders, but was met with silence. In the third case of claiming, the explanation was delivered in written form, and likewise failed to provoke a reaction. Returning to Felstiner et al.'s distinction between a claim and a dispute, the only actual dispute that this extended case entailed was thus constituted in the moment when police officers, party members, and monks entered the Mogul Shia Mosque. Thus, the dispute lasted only for as long as the meeting in the mosque lasted: after the meeting was over, the trustees immediately ordered that all black flags be taken down from the two mosques as well as from the *imambargahs* and *astanas*. When I inquired why they had complied with the order, all members I talked to said that they had not – the mourning period had come to an end and they were going to take down the flags that night in any case.

I suggest that by writing and sending a letter to the authorities, the signatories reinforced both the 'personalized anxiety' and the 'general uncertainty' that I often encountered in the local state media's portrayal of Muslims in the country. My interlocutors thereby turned a potentially threatening situation into a window of opportunity for themselves. The rumour allowed them to clearly state the legitimacy of their religious practices, reaffirm their existence as a community in the country, and add documentation to the unbroken tradition of having been granted the right to commemorate their mourning rituals in public.[19] The people with whom I discussed the removal of the flags also emphasized their own agency, asserting that they were merely upholding customary practice and not caving in to the external demand that had come from the police officers, the member of the party, and the monks. That their letter was met with silence was later claimed to be ideal by my Shia interlocutors, who said they had not wanted any direct confrontation with 'the state' and were not interested in meeting with the other parties again. They thereby reinterpreted their position in a way that helped them save face. Drawing on Modonesi's (2014) conceptual framework, I see this as an example of 'stagnated subalternity' (2014: 150), where resistance and relative autonomy occur but never lead to transgression. Such a perspective sheds new light on Spivak's argument that the subaltern 'cannot speak' – my interlocutors do speak and they regularly speak up to the state, but their words are often met with silence. Instead of viewing this silence as defeat, they interpret it as their victory.

I suggest that rather than seeing this case as orchestrated from beginning to end, or as following a typical cultural pattern, or even as being pushed by strategically acting individuals, we should understand it as the outcome of a series of side-effects that were amplified through talk and media such as newspaper articles and Facebook. I also suggest that we

---

19. I should emphasize that their point about mourning processions being a long-standing tradition in Myanmar is what differentiates their community from those of other Muslims who either lack similar 'traditional' practices (read 'the Sunnis') or have no standing as a recognized ethno-religious group as such in the country. This criticism can often be found in local media reports concerning other Muslims, particularly concerning ethnic Rohingya, who are labelled 'Bengali', thus not indigenous to Myanmar, but from Bangladesh.

should understand members' efforts to come up with rationalizations for why this case developed the way it did by drawing on gossip as an *ex post facto* explanation aimed at saving face. On the other hand, however, by tracing their practices during the various stages of the case, I could see how they began to 'belong differently' according to the situation at hand.

Belonging could be experienced in modes of 'belonging as loss' and 'territorial belonging', as well as in Sartre's first two dimensions of the body. As such, practices initially centred on the embodiment of the martyred imams continued in the alignment of members on the basis of a common fellowship in the *anjuman* according to gender, age, and individual inclination. These joint practices ceased to exist once the trustees, in their role as 'elders', began to make claims in the name of the entire community. Different modes of belonging were neither 'produced' as a result of heightened ritual activity around the mourning period, nor did they arise due to external threat. These more internal and less explicit modes, however, no longer mattered once 'community' was publicly invoked by the male elders. Acting in the name of the community, only a fraction of the senior elder members 'spoke', thereby silencing not only 'the Buddhists' who challenged 'the Muslims' but also their own younger members. My analysis cautions against assuming that 'communal' motives are necessarily a reaction to dispute and violence, as it has come to be predominantly pursued in analyses concerning Myanmar. The actual dispute during which representatives of Buddhist and Muslim communities opposed one another took place inside a mosque and lasted for not more than a few minutes. Even then it is questionable whether two monks, a party representative, a policeman, and several members of the mosque administrative team could be construed as constituting two opposing 'communities'. This leads me to the final part of my analysis.

Political belonging and the body of community

With her concept of 'political belonging', Tine Gammeltoft (2018) presents a third mode of relatedness with which she intends to convey how individuals achieve a sense of belonging by drawing on categories provided by 'the state'. This sense of belonging, however, does not come automatically with citizenship, she reminds us. Ghassan Hage (2002) has argued that '[t]o fully belong as citizens, people must feel recognized. ... It is a mode of honouring the society you belong to. And this only emerges when the society you belong to honours you' (Hage 2002: 4).[20] Relating Gammeltoft's third mode of belonging to my material from Myanmar, I encounter a dilemma: most of my interlocutors are proud citizens of Myanmar. I have described throughout the book that they consider themselves the true 'city-zens' of Yangon (as those whose ancestors helped build old Rangoon), that before the attempted military coup in February 2021, they continued to support Aung San Suu Kyi, along with the majority of the local population (see also Beyer 2017; Beyer and Girke 2019a,b), and held 'the state' in high regard, continuing to turn to its courts, its ministries, and its head of government with their pleas and claims. Yet they are not honoured by 'the state' as citizens; rather, they receive recognition only on the basis of their membership to an ethno-religious community. Myanmar has up to the aftermath of the attempted military coup been a country where possession of the 'right' identification document – that is, the pink national ID card – does no good in daily interactions if one does not 'look' Burmese. This sentiment might be changing slowly as the population continues to resist the generals and has begun to form coalitions and alternative infrastructures of governance where ethno-religious equality is considered. If we once again take a careful look at the letter that the managing trustee and the other senior men drafted, it is through foregrounding their community that they state their claims. They did not object to the derogatory treatment by the party member, the police, and the monks on the basis of being citizens of Myanmar, demanding *equal* rights; they appealed as members of an ethno-religious community, demanding *special* rights on the basis of religion and tradition instead. They could only do so as citizens, which is why they gave their ID numbers and their Burmese names (instead of their Muslim ones), and why many other Shia members who did not meet those criteria did not sign the letter. They thereby also

20. We know from Michel Foucault's work on governmentality (1998, 2003) how 'the state' governs through the body of its citizen subjects (body politic), but I do not consider his theories here, as his concept of the body remains at the level of discourse: he never observed actual physical bodies. Moreover, as his individual is rather powerless (Oksala 2005; Oliver 2010), his concept of freedom, too, is diametrically opposed to Sartre's: for Foucault, 'there is no escape from power into freedom' (Taylor 1984: 159), whereas for Sartre, that is all there is.

differentiated themselves implicitly (without mentioning it) from all 'illegal' and problematic Muslims accused by 'the state' of illegitimately residing in Myanmar.

Sartre's findings on 'the third ontological dimension of the body' helped me understand why my interlocutors continue to perceive themselves as acting independently and as having 'the state' on their side as an institution to turn to in case of need, despite the fact that they repeatedly also told me stories about how they were faced with discrimination and even racism in their everyday lives, particularly when encountering state bureaucracy. I suggest that my interlocutors remain within the delineations of the ethno-religious community because they have come to accept this disposition as the only one available to them. This is Sartre's third ontological dimension of the body, which he termed *for-itself-for-others*. Delineating the three dimensions of the body, he summarized: 'I exist my body: this is the first dimension of being. My body is utilized and known by the Other: this is its second dimension. But in so far as I am for others, the Other is revealed to me as the subject for whom I am an object' (1992: 460). He further specified this third dimension: 'I can not *be in the presence of the Other* without being that "in-the-presence" in the form of having to be it' (1992: 474; emphasis in original). In order to get his point across, Sartre draws an analogy between the three dimensions of the body and pain, suffered illness, and disease. Pain, as a physical symptom, he says, is painfully lived in the body. Suffered illness works through a process of naming (1992: 466), which stems from 'bits of knowledge which I have acquired from Others or from such knowledge as Others have of me' (ibid.). Disease, finally, describes an objectified state for which another (usually a doctor) has become responsible but which now dictates my very being.

While Modonesi's (2014) concept of stagnated subalternity, which I introduced at the beginning of this book and on which I have drawn repeatedly throughout the chapters, adequately describes the positionality of my interlocutors, with Sartre's concepts of the body we can better understand why they choose to remain in such a state. Sartre has always been adamant about choice – that humans are condemned to be free, that all we 'are' are our choices; yet he never denied that humans are embedded in intricate webs of dependencies and structural inequalities and are subjected to gross injustices. 'Having to be it', as he put it in the quote above, to me stands not for the end of choice, but for having internalized the realization that in a situation of no alternatives, there is nothing left to do but 'choose' the only option there is (see also Arendt 1943 on suicide). In the case of my interlocutors, this option is identifying as 'being Shia' (or 'Kalai', or 'Memon', or 'Indian', or 'Hindustani', or 'Muslim' or *kalar* even) – particularly when an *other* (like me) is present. As we are incapable of seeing ourselves, says Sartre, it is only through the other that we can 'see ourselves as we are' (1992: 463) – or, rather, that we can see ourselves in any way at all. When that outside perspective onto an individual, however, has been exclusively, systematically, and for a long time perceived as one in which one is looked down upon, belittled, made small, incompetent, and superfluous – made to feel like someone who does not belong, who should be elsewhere, who should remain on the sidelines at all times or only in the place the other has allocated to them – then this will have an impact on how individuals perceive themselves. 'To them, we are only *kalar* now', said Uncle Ghaffar once when I wondered how many Bama even knew that he was not simply a 'Muslim', but a Halai Memon.

On 30 September 2017, thus almost two years after the case of 'the Flag' had occurred, I had intended to join my Shia interlocutors for Ashura, but fell ill the night before my flight. Corresponding via social media with some of my younger key interlocutors, who were sorry that I could not attend, we agreed that they would make sure I could 'participate' in the processions via live recording on Facebook chat. One walked with his cell phone during the procession, one stayed at the Mogul Shia Mosque, and one remained at the Bindaneem Imambargah so that I could – with several windows on my laptop open – be present with them in several locations at once. It took a while for me to notice that apparently all the women had remained at the mosques, *imambargahs*, and *astanas*, and that only men accompanied the *zarees* and *mafa* through downtown. I immediately related this situation to a conversation I had had with U Maung Maung Ta's wife, Asma, via Facebook the night before. After sending me the three-day programme for the days around Ashura, she added, 'Tonight the flags will need to be taken down, said the government. The present trustees said they cannot do anything. This is very sad news.' I then found out that people had apparently started

Fig. 6.9: 'We have been hoisting this flag for one hundred years with the permission of the government.' Comment underneath this photograph in a Facebook post from 29 September 2017. The photograph is said to be from 1953 and shows a Shia procession in front of City Hall. Photographer unknown.

again to post photographs of Shia flags on Facebook, inciting rumours of the flags being 'dangerous' and related to ISIS. I checked the respective online pages and was surprised to find several Shia youths engaged in long conversations with those individuals who had actively begun to spread such rumours about the flags. My acquaintances came prepared and well-equipped this time: they posted historical photographs of Shia engaged in processions around downtown that dated from the mid-1950s; they educated everyone who followed along in the comments about the true meaning of the black flag; and they drew a clear connection between the white dagger depicted on the flags to the one that the Burmese kings had as part of their royal regalia.

They also referred to the situation of 2015 as 'a misunderstanding which we have already solved'. And some of the negative commentators began to change their opinion: 'I learned a lot from your comments. Thank you so much', said one. And another even conceded, 'No matter what your religion, you are a citizen of Myanmar. Thank you for describing your religion to us.'

While the rumours stopped spreading on Facebook, the flags were taken down nonetheless. In addition, Jasmine Baji told me that all women had been ordered by the men to remain inside or at the gates of the religious buildings for the entire duration of the processions. Apparently, the trustees and others in charge of organizing the processions judged the general atmosphere to be too uncertain or maybe even dangerous. Nothing untoward happened that night or during the rest of Moharram and Safar, but to me this episode – which I observed from a distance, yet strangely up close via social media – brought home the message that in addition to suffering and being proud, there lies an existential uncertainty at the core of 'being Shia'. Not allowing women to enter the public sphere of 'their' city was a drastic concession to a state and a majority population that increasingly marginalizes, restricts, and refines Muslim religious practice in the country.

Conclusion

Belonging allows us 'to capture the plural and often competing and contradictory memberships that characterize human lives' (2018: 89), argues Tine Gammeltoft. She positions her approach as an alternative to more 'conventional categories of identity – such as gender, class, ethnicity, nationality – which tend to fix people in reified social landscapes' (ibid.). When she summarizes that, for her, 'the anthropology of belonging attends to the ways in which individuals come into being through mutual relations of possession, attachment, and dependence' (2018: 88), one might be inclined to ask how this is any different from what anthropologists have tried to get at when speaking about community; she even employs the term herself and cites the established literature on community (e.g. Cohen 1985), noting that belonging can come with the surrender of some freedoms. Thus, I suggest that rather than substituting one term for another (belonging for community, in this case) or viewing belonging as independent of gender, class, ethnicity, and nationality, we need to address and pay attention to practices of individual self- and we-formation as the most basic and co-constitutive processes of human sociality. Community as an abstract (ethno-)category only covers a small fraction of human co-existence (even considering its transversal aspect in my fieldsite), as does belonging. We should, therefore, be careful not to overemphasize community in our analyses of subtler 'inner' dynamics, especially as it is so outwardly visible and even seems to be the obvious unit of analysis. For community to have such a prominent role, individual uniqueness and contradictory relations with one another – important parts of human sociality – must necessarily be downplayed. Individual experience gets sidelined once the discursive effort that I call the *work of community* is set in motion.

CONCLUSION

We-formation in times of 'communal' violence

In her article *We Refugees* (1943), the political theorist Hannah Arendt drew on Sartre's notion of freedom when she wrote about how an individual's perspective on the world changes significantly depending on whether they think of themselves as a *we* or as a singular human being:

> At the camp of Gurs [France], for instance, where I had the opportunity of spending some time, I heard only once about suicide, and that was the suggestion of a collective action, apparently a kind of protest in order to vex the French. When some of us remarked that we had been shipped there *'pour crever'* [vulgar; to die] in any case, the general mood turned suddenly into a violent courage of life. The general opinion held that one had to be abnormally asocial and unconcerned about general events if one was still able to interpret the whole accident as personal and individual bad luck and, accordingly, ended one's life personally and individually. But the same people, as soon as they returned to their own individual lives, being faced with seemingly individual problems, changed once more to this insane optimism which is next door to despair. We are the first non-religious Jews persecuted – and we are the first ones who, not only *in extremis*, answer with suicide. Perhaps the philosophers are right who teach that suicide is the last and supreme guarantee of human freedom; not being free to create our lives or the world in which we live, we nevertheless are free to throw life away and to leave the world. (Arendt 1943: 72)

In this book I have been concerned with existential questions that are similar to those Arendt poses here for stateless Jews during and after the Second World War: How does a *we* foster a 'violent courage of life' in the face of structural inequality? And how can an understanding of 'being in it together' support my interlocutors in their freedom to create

241

their individual lives? Like Arendt, I am very concerned with the political reality of where ethno-religious minorities were slotted into Burma/ Myanmar and how they managed to obtain and carve out a place for themselves. The material I discuss in this book establishes *we-formation* as a sensitizing concept that scholars should pay attention to alongside what I have called *the work of community*. I have argued that individual self-formation is intrinsically related to we-formation, and that both are anchored in material objects, as it is often through objects that subjects are created. Throughout the book I have drawn on conceptual work from ethnomethodology and existential anthropology to investigate practices of we-formation through which individuals develop a sense of self and find ways to relate to one another. While some of the practices I observed were pre-reflective and embodied and cannot, therefore, be disembedded from the situation in which they were experienced or uttered, others, I suggest, built on conscious, discursive acts of classification, and were planned well in advance. I have thus distinguished various types of we-formation that can occur entirely without community (or any of its cognates) from carefully orchestrated events that are framed or enacted in the name of community, without necessarily having an affective impact on the participants. This distinction is not meant to reify two kinds of practice, but rather to methodologically highlight that these two things do not always go together. In Chapter 3, I began with a microanalysis of a case of spirit possession that I observed inside the Śrī Kāmāchi Amman Temple. Investigating the various reactions of bystanders who witnessed the possession, I complicated the notion of membership and cautioned against rashly attributing a communal (and collective) identity to people attending a religious event together. I paid particular attention to the phenomenon of 'standing by' in order to challenge the usual overemphasis on communal action at religious sites, precisely because, historically speaking, 'communal violence' has been assumed to centre on such places (Walton and Hayward 2014). We are currently seeing a resurgence of this idea not only in Myanmar and India, but across the globe in contexts characterized by ethno-religious plurality.

The second part of this first case study investigated the subsequent downtown procession that this self-proclaimed Tamil community conducted at night as part of their celebrations marking the one-year anniversary of the renovation of the Śri Kāmāchi Amman Temple. I argued that in order to imprint their often precarious existence as a community in the public domain, the temple trustees had an interest in cultivating collective visibility and striving for at least tacit public recognition. This is achieved by literally taking up space in the cityscape, demonstrating that as an urban community they, too, belong. The question that guided my analysis was how the organizers and performers of those external dynamics intended them to be perceived by, yet again, bystanders in the street, who formed an observing audience. I also looked at the role of 'the state', which operates invisibly in the background but whose presence was clearly felt by my interlocutors. Exceptional events like this procession are carried out not only for and with the help of diverse internal audiences, I suggested, but specifically for non-members as well. In Myanmar, performances that are expressly staged as representative of a minority ethno-religious community need to be understood with the majority Burmese-Buddhist population as the *other* in mind. In the way they are orchestrated, processions and the like constitute a form of what one could call 'sensory politics', thereby mirroring the state's strategy of governance, which likewise works through the senses, thus ultimately through people's bodies (see also Kapoor 2021). In order not to upset the majority, organizers of these public events have to tread carefully by constantly making concessions in terms of timing and routes, thus remaining in a subaltern position. Still, they find themselves confronted with Buddhist counter-events that often trespass not only onto their own demarcated properties, but also challenge individual bodily integrity.

Chapter 4, 'The Making of a Community in Court', took 'processing' – the practice of carrying out a procession – away from its religious and ritualistic connotations and into the country's state courts. By means of an extended case study that spans more than a century and draws on colonial and postcolonial court case materials and my own ethnohistorical work with members of a family that classified itself as the 'Kalai community', I showed how – in what can be seen as a follow-up to Arjun Appadurai's ethnohistorical analysis of temple administration and disputes in South India – a so-called community was brought into being with the help of the judiciary. In this case, the claim of community status was successfully attained by a single individual, who managed to use colonial-era personal status laws, designed specifically to appease and govern ethno-religious communities, to ward off a civil case concerning the right to inheritance. In the process, the key figure, Daw Nu, and her descendants succeeded in keeping the Myanmar state, the Buddhist order of monks, and the Hindu Association at bay.

This chapter furthered my argument that one should exercise great caution when encountering the category of community in Myanmar (as elsewhere). The material I presented in Chapter 4, with its focus on how a single individual turned colonial-era state law to her own advantage, strengthens my assertion that our anthropological task lies in clearly distinguishing the work that is being done in the name of community from the diverse range of practices of *we-formation* that might be conducted in the very same locations and even by the very same actors. In both case studies, *the work of community* is clearly noticeable, but remains detached from the daily comings and goings of religious practitioners.

While I tried my best to avoid uncritically buying into my interlocutor's communal portrayal as the essence of their very being, my intention was never to dismiss the way they presented themselves to me. Carefully differentiating between discourse and practice required not only ethnographic attention to the details of their everyday lives, but also an ethnohistorical approach to community as a category. Only through this was I able to understand how community had acquired such a prominent role and become my interlocutors' default way of characterizing their social world to others like me. Given the long history of discrimination in the country overall, it is crucial to acknowledge the inconsistencies and contradictions inherent in an individual's struggle to realign ideology with practice. Understanding how people can be so ready to tear down their own categories when it comes to actual encounters means paying attention to the 'leftovers', as Piette (2015, 2016) has urged us to do, in other words, to that which does not add up, to that which lets us go beyond understanding people as always strategic and conscious (inter-)actors, and instead acknowledges the ambiguities inherent in being human.

But *we-formation* does not offer a 'way out' out of my interlocutors' existential dilemmas. I have rather posited it as a solution to the dilemma of 'community studies' in that it allows us to question the naturalness of community and its prevalence at particular sites. At the same time, I have sought to demonstrate that in my fieldsite, my interlocutors primarily *existed* their individuality and shaped their selves in relation to and as part of a *we* in or around religious buildings, a finding that highlights the material and bodily aspects of we-formation.

Throughout this book I have drawn on the work of Jean-Paul Sartre, who has always engaged with individual freedom, intersubjective human relations, and the coercive power of institutions in perpetual and, in the end, irreconcilable conflict. Others have criticized his work for being internally contradictory. Herbert Marcuse, for example, took issue with the fact that Sartre continued to speak of 'freedom' even in the direst of possible circumstances:

> Established as the locus of freedom in the midst of a world of totalitarian oppression, the *Pour-soi*, the Cartesian *Cogito*, is no longer the jumping-off point for the conquest of the intellectual and material world, but the last refuge of the individual in an 'absurd world' of frustration and failure. In Sartre's philosophy this refuge is still equipped with all the paraphernalia which characterised the heyday of individualistic society. (Marcuse 1948: 322–323)

I find it probable that Sartre might even have agreed with Marcuse on this. He never offered a solution regarding how to bridge the for-itself (*pour-soi*, where I exist my body), the for-others (*pour-autrui*, where my body is known by the other), and the for-itself-for-others (where I become an object for others who only thereby are revealed as subjects to me). It is in this last mode of existing that 'the common freedom constitutes itself as terror' (Sartre [1960] 2004: 431) and 'the individual disappears from historical categories' (ibid.: 51), as Sartre clearly acknowledged in his later work.[1] One reason I have drawn on Sartre throughout my chapters is that I have encountered in the way my interlocutors comport themselves the same kind of existential *habitus*, here understood in the Bourdieuian sense not as 'habit', but as the way people unconsciously use their physical bodies, as well as abstract schemes of classification, to navigate and negotiate their being in the world. They have come to terms with the realization that much of who they are allowed to 'be' is defined by others to such an extent that there is no complete 'way out'. Yet at the same time they yearn to be free from such dispositions, as all individuals do. Sullivan and Palitsky (2018) have summarized Sartre's contradictory stance, which he himself termed the 'progressive-regressive method', as follows:

---

1. See also Fleming (2011).

All activity is, at one and the same time, progression toward an as-yet unrealized (but envisioned) prospect, and a simultaneous regression to a pre-existing 'field of possibilities' set by one's cultural and material circumstances. It is in this sense that the concept of freedom in existentialism is vital but tragic; it is always accompanied by the shadow of threat. This is why Sartre said we are 'condemned to be free'. (Sullivan and Palitsky 2018: 28–29)

By way of analogy to Sartre, I suggest that, from my interlocutors' perspectives, 'community' must be understood as a 'field of possibilities' in the cultural and material circumstances of which they have become embedded and entangled from early childhood and from which each of them tries to progress to existing their very own – always 'as yet unrealized' – individual lives. On the one hand, community allows people to huddle under a common shield (Bauman 2001) and protect one another from the harsh conditions of living marginalized lives, just as Arendt has described for the Jews in the camps. My interlocutors have portrayed community in the brightest of terms, linking it in particular to the religious buildings where I conducted much of my ethnographic work: to be near 'our culture' means to be near 'our mosque', as Uncle Ghaffar put it. On the other hand, I have shown that while community significantly shapes an individual's experience and sense of self, it never entirely trumps it. My interlocutors in Yangon never entirely defined themselves through their communal identity alone, but always held on to their individuality. They are always individuals first and members second, something that has been particularly neglected in studies on minorities in Myanmar. I have also hinted at Freud's 'narcissism of minor differences', according to which the fault lines *within* ethno-religious communities are experienced as harsher than those between clearly separable communities – an observation that resonates with my own experiences in Myanmar, particularly in regard to internal differentiations among Shia along class and factional lines, as I developed in Chapter 5. I approached my interlocutors' family and community histories in light of the realities of intermarriage, understood here as *within* rather than across the religious denomination of Shia Islam, exemplified by a case study of a Hindustani Shia man who married an Iranian Shia woman, both born in Burma.

I have also drawn attention to the possibility that it is our very presence as *other* that might encourage such strong communal ways of identification among our interlocutors – for example, when Mukhtar Bhai would speak disparagingly of 'the Sunni' in my presence, whereas in his everyday life he cooperated with and befriended several Sunni and worked for others himself. Or when I became Sartre's *third*, under whose eyes my interlocutors felt the need to reify their sameness in stating the obvious 'We are Shia!' In the first two chapters of this book I demonstrated that such communal portrayal had been the predominant way of characterizing subalterns in the British empire, and I have detailed the continuation of these policies through the various regimes in Burma and Myanmar, where community has retained its distinct characterization as a marker of ethno-religious *others*, most recently enshrined in the Race and Religion Laws.

Throughout the book, I have presented new ethnographic material on Muslim and Hindu lives in Yangon. My data complicate the image of them as a collective *other* who, in academic publications that criticize contemporary Myanmar politics in general and the Race and Religion Laws in particular, is often written *about* but rarely listened *to* or accompanied throughout daily life. For example, to date we still have no ethnographic literature that focuses on Muslims in Myanmar, who make up somewhere between 4 and 10 per cent of the country's population. If Muslims are portrayed, then it is in their role as *others*, usually vis-à-vis the majority Buddhist Bama population. I suggest that, as a result of this exclusive focus on the opposition between Muslims and Buddhists, even those authors who aim at deconstructing the portrayal of Muslims as a 'communal bloc' (Schonthal 2016: 236; see also Wade 2017) indirectly reinforce community as an essentialized category. I offer a corrective to this tendency with my concept of *we-formation*, which always begins with individuals and observes the various ways in which they *exist* themselves, are co-present in a situation, or form temporary groups that do not need to rely on higher-order classifications.

I have put forward Modonesi's concept of 'stagnated subalternity' (2014) as an evocative description of a particular disposition I found prevalent among many of my interlocutors. On the one hand, a basis for it lies in their ongoing structural marginality in Myanmar society; on the other hand, they themselves cultivate a disposition according to which they are recognized first and foremost not as individuals, but as members of ethno-religious communities. While this categorization targets and victimizes them, it also shelters: they live in a state that oppresses them, but they know that they are not targeted as individuals. I have empha-sized that in this context, the question of whether one is able to 'speak' or not might not be precise enough. While 'Burmese Indians' have been silenced by the majority population and 'the state', my interlocutors were never passively silent. Beginning with Ma Yait and Daw Nu in the historical Mahapeinne Temple case, we see that even those most mar-ginalized – dark-skinned, 'half-breed' women – were able to successfully and cunningly navigate the colonial legal system and turn it to their own advantage by letting the courts speak for them. And in the case of 'the Flag' (discussed in Chapter 6), silence was reinterpreted as victory by my Shia interlocutors, who had likewise addressed 'the state' – explicitly as members marked by belonging to a community. A methodologically relevant conclusion, then, is that we need to look more closely into the ways and motives of individuals, groups, and 'states' whenever they invoke communal identities, traditions, and histories.

An attempted coup and the empire's endgame

The findings of this book shed light on the recent attempted military coup in Myanmar, as well as the politics of the contemporary British state. In their collaboratively written book *Empire's Endgame: Racism and the British State* (Bhattacharyya et al. 2021), the authors ask the pertinent question: '[W]hat kind of state do we have now, and how is its programme of cruelty, neglect and expulsion justified ideologically?' (3) They answer their own question by arguing that

> [w]hen trying to understand race and racism in Britain today, we need to analyse how racist state practices – immigration controls, counter-terror measures and criminal justice policies – *seem* to address people's real problems and lived experiences. In other words, we need to think about the relationship between state racism and the making of political subjectivities. (Bhattacharyya et al. 2021: 3; emphasis in original)

The authors put forward the argument that the state has retreated from all public domains in contemporary Great Britain and only exerts its power in the form of punishment. As a consequence, the wider popu-lation has begun to associate 'belonging' with being pooled together simply because they were 'those who were not being punished and who were therefore invited to identify with the state that acted to exclude

Others in their name' (9). In this context, 'belonging' has acquired entirely negative characteristics and is combined with an 'internalized fear of abjection' (11) – of being *othered* by the punitive state – that ensures that people remain submissive. If one follows Bhattacharyya et al. in their argumentation, as I am inclined to do, it is not hard to see that Great Britain is now perpetuating the very policies within its own state territory and against its own population that colonial Britain had imposed on its overseas peoples in the past. Categorizations on the basis of 'community' that have been so skilfully crafted for Britain's colonial *others* can now potentially be turned against every British citizen. Continuation of such politics of *othering* is particularly evident when the state deprives citizens of their nationality and thereby pushes them out of the body politic, or when immigrants are prevented from obtaining citizenship or even a minimal *de jure* status as stateless.

As a so-called country-of-origin expert in cases involving individuals seeking protection because they fear they will be persecuted in Myanmar for being stateless Rohingya (Beyer 2022a; Beyer 2022b), I have by now acquired enough insight into the dystopia that is the British immigration system. Roughly one and a half million stateless Rohingya have been shuffled back and forth between Myanmar and Bangladesh in the last five decades, with the most recent 'wave' occuring in 2016. As a result, hundreds of thousands are now displaced and many have come to Europe to seek refuge. Even in their first interaction with the British Home Office, their very existence as a Rohingya is called into doubt: they cannot be who they claim to be because they have no documents to prove it. In the absence of written evidence, asylum claims are subsequently denied because the person does not speak Rohingya, does not know about 'Rohingya culture', or does not remember particular Rohingya holidays, sports, or even culinary recipes. While only individuals can claim asylum, stateless Rohingya need to perform their 'groupism' for state authorities in the most essentializing way imaginable in order to meet the presumptions of what constitutes their 'community'. Besides such folklorization and upholding of the belief that one can only belong to a community if one speaks 'its' language, I have also encountered biological determinism both in official interviews conducted by the Home Office and among well-meaning lawyers fending for their clients. For example, I have heard of people being asked to deliver DNA results to prove the nationality of their grandparents, and have even been presented with frontal and side-view photographs of a person's head in the expectation that I should, on that basis, be able to determine whether that person is 'really' a Rohingya or not.

While in Great Britain recognition as a Rohingya is only possible on the basis of proving one's belonging to a 'community', in Myanmar Rohingya have been denied precisely such a 'communal' categorization for decades. And while Myanmar has dehumanized Rohingya by rendering them stateless, internationally, Rohingya do not matter as individuals on the international stage either, as long as their existence is reduced to forming part of a 'wave' or an 'influx' of migrants. Every personal story of flight, every eyewitness account of unimaginable suffering, only pretends to foreground the individual, whereas in reality, it is only through body counts that individuals come to matter – bodies mutilated, raped, disabled, and emaciated; bodies traversing borders, crossing rivers, and collapsing; dead bodies. But counting and accountability are intrinsically connected. There is an ethical dimension to the numerical and the representational that has less to do with categorizations and numbers and more with how one comes to value another human being. The atrocities are what they are the moment they are committed, but the labelling shifts over time in the most unfortunate ways. Rohingya are now doubly excluded: they do not count as a 'community' nor as individuals. Since December 2019, Myanmar stands accused at the International Court of Justice (ICJ) in The Hague for having violated the UN Genocide Convention (Beyer and Girke 2019a, b). With the attempted military coup of 1 February 2021, the court has become a stage for the military to perform 'as a state', thereby trying to legitimize the attempted coup, using the court case as a mere opportunity (Beyer 2022c). This is strategic litigation taken to its extreme.

But the attempted military coup and generals' illegal power grab has not only ended two decades of quasi-democratic rule, it has also united the population in a novel way. As an unintended consequence, it has opened up possibilities of we-formation and enabled new debates about the meaning of community beyond ethno-religious identity (see also Prasse-Freeman and Ko Kabya 2021). In the words of Bhattacharyya et al., one could say that the *Empire's endgame* is not only taking place in contemporary Britain, but also in contemporary Myanmar.

From the first day of the attempted coup the population has taken to the streets throughout the country in millions, forming what has come to be called the Civil Disobedience Movement (CDM), raising awareness internationally for their cause, and demonstrating their will to not give in. When the initial international attention waned and there was no end in sight to the military terror, many began joining one or another of the armed ethnic groups or received training from them to enroll as soldiers in the newly formed People's Defense Movement (PDF). Some of my interlocutors and some of the students I taught at Yangon University are now actively engaged in combat, while others had to flee the country and are trying to support the resistance in exile. None of the locals I interacted with in the last decade has taken a neutral stance. While some resist with a rifle in hand, for others protesting means no longer drinking 'Myanmar' beer or consuming any other product manufactured by the generals and their extended families. These practices might not seem comparable at the outset, but when one looks at them from an individual perspective, they all centre on the body, which is thereby turned into an instrument of resistance.

Antonio De Lauri (2022), a specialist in the anthropology of war, has recently argued that for one person to be able to kill another in combat, the target person's identity needs to be transformed 'from the status of an individual to a member of a defined and hated enemy group'. War, like community, is an *other*-making category. But De Lauri interviewed foreign fighters at the Ukrainian border who had joined the army for money. These men have no need to identify with the country or the people they are fighting for or develop a hatred for the country and the people they are fighting against. They only need to deindividualize the other soldiers so that, in the end, they are no longer in combat with individual human beings, but a category. The situation in Myanmar could not be more different. In the first months, protestors staged loud, colourful, and sometimes even shrill performances in the streets of Yangon, Mandalay, and hundreds of smaller cities and even villages. These were orchestrated along the lines of groups: workers, teachers, lawyers, university staff, doctors, religious representatives, the LGBTQI+ community, spirit mediums, and artists. The outpouring of creativity seemed endless, as was people's innovative group-making capacities: pregnant mothers, couples playing bride and groom, adolescents in superhero costumes, and many more. Most strikingly, however, was the public appearance of stateless Rohingya, who identified themselves by holding up signs that stated their ethnicity and their resistance. What had been unthinkable – and dangerous – just months before, was now possible. In a way, the beginning of the resistance movement saw an increasing pluralization that initially drew on the well-established category of community. As such, it allowed for ever more groups to appear in public, including those that had been invisibilized before. One sign had altered the famous quote by the German pastor Martin Niemöller in the following way: 'First they came for the Karens and we didn't speak out. Then they came for the Rohingya and we didn't speak out. Now they are coming for all of us.'[2]

How far can a *we* go?

Rather than declaring defeat and resigning themselves to the new regime as an illegitimate successor of the previous one, people in Myanmar acknowledged that each and every one of them has become part and parcel of the war. Now it is not only those living in armed ethnic territories in the border zones who are facing this existential situation, it is also my interlocutors in downtown Yangon. While Furnivall (1948) declared in a condescending tone that in colonial Burma the individual will of the people was more important than their community interests, it turns out that it is this exact individual will that might now be the key to why the generals have not succeeded. What motivates all of my interlocutors and, as far as I can tell, what lends the resistance movement its force is not only having a common enemy. It also stems from every individual's determination to live freely. This includes soldiers who are defecting from the army, and even those who remain but use their insider knowledge to support the resistance (Kyed and Ah Lynn 2021). That they are referred to as 'watermelons' (*hpe-ye: thi:*, 'green outside [because of their uniforms], but red inside [because of their allegiance to the democracy movement]') demonstrates an emic un-

---

2. Among the many versions of the original poem that are known, this is probably the most famous one: 'First they came for the socialists, and I did not speak out because I was not a socialist. Then they came for the trade unionists, and I did not speak out because I was not a trade unionist. Then they came for the Jews, and I did not speak out because I was not a Jew. Then they came for me – and there was no one left to speak for me.'

derstanding of the unreliability of appearances and the possibility that people can transcend the corporate group to which they belong. Within the resistance movement it is also hotly debated whether it is ethical to use violence as a means of resistance at all, despite the fact that soldiers are murdering civilians. Moreover, very diverse and often emotionally articulated opinions regarding who should rightfully be in charge once Myanmar is freed from the military dictatorship shows that even in the middle of an ongoing nationwide war, people have existential debates over the conditions under which they will choose their freedom. This proves, to me at least, that no matter how difficult the situation in which they find themselves might be, they have already decided that there is no other way but to traverse it.

Since the attempted coup, my Shia, Memon, and Tamil interlocutors have not changed their practice of going to the mosque or the temple regularly. They continue to meet one another, exchange news, celebrate, commemorate, organize, and simply enjoy drinking tea together, while the world around them has changed. Nowadays, structural constraints that have been experienced predominantly by them and other minorities in the country weigh heavily on every single individual, regardless of their ethno-religious identification or classification. And it is as individuals that the people of Myanmar continue *existing themselves* in these dire circumstances, demonstrating 'a violent courage of life' in the face of terror. Whereas in Great Britain, 'the people' are careful not to be positioned by the state or observing Thirds as part of the exluded *others*, in Myanmar there is a collective embrace of one's (newly) marginalized positionality. Since the generals began to wage war on the entire population, including the ethnic majority, they have in fact lost power. As I have laid out in this book, the power to dictate an individual's very being depends not only on the *other*, but on oneself accepting an objectified state for which one declares the *other* responsible. What we have been seeing since the very beginning of the resistance movement is that people in Myanmar are refusing to let their being be dictated by the *other*. Some have had to go into exile and continue supporting the resistance from there. Others have left the country on their own terms, refusing to be suffocated by a military dictatorship that threatens their livelihoods and destroys their property and everything else they have achieved for themselves over the past decades. Yet others, while remaining separated from one another in different countries, have established new modes of communicating and staying in touch, inquiring about each other's state of being, solving disputes among friends and lovers via long-distance calls, and trying to keep their business going across the oceans. Most inhabitants of Myanmar, however, are going about their everyday lives and are keeping up established routines in exactly the same places where they lived before February 2021. This, however, does not mean that they have given in or have accepted a new status quo. It also should not be read as a 'normalization' of the political situation. When asked directly, my older interlocutors will go to great lengths to explain that while they are very familiar with 'all this', they, like the younger generation that until recently only had indirect knowledge about what it means to live in a military dictatorship, adamantly refuse to accept the situation. Thus, I argue, with each 'not relevant, not noticed or barely noticed ... "lesser" way of performing actions' (Piette 2015a: 40), my interlocutors and millions of other residents of Myanmar engage in practices of we-formation that are at the same time acts of refusal.[3] These practices always begin with an individual's body and are often barely noticeable as they require attention to what Piette has called reality's 'minor mode' (Piette 2012, 2016). With each individual acting out who they imagine themselves to be, it is through such practices of we-formation that the people of Myanmar might already be in the middle of building an alternative form of society.

---

3. On the the intertwining of and subtle nuances between the concepts of refusal and resistance, see Elliott Prasse-Freeman (2022).

References

Abraham, Delna and Ojaswi Rao. 2017. 86% dead in cow related violence since 2010 are Muslims; 97% attacks after 2014. *Indiaspend*, 28 June 2017. http://www.indiaspend.com/cover-story/86-dead-in-cow-related-violence-since–2010-are-muslim–97-attacks-after–2014–2014 (accessed 22 September 2019, link no longer available).

Adcock, Cassie and Radhika Govindrajan. 2019. Bovine politics in South Asia. Rethinking religion, law and ethics. *South Asia. Journal of South Asian Studies* 42 (6): 1095–1107.

Afsheen, Karmel. 2011. *Under five flags. Life like a turbulent river flows*. Xlibris Corporation.

Aguirre, Daniel. 2018. Rule by law and impunity undermine prevention of and accountability for human rights violations in Myanmar. Tea Circle Blog. 4 June 2018. https://teacircleoxford.com/2018/06/04/rule-by-law-and-impunity-undermine-prevention-of-and-accountability-for-human-rights-violations-in-myanmar/ (accessed 18 July 2022).

Alex, Gabriele. 2008. A sense of belonging and exclusion. 'Touchability' and 'untouchability' in Tamil Nadu. *Ethnos. Journal of Anthropology* 73 (4): 523–543.

Alexander, Catherine, Maja Bruun and Insa Koch. 2018. Political economy comes home. On the moral economies of housing. *Critique of Anthropology* 38 (1): 121–139.

Amit, Vered. 2002. *Realizing community. Concepts, social relationships and sentiments*. London and New York: Routledge.

———. 2020. Rethinking anthropological perspectives on community. Watchful indifference and joint commitment. In *Rethinking community through transdisciplinary research*, edited by Bettina Jansen. Cham Imprint: Palgrave Macmillan, 49–67.

Amit, Vered and Nigel Rapport. 2002. *The trouble with community. Anthropological reflections on movement, identity and collectivity*. London: Pluto Press.

Amrith, Sunil. 2013. *Crossing the Bay of Bengal. The furies of nature and the fortunes of migrants*. Cambridge, Massachusetts: Harvard University Press.

Anderson, Clare. 2016. *New histories of the Andaman Islands. Landscape, place and identity in the Bay of Bengal, 1790–2012*. Cambridge: Cambridge University Press.

Andrew, E.J.L. 1933. *Indian labour in Rangoon*. Bombay: Oxford University Press.

Antweiler, Christoph. 2004. Urbanität und Ethnologie. Aktuelle Theorietrends und die Methodik ethnologischer Stadtforschung [Urbanity and anthropology. Recent theoretical trends and the methodology of anthropological urban research]. *Zeitschrift für Ethnologie* 129: 285–307.

———. 2012. *Inclusive humanism. Anthropological basics for a realistic cosmopolitanism*. Taipeh: National Taiwan University Press.

Appadurai, Arjun. 1981. *Worship and conflict under colonial rule. A South Indian case*. Cambridge: Cambridge University Press.

———. 1998. Number in the colonial imagination. In *Orientalism and the postcolonial predicament. Perspectives on South Asia*, edited by Carol Breckenridge and Peter van der Veer. Philadelphia: University of Pennsylvania Press, 314–339.

———. 2006. *Fear of small numbers. An essay on the geography of anger*. Durham and London: Duke University Press.

Appleton, George. 1947. Burma two years after liberation. *International Affairs* 23 (4): 510–521.

Arendt, Hannah. 1943. We refugees. *The Menorah Journal* XXXI: 69–77.

AWID. 2014. Women's rights activists resist Myanmar's proposed 'Laws on Protection of Race & Religion'. *Association for Women's Rights in Development*. 12 November 2014. https://www.awid.org/news-and-analysis/womens-rights-activists-resist-myanmars-proposed-law-protection-race-and-religion (accessed 18 July 2022).

Aye Kyaw. 1994. Religion and family law in Burma. In *Tradition and modernity in Myanmar. Culture, social life and languages*, edited by Uta Gärtner and Jens Lorenz. Hamburg: LIT, 237–250.

Bailey, F.G. 1971. Gifts and poison. The management of reputations and the process of change. In *Gifts and poison. The politics of reputation*, edited by F.G. Bailey. Oxford: Basil Blackwell, 1–25.

Barth, Fredrik (ed.) 1969. *Ethnic groups and boundaries. The social organization of culture difference*. Bergen: Universitetsforlaget.

Basu, Amrita. 1994. When local riots are not merely local. Bringing the state back in, Bijnor 1988–92. *Economic and Political Weekly* 29 (40): 2605–2621.

Bataille, Georges. 1985 [1929]. Formless. In *Vision of excess. Selected writings, 1927–1939*, edited and translated by Allan Stoekl with Carl Lovitt and Donald Leslie Jr. Manchester: University of Manchester Press, p. 31.

Bates, Crispin. 2001. Introduction. Community and identity among South

Asians in diaspora. In *Community, empire and migration. South Asians in diaspora*, edited by Crispin Bates. Houndmills and New York: Palgrave Macmillan, 1–45.

Bauman, Zygmunt. 2001. *Community. Seeking safety in an insecure world.* Cambridge: Polity.

Becci, Irene, Marian Burchardt and José Casanova (eds). 2013. *Topographies of faith. Religion in urban spaces.* Leiden and Boston: Brill.

Belk, Russell. 1988. Possessions and the extended self. *Journal of Consumer Research* 15 (2): 139–168.

Behm, Amanda. 2018. *Imperial history and the global politics of exclusion. Britain, 1880–1940.* Cambridge: Cambridge University Press.

Benda-Beckmann, Keebet von. 1984. *The broken stairways to consensus. Village justice and state courts in Minangkabau.* Dordrecht: Foris.

Benda-Beckmann, Franz von. 2001. Between free riders and free raiders. Property rights and soil degradation in context. In *Economic policy and sustainable land use. Recent advances in quantitative analysis for developing countries*, edited by N van Heerink and M Kuiper. Heidelberg: Physica-Verlag, 293–316.

Benda-Beckmann, Franz von, Keebet von Benda-Beckmann and Melanie Wiber. 2006. The properties of property. In *Changing properties of property*, edited by Franz von Benda-Beckmann, Keebet von Benda-Beckmann and Melanie Wiber. New York: Berghahn, 1–39.

Benjamin, Walter. 1999. *The arcades project*, translated by Howard Eiland and Kevin McLaughlin. Cambridge, MA and London: The Belknap Press of Harvard University Press.

Berger, John. 1968. The nature of mass demonstrations. *New Society* 295: 754–755.

Bergmann, Jörg. 1993 [1987]. *Discreet indiscretion. The social organization of gossip*, translated by John Bednarz, Jr. New York: Aldine De Gruyter.

———. 1988. *Ethnomethodologie und Konversationsanalyse* [Ethnomethodology and conversation analysis]. Studienbrief. Kurseinheit 1. Hagen: Fern-Universität Hagen.

Bergmann, Jörg and Christian Meyer (eds). 2021. *Ethnomethodologie reloaded – Neue Werkinterpretationen und Theoriebeiträge zu Harold Garfinkels Programm.* Bielefeld: Transcript.

Berlie, Jean. 2008. *The Burmanization of Myanmar's Muslims.* Bangkok: White Lotus.

Beyer, Judith. 2014. Houses of Islam. Muslims, property rights, and the state in Myanmar. In *Islam and the state in Myanmar. Muslim-Buddhist relations and the politics of belonging*, edited by Melissa Crouch. New Delhi: Oxford University Press, 127–155.

————. 2016. *The force of custom. Law and the ordering of everyday life in Kyrgyzstan.* Pittsburgh: University of Pittsburgh Press.

————. 2017. Saints in politics. Aung San Suu Kyi and the dilemmas of political desire. *openDemocracy.* 24 September 2017. https://www. opendemocracy.net/en/transformation/saints-in-politics-aung-san-suu-kyi-and-dilemmas-of-political-desire (accessed 17 July 2022).

————. 2019a. Das Recht der Anderen. Rechtsethnologie zwischen Pluralität, Indigenität und Alterität [The law of others. Legal anthropology between plurality, indigeneity and alterity]. In *Interdisziplinäre Rechtsforschung. Eine Einführung in die geistes- und sozialwissenschaftliche Befassung mit dem Recht und seiner Praxis,* edited by Christian Boulanger, Julika Rosenstock and Tobias Singelnstein. Wiesbaden: Springer, 91–108.

————. 2019b. Recentering the sidelines. On the politics of 'standing by'. Blog-post for *Public Anthropologist.* 4 May 2019 (accessed 10 January 2020).

————. 2021. 'You messed with the wrong generation'. The young people resisting Myanmar's military. *openDemocracy.* 11 February 2021. https:// www.opendemocracy.net/en/you-messed-with-the-wrong-generation-the-young-people-resisting-myanmars-military/ (accessed 16 July 2022).

————. 2022a. The common sense of expert activists. Practitioners, scholars, and the problem of statelessness in Europe. *Dialectical Anthropology.* https://doi.org/10.1007/s10624-022-09666-5.

————. 2022b. Statelessness, expert activists and the 'practitioner-scholar dilemma'. *Critical Statelessness Studies (CSS) Blog* series. https://law. unimelb.edu.au/centres/statelessness/resources/critical-statelessness-studies-blog/statelessness-expert-activists-and-the-practitioner-scholar-dilemma (accessed 27 December 2022).

————. 2022c. Who gets to be 'Myanmar' at the ICJ? *Allegra Lab.* February 2022. https://allegralaboratory.net/who-gets-to-be-myanmar-at-the-icj/ (accessed 17 July 2022).

Beyer, Judith and Felix Girke. 2015. Practicing harmony ideology. Ethnographic reflections on community and coercion. *Common Knowledge* 21 (2):196–235.

————. 2019a. Aung San Suu Kyi at the International Court of Justice. When the personal is political. *openDemocracy.* 8 December 2019. https://www. opendemocracy.net/en/transformation/aung-san-suu-kyi-international-court-justice-when-personal-political/ (accessed 17 July 2022).

————. 2019b. Harmony ideology at The Hague. Myanmar before the International Court of Justice. *Public Anthropologist.* 14 December 2019. http://publicanthropologist.cmi.no/2019/12/14/harmony-ideology-at-the-hague-myanmar-before-the-international-court-of-justice/ (accessed 17 July 2022).

Beyer, Judith and Nina Johnen. 2014. Almost Englishmen. Baghdadi Jews in Yangon. 24 June 2014. https://allegralaboratory.net/review-almost-englishmen/ (accessed 17 July 2022).

Beyer, Judith and Peter Finke (eds). 2019. Introduction. In *Central Asian Survey*. Special Issue "Practices of traditionalization in Central Asia", edited by Judith Beyer and Peter Finke. 38 (3): 310–328.

Bhabha, Homi. 1984. Of mimicry and man. The ambivalence of colonial discourse. *October* 28: 125–133.

Bhattacharya, Swapna. 2007. *India-Myanmar relations 1886–1948*. Kolkata: Bagchi and Company.

Bhattacharyya, Gargi, Adam Elliott-Cooper, Sita Balani, Kerem Nisancioglu, Kojo Koram, Dalia Gebrial, Nadine El-Enany, Luke De Noronha. 2021. *Empire's endgame. Racism and the British state*. London: Pluto Press.

Bhaumik, Parthasarathi. 2022. *Bengalis in Burma. A colonial encounter (1886–1948)*. London and New York: Routledge.

Boddy, Janice. 1989. *Wombs and alien spirits. Women, men, and the Zar cult in Northern Sudan*. Madison: University of Wisconsin Press.

Boissevain, Jeremy. 1965. *Saints and fireworks. Religion and politics in rural Malta*. London: Berg.

Bourdieu, Pierre. 1977 [1972]. *Outline of a theory of practice*, translated by Richard Nice. Cambridge et al.: Cambridge University Press.

Bowman, Glenn. 1997. Identifying vs. identifying with 'the Other.' Reflections on the siting of the subject in anthropological discourse. In *After writing culture. Epistemology and praxis in contemporary anthropology*, edited by Alison James, Jenny Hockey and Andrew Dawson. London and New York: Routledge, 34–50.

Brac de la Perrière, Bénédicte. 2015. Ma Ba Tha, les trois syllabes du nationalisme religieux birman [Ma Ba Tha. The three syllables of Burmese religious nationalism]. *L'Asie du Sud-Est*, 31–44.

———. 2016. Spirit possession: An autonomous field of practice in the Burmese Buddhist culture. *Journal of Burma Studies*, 20 (1): 1–29.

———. 2017a. About Buddhist Burma. Thathana or 'religion' as social space. In *Encountering 'religion' in Southeast Asia. Anthropological explorations of religion, politics and the spiritual*, edited by Michel Picard. London and New York: Routledge, 39–66.

———. 2017b. Initiations in the Burmese ritual landscape. *Journal of Ethnology and Folkloristics* 11 (1): 65–82.

Breckenridge, Carol. 1976. The Sri Minaksi Sundaresvarar Temple. Worship and endowments in South India, 1833 to 1925. PhD Thesis. Ann Arbor and London: University Microfilms International.

Breman, Jan. 1989. *Taming the coolie beast. Plantation society and the colonial order in Southeast Asia.* Delhi: Oxford University Press.

Brint, Steven. 2001. Gemeinschaft revisited. A critique and reconstruction of the community concept. *Sociological Theory* 19 (1): 1–23.

Brooke, Tal. 1982. *Avatar of night. The hidden side of Sai Baba.* Ghaziabad: Vikas.

Brouwer, Jan. 1995. *The makers of the world. Caste, craft and mind of artisans in South India.* Delhi: Oxford University Press.

———. 2016. In conversation with Jan Brouwer. 3 November 2016. https://www.sahapedia.org/conversation-jan-brouwer (accessed 17 July 2022).

Brown, Bill. 2001. Thing theory. *Critical Inquiry* 28 (1): 1–22.

Brown, Ian. 2005. *A colonial economy in crisis. Burma's rice cultivators and the world depression of the 1930s.* London: Routledge-Curzon.

Brubaker, Rogers. 2002. Ethnicity without groups. *European Journal of Sociology* 43 (2): 163–189.

Brumann, Christoph. 1998. *Die Kunst des Teilens. Eine vergleichende Untersuchung zu den Überlebensbedingungen kommunitärer Gruppen* [The art of sharing. A comparative study on conditions of survival of communitarian groups]. Hamburg: LIT.

Buchli, Victor (eds) 2002. *The material culture reader.* Oxford: Berg.

Burchardt, Marian and Irene Becci. 2013. Introduction. Religion takes place – producing urban locality. In *Topographies of faith. Religion in urban spaces,* edited by Irene Becci, Marian Burchardt and Jose Casanova. London: Brill, 1–21.

Burnes, Alexander. 1835. *Travels into Bokhara. Containing the narrative of a voyage on the Indus from the sea to Lahore with presents from the King of Great Britain and an account of a journey from India to Cabool, Tartary, and Persia.* London: Murray. https://archive.org/details/travelsintobokh02burngoog (accessed 18 July 2022).

Butler, Judith. 2008. Violence, nonviolence. Sartre on Fanon. In *Race after Sartre. Antiracism, Africana existentialism, postcolonialism,* edited by Jonathan Judaken. Albany: State University of New York Press, 211–231.

Calcagno, Antonio. 2012. Gerda Walther. On the possibility of a passive sense of community and the inner time consciousness of community. *Symposium. Canadian Journal of Continental Philosophy* 16 (2): 89–105.

Carstens, Charles. 2018. Religion. In *Routledge handbook of contemporary Myanmar,* edited by Adam Simpson, Nicholas Farrelly and Ian Holliday. London and New York: Routledge, 126–145.

Carter, Marina and Khaleel Torrabully (eds). 2002. *Coolitude. An anthology of the Indian labour diaspora.* London: Anthem.

Carter, Marina. 1996. *Voices from indenture. Experiences of Indian migrants in the British Empire.* London: Leicester University

Casanova, José. 1994. *Public religions in the modern world*. Chicago and London: University of Chicago Press.

Casimir, Michael J. 2009. 'Honor and dishonor' and the quest for emotional equivalents. In *Emotions as bio-cultural processes*, edited by Birgitt Röttger-Rössler and Hans Jürgen Markowitsch. New York: Springer, 281–316.

Charney, Michael. 2009. *A history of modern Burma*. Cambridge: Cambridge University Press.

Chakravarti, Nalini Ranjan. 1971. *The Indian minority in Burma. The rise and decline of an immigrant community*. London: Oxford University Press for the Institute of Race Relations.

Chandra, Bipan. 1984. *Communalism in modern India*. New Delhi: Vikas (Vani Educational Books).

Chatterjee, Partha. 1993. *The nation and its fragments. Colonial and postcolonial histories*. Princeton, N.J.: Princeton University Press.

———. 2004. *The politics of the governed. Popular politics in most of the world*. New York: Columbia University Press.

Chatterjee, Nandini. 2011. *The making of Indian secularism. Empire, law and Christianity, 1830–1960*. New York: Palgrave Macmillan.

Chatterjee, Saheli. 2021. From circular migrants to repatriates. Burmese-Indians of West Bengal, India. Unpublished Master's Thesis. Department of International History and Politics. Graduate Institute of International and Development Studies. Geneva.

Cernea, Ruth Fredman. 2006. *Almost Englishmen. Baghdadi Jews in British Burma*. Lexington Books.

Chattopadhyaya, Saratchandra. 1993. *Srikanta*, translated by Aruna Chakravarti. Delhi: Penguin Books.

Cherry Thein. 2014. Myanmar women object to proposed restrictions on interfaith marriage. *Religion News Service*. 18 December 2014. https://religionnews.com/2014/12/18/myanmar-women-object-proposed-restrictions-interfaith-marriage/ (accessed 18 July 2022).

Cheesman, Nick. 2015. *Opposing the rule of law. How Myanmar's courts make law and order*. Cambridge: Cambridge University Press.

———. 2017. How in Myanmar 'national races' came to surpass citizenship and exclude Rohingya. *Journal of Contemporary Asia* 47 (3): 461–483.

Chicago Memons. 2014. A brief Memon history. www.chicagomemons.com/history.htm (accessed 17 July 2022).

Chidester, David. 1996. *Savage systems. Colonialism and comparative religion in Southern Africa*. Cape Town: University of Cape Town Press.

Coast, David and Jo Fox. 2015. Rumour and politics. *History Compass* 13 (5): 222–234.

Coates, Jennifer. 2013 [2004]. *Women, men and language. A sociolinguistic account of gender differences in languages.* 3rd edition. London and New York: Routledge.

Coconuts Yangon. 2015. Authorities ask Shi'ite Muslims in Yangon to take down 'ISIS' flag. 14 December 2015. http://yangon.coconuts.co/2015/12/14/authorities-ask-shiite-muslims-yangon-take-down-isis-flag (accessed 17 July 2022).

Coderey, Céline. 2015. The healing power of the gift healing services and remuneration in Rakhine (Western Myanmar). *Religion Compass* 9 (11): 404–422.

Cohen, Anthony. 1985. *The symbolic construction of community.* Chichester: Ellis Horwood Limited.

Cohn, Bernard. 1965. Anthropological notes on disputes and law in India. *American Anthropologist* 67 (6/2): 82–122.

———. 1983. Representing authority in Victorian India. In *The invention of tradition,* edited by Eric Hobsbawm and Terrence Ranger. London: Verso, 165–209.

———. 1987. The census, social structure and objectification in South Asia. In *An anthropologist among the historians and other essays,* edited by Bernard Cohn. Delhi: Oxford University Press, 224-254.

Cole, David and Joff Bradley. 2018. *Principles of transversality in globalization and education.* Singapore: Springer.

Collis, Maurice. 1955. *Trials in Burma.* London: Faber and Faber.

Comaroff, Jean and John Comaroff (eds). 2001. Millennial capitalism. First thoughts on a second coming. In *Millennial capitalism and the culture of neoliberalism,* edited by Jean and John Comaroff. Durham and London: Duke University Press, 1–56.

Cooler, Richard. 2002. *The art and culture of Burma.* Center for Southeast Asian Studies. Northern Illinois University. http://seasite.niu.edu/burmese/Cooler/BurmaArt_TOC.htm (accessed 17 July 2022).

Corin, Ellen. 1998. Refiguring the person. The dynamics of affects and symbols in an African spirit possession cult. In *Bodies and persons. Comparative perspectives from Africa and Melanesia,* edited by Michael Lambek and Andrew Strathern. Cambridge: Cambridge University Press, 80–102.

Cox, Harvey. 1965. *The secular city. Secularization and urbanization in theological perspective.* New York: Collier Books.

Crapanzano, Vincent. 1980. *Tuhami. Portrait of a Moroccan.* Chicago and London: Chicago University Press.

Creed, Gerald. 2006a. Reconsidering community. In *The seductions of community. Emancipations, oppressions, quandaries,* edited by Gerald Creed. Santa Fe and Oxford: School of American Resarch Press, 3–22.

————. (ed.). 2006b. *The seductions of community. Emancipations, oppressions, quandaries.* Santa Fe and Oxford: School of American Resarch Press.

Crouch, Melissa. 2015. Constructing religion by law in Myanmar. *The Review of Faith and International Affairs* 13(4): 1–11.

————. 2016. Promiscuity, polygyny and the power of revenge. The past and future of Burmese Buddhist law in Myanmar. *Asian Journal of Law and Society* 3: 85–104.

Csíkzentmihályi, Mihály and Eugene Rochberg-Halton. 1981. *The meaning of things. Domestic symbols and the self.* Cambridge: Cambridge University Press.

Csordas, Thomas. 2002. *Body, meaning, healing.* Basingstoke and New York: Palgrave McMillan.

————. 2007. Introduction. Modalities of transnational transcendence. *Anthropological Theory* 7 (3): 259–272.

Dant, Tim. 2006. Material civilization. Things and society. *British Journal of Sociology* 57 (2): 289–308.

Das, Veena. 2010. Engaging the life of the other. Love and everyday life. In *Ordinary ethics. Anthropology, language, and action,* edited by Michael Lambek. New York: Fordham University Press, 376–399.

De Lauri, Antonio. 2022. The idea of a clean and efficient war is a dangerous lie. *Common Dreams.* 8 April 2022. https://www.commondreams.org/views/2022/04/08/idea-clean-and-efficient-war-dangerous-lie (accessed 7 May 2022).

Deprez, Stanislas. 2014. The minor mode. Albert Piette and the reshaping of anthropology. *Sociologus* 64 (1): 87–95.

Dirks, Nicholas. 2001. *Castes of mind. Colonialism and the making of modern India.* Princeton and Oxford: Princeton University Press.

Dogra, Sufyan Abid. 2019. Living a piety-led life beyond Muharram. Becoming or being a South Asian Shia Muslim in the UK. *Contemporary Islam* 13: 307–324.

Douglas, Mary. 1966. *Purity and danger. An analysis of concepts of pollution and taboo.* London: Routledge.

Dumont, Louis. 1980 [1966]. *Homo hierarchicus. The caste system and its implications.* Chicago: University of Chicago Press.

Dwyer, Kevin. 1979. The dialogic of ethnology. *Dialectical Anthropology* 4 (3): 205–224.

Edgar, Iain. 2011. *The dream in Islam. From Qur'anic tradition to Jihadist inspiration.* Oxford: Berghahn.

Edwards, Jeanette, and Marilyn Strathern. 2000. Including our own. In *Cultures of relatedness. New approaches to the study of kinship,* edited by Janet Carsten. Cambridge: Cambridge University Press, 149–166.

Edwards, Jeanette. 1998. The need for 'A bit of history.' Place and past in English identity. In *Locality and belonging*, edited by Nadia Lovell. London: Routledge, 147–167.

Egreteau, Renaud. 2011a. A passage to Burma? India, development and democratization in Myanmar. *Contemporary Politics* 17 (4): 467–486.

———. 2011b. Burmese Indians in contemporary Burma. Heritage, influence, and perceptions since 1988. *Asian Ethnicity* 12 (1): 33–54.

———. 2013. India's vanishing 'Burma colonies.' Repatriation, urban citizenship, and (de)mobilization of Indian returnees from Burma (Myanmar) since the 1960s. *Moussons* 22: 11–34.

———. 2014. The idealization of a lost paradise. Narratives of nostalgia and traumatic return migration among Indian repatriates from Burma since the 1960s. *Journal of Burma Studies* 18 (1): 137–180.

Emmer, Pieter. 1986. The meek Hindu. The recruitment of Indian indentured labourers for service overseas, 1870–1916. In *Migration, indentured labour before and after slavery*, edited by Pieter Emmer. Amsterdam: Dordrecht, 187–207.

———. 1990. The great escape. The migration of female indentured servants from British India to Surinam 1873–1916. In *South Asians overseas*, edited by Colin Clark, Ceri Peach and Steven Vertovec. Cambridge: Cambridge University Press, 245–266.

Engelke, Matthew. 2008. The objects of evidence. *Journal of the Royal Anthropological Institute* 14: 1–21.

Esposito, Roberto. 2010 [1998]. *Communitas. The origin and destiny of community*. Stanford: Stanford University Press.

Evens, Terry and Don Handelman (eds). 2008. *The Manchester school. Practice and ethnographic praxis in anthropology*. Oxford and New York: Berghahn.

Falk Moore, Sally. 2005. Certainties undone. Fifty turbulent years of legal anthropology, 1949–1999. In *Law and Anthropology. A reader*, edited by Sally Falk Moore. Oxford: Blackwell, 346–367.

Felek, Özgen and Alexander Kynsh (eds) 2012. *Dreams and visions in Islamic societies*. New York: SUNY.

Felstiner, William, Richard Abel and Austin Sarat. 1980–1981. The emergence and transformation of disputes. Naming, blaming, claiming. *Law* and *Society Review*. Special Issue on Dispute Processing and Civil Litigation, 15 (3–4): 631–654.

Ferguson, Jane. 2015. Who's counting? Ethnicity, belonging and the national census in Burma/Myanmar. *Bijdragen* 171 (1): 1–28.

Fine, Gary Alan, Véronique Campion-Vincent, Chip Heath (eds). 2017 [2005]. *Rumor mills. The social impact of rumor and legend*. Milton Park and New York: Routledge.

Firth, Raymund. 1964 [1954]. Foreword to Edmund Leach. *Political systems of highland Burma. A study of Kachin social structure.* London: Athlone, v–viii.

Fisher, William. 1997. Doing good? The politics and antipolitics of NGO practices. *Annual Review of Anthropology* 26: 439–464.

Foucault, Michel. 1998. *Will to knowledge,* translated by Robert Hurley. London: Penguin.

———. 2003. The subject and power. In *The essential Foucault,* edited by Paul Rabinow and Nikolas Rose. New York: New Press, 126–144.

Foxeus, Niklas. 2019. The Buddha was a devoted nationalist. Buddhist nationalism, *ressentiment,* and defending Buddhism in Myanmar. *Religion* 49 (4): 661–690.

Freitag, Sandria. 1989. *Collective action and community. Public arenas and the emergence of communalism in North India.* Berkeley: University of California Press.

Freud, Sigmund. 1914. Der Moses des Michelangelo [The Moses of Michelangelo]. *Imago. Zeitschrift für Anwendung der Psychoanalyse auf die Geisteswissenschaften* III: 15–36.

———. 1930. *Das Unbehagen in der Kultur* [Civilization and its discontents]. Wien: Internationaler Psychoanalytischer Verlag.

Fuerst, Ilyse Morgenstein. 2017. *Indian Muslim minorities and the 1857 rebellion. Religion, rebels and jihad.* London and New York: I.B. Tauris.

Frydenlund, Iselin. 2017a. The birth of Buddhist politics of religious freedom in Myanmar. *Journal of Religious and Political Practice* 4 (1): 107–121.

———. 2017b. Religious liberty for whom? The Buddhist politics of religious freedom during Myanmar's transition to democracy. *Nordic Journal of Human Rights* 35 (1): 55–73.

Furnivall, John. 1948. *Colonial policy and practice. A comparative study of Burma and Netherlands India.* Cambridge: Cambridge University Press.

Fytche, Albert. 1878. *Burma past and present. With personal reminiscences of the country.* London: Kegan Paul.

Galanter, Marc. 1974. Why the 'haves' come out ahead. Speculations on the limits of legal change. *Law and Society Review* 9 (1): 95–160.

Gammeltoft, Tine. 2014. *Haunting images. A cultural account of selective reproduction in Vietnam.* Berkeley et al: University of California Press.

———. 2018. Belonging. Comprehending subjectivity in Vietnam and beyond. *Social Analysis* 62 (1): 76–95.

Garfinkel, Harold. 1967. *Studies in ethnomethodology.* Englewood Cliffs, NJ: Prentice Hall.

Gell, Alfred. 1998. *Art and agency. An anthropological theory.* Oxford: Oxford University Press.

Ghosh, Amitav. 2011. Exodus from Burma, 1941. A personal account, Parts 1, 2, & 3. 21 June 2011. http://amitavghosh.com/blog/?p=432 (accessed 17 July 2022).

Girke, Felix. 2018. Das Bildnis des General Aung San [The portrait of General Aung San]. In *Dinge als Herausforderung. Kontexte, Umgangsweisen und Umwertungen von Objekten*, edited by Hans-Peter Hahn und Friedemann Neumann. Bielefeld: Transcript. https://www.degruyter.com/document/doi/10.1515/9783839445136-008/html (accessed 17 July 2022), 143–166.

———. 2020. Shared field, divided field. Expectations of an anthropological couple in Southeast Asia. In *Being a parent in the field. Implications and challenges of accompanied fieldwork*, edited by Fabienne Braukmann et al. Bielefeld: Transcript, 259–278.

———. forthcoming. Subjects of Heritage. Transforming people and their past in contemporary Myanmar. Habilitation Thesis. Department of History and Sociology. University of Konstanz.

Girke, Felix and Judith Beyer. 2018. 'Transition' as a migratory model in Myanmar. *Journal of Burma Studies* 22 (2): 215–241.

Gluckman, Max. 1963. Gossip and scandal. *Current Anthropology* 4 (3): 307–316.

Goffman, Erving. 1966 [1963]. *Behavior in public places. Notes on the social organization of gatherings*. New York: The Free Press.

Gómez-Ibanez, José, Derek Bok and Nguyen Xuan Thành. 2012. Yangon's development challenges. Report prepared for Proximity Designs. March. https://ash.harvard.edu/files/yangon.pdf (accessed 17 July 2022).

Good, Mari-Jo Delvecchio and Byron Good. 1988. Ritual, the state, and the transformation of emotional discourse in Iranian society. *Culture, Medicine, and Psychiatry* 12 (1): 43–66.

Gouldner, Alvin. 1971. *The coming crisis of Western sociology*. London: Heinemann.

Gramsci, Antonio. 1971 [1935]. *Selections from the Prison Notebooks*, edited and translated by Quintin Hoare and Geoffrey Nowell Smith. New York: International Publishers.

———. 1975. *Quaderni del carcere* [The prison notebooks]. 4 vols, edited by Valentino Gerratana. Turin: Einaudi Editore.

Guattari, Félix. 1984. *Molecular revolution. Psychiatry and politics*, translated by Rosemary Sheed. Harmondsworth, UK and New York: Penguin.

———. 2015 [1972]. *Psychoanalysis and transversality. Texts and interviews 1955–1971*, translated by Ames Hodges. South Pasadena, CA: Semiotext(e).

Hage, Ghassan. 2002. Citizenship and honourability. Belonging to Australia today. In *Arab-Australians today. Citizenship and belonging,* edited by Ghassan Hage. Melbourne: Melbourne University Press, 1–15.

Hall, D.G.E. 1960. Studies in Dutch relations with Arakan, Part I, Dutch Relations with King Thirithudhamma of Arakan. *Burma Research Society Fiftieth Anniversary Publications* 2.

Hamilton, Peter. 1985. Foreword. In *The symbolic construction of community,* written by Anthony Cohen. Chichester: Ellis Horwood Limited, 7–9.

Harriden, Jessica. 2012. *The authority of influence. Women and power in Burmese history.* Copenhagen: NIAS Press.

Harrisson, Annika. 2018. Everyday justice for Muslims in Mawlamyine. Subjugation and skilful navigation. In *Everyday justice in Myanmar. Informal resolutions and state evasion in a time of contested transition,* edited by Helene Kyed. Copenhagen: NIAS Press, 255–281.

Harvey, G.E. 1925. *History of Burma. From the earliest times to 10 March 1824.* London: Frank Cass.

———. 1934. Indian labour in Rangoon by E. J. L. Andrew (1933). *The Economic Journal* 44 (175): 501–503.

Hauschild, Thomas, 2002. *Magie und Macht in Italien* [Magic and power in Italy]. Gifkendorf: Merlin-Verlag.

Haviland, John. 1977. *Gossip, reputation, and knowledge in Zinacantan.* Chicago and London: The University of Chicago Press.

Hayden, Robert. 2002. Antagonistic tolerance. Competitive sharing of religious sites in South Asia and the Balkans. *Current Anthropology* 43 (2): 205–231.

Heath, Christian. 2006. Body work. The collaborative production of the clinical object. In *Communication in medical care. Interaction between primary care physicians and patients,* edited by John Heritage and Douglas W. Maynard. Cambridge: Cambridge University Press, 185–213.

Hegner, Victoria and Peter Margry. 2017. *Spiritualizing the city. Agency and resilience of the urban and urbanesque habitat.* London: Routledge.

Heidemann, Frank. 1992. *Kanganies in Sri Lanka and Malaysia. Tamil recruiter-cum-foreman as a sociological category in the nineteenth and twentieth century.* München: Anacon.

———.2018. Dorfatmosphären. Hatti und keri der Badaga in Südindien [Village atmospheres. Hatti and keri of the Badaga in South India]. *Paideuma* 64: 51–73.

Heidemann, Frank and Philipp Zehmisch (eds). 2016. *Manifestations of history. Time, space, and community in the Andaman Islands.* Delhi: Primus Books.

Heminway, Sarah. 1992. The resemblance in external appearance. The colonial project in Kuala Lumpur and Rangoon. PhD Dissertation. Ann Arbor: UMI.

Henare, Amiria, Martin Holbraad and Sari Wastell (eds). 2007. *Thinking through things. Theorizing artefacts ethnographically.* London: Routledge.

Heritage, John. 1984. *Garfinkel and ethnomethodology.* Cambridge: Polity Press.

———. 1988. Explanations as accounts. A conversation analytic perspective. In *Analyzing everyday explanation. A casebook of methods,* edited by Charles Antaki. London, SAGE, 127–144.

Hillery, George. 1955. Definitions of community. Areas of agreement. *Rural Sociology* 20 (2): 111–123.

Ho, Engseng. 2006. *The graves of Tarim. Genealogy and across the Indian Ocean.* Berkeley et al: University of California Press.

Holbraad, Martin and Axel Pedersen (eds). 2017. *The ontological turn. An anthropological exposition.* Cambridge: Cambridge University Press.

Holder, Jane und Carolyn Harrison (eds). 2003. *Law and geography. Current legal issues.* No. 5. Oxford: Oxford University Press.

Holleman, John. 1973. Trouble-cases and trouble-less cases in the study of customary law and legal reform. *Law and Society Review* 7 (4): 585–610.

Htoo Thant. 2016. Mone Wun (Bamar) national cards debated. Myanmar Times. 5 May. https://www.mmtimes.com/national-news/20123-mone-wun-bamar-national-cards-debated.html (accessed 17 July 2022).

Husserl, Edmund. 1980 [1928]. Die doppelte Intentionalität der Retention und die Konstitution des Bewußtseinsflusses [The double intentionality of retention and the constitution of the flow of consciousness]. In: ibid. *Vorlesungen zur Phänomenologie des inneren Zeitbewußtseins,* edited by Martin Heidegger. Second edition. Tübingen: Max Niemeyer, 433–437.

Huxley, Andrew. 1990. How Buddhist is Theravada Buddhist law? A survey of legal literature in Pali-land. *The Buddhist Forum* 1: 41–85

———. 1998. The last fifty years of Burmese law. E Maung and Maung Maung'. *Lawasia*: 9–20.

———. 2006. Buddhist law, Asian law, Eurasian law. *Journal of Comparative Law* 1: 158–64.

Ikeya, Chie. 2006. The 'traditional' high status of women in Burma. *Journal of Burma Studies* 10: 51–77.

———. 2011. *Refiguring women, colonialism, and modernity in Burma.* Honolulu: University of Hawai'i Press.

———. 2013. Colonial intimacies in comparative perspective. Intermarriage, law and cultural difference in British Burma. *Journal of Colonialism and Colonial History* 14 (1). doi:10.1353/cch.2013.0014.

———. 2017. Transcultural intimacies in British Burma and the Straits settlements. A history of belonging, difference, and empire. In *Belonging across the Bay of Bengal. Religious rites, colonial migrations, national rights,* edited by Michael Laffin. London and New York: Bloomsbury, 117–137.

Ingold, Tim. 2000. *The perception of the environment. Essays on livelihood, dwelling and skill.* New York: Routledge.

———. 2007. Materials against materiality. *Archaeological Dialogues* 14 (1): 1–16.

———. 2011. *Redrawing anthropology. Materials, movements, lines.* Ashgate: Farnham.

Jackson, Michael. 2005. *The politics of storytelling. Violence, transgression and intersubjectivity.* University of Copenhagen: Museum Tusculanum Press.

———. 2012. *Between one and one another.* Berkeley et.al.: University of California Press.

Jackson, Michael and Albert Piette (eds). 2017 [2015]. *What is existential anthropology?* New York and Oxford: Berghahn.

Jaiswal, Ritesh. 2014. Indian labour emigration to Burma (c. 1880–1940). Rethinking Indian migratory patterns. *Proceedings of the Indian History Congress* 75: 911–919.

Jameson, Fredric. 1974 [1971]. *Marxism and form. Twentieth-century dialectical theories of literature.* New Jersey: Princeton University Press.

Joshi, Vibha. 2012. *A matter of belief. Christian conversion and healing in North-East India.* New York and Oxford: Berghahn.

Kahn, Joel. 2008. Other cosmopolitans in the making of the modern Malay world. In *Anthropology and the new cosmopolitanism*, edited by Pnina Werbner. Oxford: Berg, 261–280.

Kapadia, Karin. 1996. Dancing the goddess. Possession and class in Tamil South India. *Modern Asian Studies* 30 (2): 423–445.

———. 2000. Pierced by love. Tamil possession, gender, and caste. In *Invented identities. The interplay of gender, religion, and politics in India*, edited by Julia Leslie and Mary McGee. New Delhi: Oxford University Press, 181–202.

Kapferer, Jean-Noël. 1990 [1987]. *Rumors. Uses, interpretations and images*, translated by Bruce Fink. London and New York: Routledge.

Kapferer, Bruce. 2014. A note on Gluckman's 1930's fieldwork in Natal. *History in Africa* 41: 147–154.

Kapoor, Shivani. 2021. The violence of odors. Sensory politics of caste in a leather tannery. *The Senses and Society* 16 (2). https://doi.org/10.1080/17458927.2021.1876365.

Kant, Immanuel. 2003 [1797]. *The metaphysics of morals*, translated by Mary Gregor. Cambridge: Cambridge University Press.

Kaur, Amarjit. 2006. Indian labor, labor standards, and workers' health in Burma and Malaya, 1900–1940. *Modern Asian Studies* 40 (2): 89–115.

Keane, Webb. 2005. Signs are not the garb of meaning. On the social analysis of things. *Materiality*: 182–205.

———. 2003. Self-interpretation, agency, and the objects of anthropology.

Reflections on a genealogy. *Comparative Studies in Society and History* 45 (2): 222–248.

Khazeni, Arash. 2020. *The city and the wilderness. Indo-Persian encounters in Southeast Asia.* Berkeley: University of California Press.

Khosronejad, Pedram. 2006. Being a martyr in Iran. *Anthropology News* 47 (8): 20.

———. 2013. *Unburied memories. The politics of bodies of sacred defence martyrs in Iran.* London: Routledge.

Kidwell, Mardi. 2005. Gaze as social control. How very young children differentiate 'the look' from a 'mere look' by their adult caregivers. *Research on Language and Social Interaction* 38 (4): 417–449.

Kierkegaard, Søren. 1997. *Without Authority. Kierkegaard's Writings, XVIII,* edited and translated by Howard Hong and Edna Hong. With introduction and notes. Princeton, NJ: Princeton University Press.

Kirsch, Thomas G. 2002. Performance and the negotiation of charismatic authority in an African indigenous church of Zambia. *Paideuma* 48: 57–76.

Kirsch, Stuart. 2002. Rumour and other narratives of political violence in West Papua. *Critique of Anthropology* 22 (1): 53–79.

Kohut, Heinz. 1971. *The analysis of the self. A systematic approach to the psychoanalytic treatment of narcissistic personality disorders.* Chicago: University of Chicago Press.

Kong, Lily. 2005. Religious processions. Urban politics and poetics. *Temenos* 41 (2): 225–249.

———. 2010. Global shifts, theoretical shifts. Changing geographies of religion. *Progress in Human Geography* 34 (6): 755–776.

Kraas, Frauke, Yin May and Zin New Myint. 2010. Yangon/Myanmar. Transformation processes and mega-urban developments. *Geographische Rundschau* 6 (2): 26–37.

Kroeger, Karen. 2003. AIDS rumours, imaginary enemies, and the body politic in Indonesia. *American Ethnologist* 30 (2): 243–257.

Kumar, Mukesh. 2022. Cooperative segregation and the culture of co-existence at an integrated religious shrine. *History and Anthropology.* DOI: 10.1080/02757206.2022.2129631.

Kyaw Latt. 2015. Yangon. Issues and challenges. Powerpoint presentation at "Vivre ensemble en transition." Organized by the French Institute, Yangon. 2 December 2015.

Kyaw Hsu Mon. 2014. UNICEF rents Rangoon office from former general. *The Irrawaddy* 20 May 2014. https://www.irrawaddy.com/news/burma/unicef-rents-rangoon-office-former-general.html (accessed 17 July 2022).

Kyed, Helene. 2018. Introduction to the special issue on everyday justice. *Independent Journal of Burmese Scholarship.* 1 (2): ii–xxii.

Kyed, Helene and Ah Lynn. 2021. Soldier defections in Myanmar. Motivations and obstacles following the 2021 military coup. Danish Institute for International Studies Report. https://pure.diis.dk/ws/files/ 4827622/ Soldier_defections_in_Myanmar_DIIS_Report_2021_06.pdf (accessed 30 June 2022).

Ladwig, Patrice. 2012. Feeding the dead. Ghosts, materiality and merit in a Lao Buddhist festival. In *Buddhist funeral cultures of Southeast Asia and China*, edited by Paul Williams and Patrice Ladwig. Cambridge: Cambridge University Press, 119–142.

Lambek, Michael. 1981. *Human spirits. A cultural account of trance in Mayotte.* Cambridge: Cambridge University Press.

———. 1993. *Knowledge and practice in Mayotte.* Toronto: University of Toronto Press.

———. 1997. Knowledge and practice in Mayotte. An overview. *Cultural Dynamics* 9 (2): 131–148.

———. 1998. Body and mind in mind, body and mind in body. Some anthropological interventions in a long conversation. In *Bodies and persons. Comparative perspectives from Africa and Melanesia*, edited by Michael Lambek and Andrew Strathern. Cambridge: Cambridge University Press, 103–123.

———. 2010. How to make up one's mind. Reason, passion, and ethics in spirit possession. In *Models of mind*, edited by Marlene Goldman and Jill Matus. Special issue of *University of Toronto Quarterly* 79/2: 720–741.

———. 2017. Both/and. In *What is existential anthropology?* Edited by Michael Jackson and Albert Piette, 58–83.

Lammerts, Christian. 2018. *Buddhist law in Burma. A history of Dhammasattha texts and jurisprudence, 1250–1850.* Honolulu: University of Hawai'i Press.

Larkin, Emma. 2007. One monk for every soldier. *The Guardian.* 30 September. https://www.theguardian.com/commentisfree/2007/sep/30/comment. burma1 (accessed 17 July 2022).

Laurie, William. 1853. *The Second Burmese War. A narrative of the operations of at Rangoon in 1852–1853.* London: Smith, Elder & Co.

Leach, Edmund. 1964 [1954]. *Political systems of highland Burma. A study of Kachin social structure.* London: G. Bell and Son.

Légrand, Dorothée. 2007. Pre-reflective self-consciousness. On being bodily in the world. *Janus Head* 9 (2): 493–519.

Lehman, F.K. 1967. Ethnic categories in Burma and the theory of social systems. In *Southeast Asian tribes, minorities, and nations*, edited by Peter Kunstadter. Princeton, New Jersey: Princeton University Press: 93–124.

Levenson, Edgar. 1998. Awareness, insight and learning. *Contemporary Psychoanalysis* 34 (2): 239–249.

————. 2018. *Interpersonal psychoanalysis and the enigma of consciousness.* Routledge: Milton Park.

LeVine, Mark and Bryan Reynolds. 2018. Fugitive pedagogy. Guattari's ecosophy in the mural discourse of the Zapatistas. In *Principles of transversality in globalization and education,* edited by David Cole and Joff Bradley. Singapore: Springer, 149–172.

Lovell, Nadia (ed.). 1998. *Locality and belonging.* London: Routledge.

Louw, Maria. 2010. Dreaming up futures. Dream omens and magic in Bishkek. *History and Anthropology* 21 (3): 277–292.

Lutgendorf, Philip. 2007. *Hanuman's tale. The messages of a divine monkey.* Oxford: Oxford University Press.

Lyall, Alfred. 1894. *Rise and expansion of British dominion of India.* 3rd edition. London: John Murray.

Lydall, Jean and Ivo Strecker. 1979. *The Hamar of Southern Ethiopia.* Vols 1–3. Hohenschäftlarn: Klaus Renner.

Macaulay, Thomas Babington. 1965 [1835]. Minute by the Hon'ble T.B. Macaulay, dated the 2nd February 1835. In *Bureau of Education. Selections from Educational Records, Part I (1781–1839),* edited by H. Sharp. Delhi: National Archives of India, 107–117.

Maine, Henry Sumner. 1861. *Ancient law. Its connection with the early history of society, and its relation to modern ideas.* London: John Murray.

————. 1871. *Village communities in the East and West. Six lectures delivered at Oxford.* London: John Murray.

Mahajani, Usha. 1960. *The role of Indian minorities in Burma and Malaya.* Bombay: Vora.

Mantena, Karuna. 2010. *Alibis of empire. Henry Maine and the ends of liberal imperialism.* Princeton and Oxford: Princeton University Press.

Marcuse, Herbert. 1948. Existentialism. Remarks on Jean-Paul Sartre's *L'être et le néant. Philosophy and Phenomenological Research. A Quarterly Journal* 8 (3): 309–336.

Masquelier, Adeline. 2000. Of headhunters and cannibals. Migrancy, labor, and consumption in the Mawri imagination. *Cultural Anthropology* 15 (1): 84–126.

Maung Maung Kyi. 1987. *The people and law.* Rangoon: Thaunglonhteiktin Press.

Maung Maung Ta, Haji. 2004. *Myanmar and the Shiah Muslims in Myanmar. The development of the Shiah Muslims in the Union of Myanmar.* Bangkok: The Islamic Cultural Center.

Mauss, Marcel. 1990 [1902]. *The gift. The form and reason for exchange in archaic societies,* translated by W.D. Halls. New York and London: W.W. Norton.

Maynard, Douglas and Steven Clayman. 1991. The diversity of ethnomethodology. *Annual Review of Sociology* 17: 385–418.

Mazumder, Rajashree. 2013. Constructing the Indian immigrant to colonial Burma, 1885–1948. PhD Dissertation. Los Angeles: University of California.

———. 2014. 'I do not envy you.' Mixed marriages and immigration debates in the 1920s and 1930s Rangoon, Burma. *The Indian Economic and Social History Review* 51 (4): 497–527.

McCrae, Alister. 1990. *Scots in Burma. Golden times in a golden land.* Edinburgh: Kiscadale Publications.

McLeod, Hugh. 1978. Religion in the city. *Urban History* 5: 7–22.

McMillan, David and David Chavis. 1986. Sense of community. A definition and a theory. *Journal of Community Psychology* 14: 6–23.

McNamara, Roger. 2006. Re-narrating the nation. Race, sexuality and hybridity in Aubrey Menen's autobiographies, In *New hybridities. Societies and cultures in transition*, edited by Frank Heidemann and Alfonso de Toro. Hildesheim: Olms, 207–222.

Medin, Douglas. 1989. Psychological essentialism. In *Similarity and analogical reasoning*, edited by Stella Vosniadou and Andrew Ortony. Cambridge: Cambridge University Press, 179–195.

Merleau-Ponty, Maurice. 1962 [1945]. *Phenomenology of perception*, translated by Colin Smith. London: Routledge and Kegan Paul.

———. 2007. The primacy of perception and its philosophical consequences. In *The Merleau-Ponty reader*, edited by Ted Toadvine and Leonard Lawlor. Evanston: Northwestern University Press, 89–118.

Mersan, Alexandra de. 2016. Comment les musulmans d'Arakan sont-ils devenus étrangers à l'Arakan? [How did the Muslims of Arakan become foreigners of Arakan] *Moussons* 28 (1): 123–146.

Meyer, Christian. 2018. *Culture, practice, and the body. Conversational organization and embodied culture in Northwest Senegal.* Stuttgart: Metzler.

———. 2016. Ethnomethodologie als Kultursoziologie [Ethnomethodology as cultural sociology]. In *Handbuch Kultursoziologie*, edited by Stephan Moebius, Frithjof Nungesser and Katharina Scherke (eds). Wiesbaden: Springer, 3–27.

Meyer, Christian, Jürgen Streeck and Scott Jordan (eds). 2018. *Intercorporeality. Emerging socialities in interaction.* Oxford: Oxford University Press.

Miguens, Sofia, Magueys Sofia and Gerhard Preyer (eds) 2016. *Pre-reflective consciousness. Sartre and contemporary philosophy of mind.* Milton Park and New York: Routledge.

Mill, John Stuart. 1848. *Principles of political economy.* London: John W. Parker.

Miller, Daniel. 2008. *The comfort of things.* Cambridge: Polity.

Mitchell, Jon. 1997. A moment with Christ. The importance of feelings in the analysis of belief. *Journal of the Royal Anthropological Institute* 3(1): 79–94.

Mittermaier, Amira. 2011. *Dreams that matter. Egyptian landscapes of the imagination*. Berkeley: University of California Press.

Modonesi, Massimo. 2014. *Subalternity, antagonism, autonomy*. London: Pluto.

Moerman, Michael. 1965. Ethnic identification in a complex civilization. Who are the Lue? *American Anthropologist* 67 (5):1215–1230.

———. 1968. Accomplishing ethnicity. In *Ethnomethodology. Selected readings*, edited by Roy Turner. Harmondsworth: Penguin, 54–68

———. 1993. Ariadne's thread and Indra's net. Reflections on ethnography, ethnicity, identity, culture, and interaction. *Research on Language and Social Interaction* 26 (1): 85–98.

Moomal, Ebrahim. 1996. *The end of the world. Random, rampant and runaway thoughts on the ultimate journey*. Pretoria: Laudium.

Moorthy, Shanti and Ashraf Jamal. 2010. Introduction. In *Indian Ocean studies. Cultural, social and political perspectives*, edited by Shanti Moorthy and Ashraf Jamal. New York: Routledge, 1–31.

Morgenstein Fuerst, Ilyse. 2017. *Indian Muslim minorities and the 1857 rebellion. Religion, rebels, and jihad*. London and New York: I.B. Tauris.

Morton, Christopher. 2005. Fieldwork and the participant-photographer: E. E. Evans-Pritchard and the Nuer rite of Gorot. *Visual Anthropology* 22 (4): 252–274.

Münster, Daniel. 2007. *Postkoloniale Traditionen. Eine Ethnographie über Dorf, Kaste und Ritual in Südindien* [Postcolonial traditions. An ethnography of village, caste and ritual in South India]. Bielefeld: Transcript.

Nader, Laura. 1990. *Harmony ideology. Justice and control in a Zapotec mountain village*. Stanford, CA: Stanford University Press.

———. 2004 [2001]. Harmony coerced is freedom denied. In *Anthropologists in the public sphere. Speaking out on war, peace, and American power*, edited by Roberto González. Austin: University of Texas Press, 252–255.

Nader, Laura and Elizabeth Grande. 2002. Current illusions and delusions about conflict management in Africa and elsewhere. *Law and Social Inquiry* 27 (3): 631–633.

Nancy, Jean-Luc. 2015 [1991]. *The inoperative community*. Edited by Peter Connor, translated by Peter Connor et al. Minneapolis and London: University of Minnesota Press.

Nandy, Ashis. 1990. The politics of secularism and the recovery of religious tolerance. In *Mirrors of violence. Communities, riots and survivors in South Asia*, edited by Veena Das. Delhi: Oxford University Press, 69–90.

———. 1991[1983]. *The intimate enemy. Loss and recovery of self under colonialism*. Delhi: Oxford University Press.

———.1993. Three positions. *Seminar* 402: 15–17.

Narayanan, Yamini (ed.). 2016. *Religion and urbanism. Reconceptualising sustainable cities for South Asia.* London and New York: Routledge.

Nemoto, Kei. 2000. The concepts of dobama ("our Burma") and thudo-Bama ("their Burma") in Burmese nationalism, 1930–1948. *The Journal of Burma Studies* 5: 1–16.

———. 2014. The Anglo-Burmese in the 1940s. To become Burmese or not. *The Journal of South Asian Studies* 32: 1–23.

Nietzsche, Friedrich. 1997 [1874]. On the uses and disadvantages of history for life. In *The untimely meditations,* edited by Daniel Breazeale, translated by R. Hollingdale. Cambridge: Cambridge University Press, 57–124.

Niezen, Ron. 2003. Culture and the judiciary. The meaning of the culture concept as a source of Aboriginal rights in Canada. *Canadian Journal of Law and Society* 18 (2): 1–26.

Niezen, Ron and Maria Sapignoli (eds). 2016. *Palaces of hope. The anthropology of global organizations.* New York et al: Cambridge University Press.

Noor, Farish. 2016. *The discursive construction of Southeast Asia in 19th century colonial-capitalist discourse.* Amsterdam: Amsterdam University Press.

Nyi Nyi Kyaw. 2018a. *Freedom of religion, the role of the state, and interreligious relations in Myanmar.* Report for: International Centre for Ethnic Studies & Equitas – International Centre for Human Rights Education. Kottawa: Horizon Printing. https://equitas.org/wp-content/uploads/2018/10/Freedom-of-Religion-Myanmar.pdf (accessed 17 July 2022).

———. 2018b. Adulteration of pure native blood by aliens? Mixed race *kapya* in colonial and post-colonial Myanmar. *Social Identities. Journal for the Study of Race, Nation and Culture.* 25 (3): 345–359.

Obeyesekere, Gananath. 1981. *Medusa's hair. An essay on personal symbols and religious experience.* Chicago: The University of Chicago Press.

Oksala, Johanna. 2005. *Foucault on freedom.* Cambridge: Cambridge University Press.

Oliver, Paul. 2010. *Foucault. The key ideas. Teach yourself.* London: John Murray.

Ooi, Gin Keat. 2004. *Southeast Asia. A historical encyclopaedia from Angkor Wat to East Timor.* Santa Barbara: ABC-Clio.

Orsi, Robert. 1985. *The Madonna of 115th street: Faith and community in Italian Harlem, 1880–1950.* New Haven: Yale University Press.

———. (ed.). 1999. *Gods of the city: Religion and the American urban landscape,* Bloomington: Indiana University Press.

Ortner, Sherry. 1984. Theory in anthropology since the sixties. *Comparative Studies in Society and History* 26 (1): 126–166.

———. 2010. Access. Reflections on studying up. *Ethnography* 11(2): 211–233.

Orwell, George. 1936. Shooting an elephant. *New Writing* 2.

Paine, Robert. 1967. What is gossip about? An alternative hypothesis. *Man* 2 (2): 278–285.

Pandey, Gyanendra. 1990. *The construction of communalism in colonial north India*. Delhi: Oxford University Press.

———. 2006. The subaltern as subaltern citizen. *Economic and Political Weekly* 41 (46): 4735–4741.

Park, Robert. 1928. Human migration and the marginal man. *The American Journal of Sociology* 33 (6): 881–893.

Pearn, Bertie Reginald. 1939. *A history of Rangoon*. Rangoon: American Baptist Mission Press.

Pemberton, Robert. 1835. *Report on the Eastern frontier of British India*. Calcutta: Baptist Mission Press.

———. 1946. *The Indian in Burma*. Ledbury: Le Play House Press.

Pennington, Brian. 2005. *Was Hinduism invented? Britons, Indians and the colonial construction of religion*. New York: Oxford University Press.

Piette, Albert. 1996. *Ethnographie de l'action. L'observation des details* Ethnography of action. On the observation of details]. Paris: Métailié.

———. 1999. *La religion de près. L'activité religieuse en train de se faire* [Religion up close. Religious activity in the making]. Paris: Métailié.

———. 2011. *Fondements à une anthropologie des hommes* [Foundations for an anthropology of humans]. Paris: Hermann.

———. 2012. *De l'ontologie en anthropologie* [On ontology in anthropology]. Paris: Berg International Papers.

———. 2015. *Existence in the details. Theory and methodology in existential anthropology*, translated by Matthew Cunningham. Berlin: Duncker & Humblot.

———. 2017 [2015]. Existence, minimality, and believing. In *What is existential anthropology?* Edited by Michael Jackson and Albert Piette. New York and Oxford: Berghahn, 178–214.

———. 2016. *Separate humans. Anthropology, ontology, existence*. Szczecin: Mimesis International.

Pina-Cabral, João. 2013. The two faces of mutuality. Contemporary themes in anthropology. *Anthropological Quarterly* 86, 1: 257–274.

———. 2017. *World. An anthropological examination*. Chicago: HAU Books.

Poojari, Omkar. 2021. The tiger changes stripes. *The Telegraph India Online*. 15 December. https://www.telegraphindia.com/opinion/shiv-sena-the-tiger-changes-stripes/cid/1843315 (accessed 4 June 2022).

Prakash, Gyan. 2002. The colonial genealogy of society. Community and political modernity in India. In *The social in question. New bearings in history and the social sciences,* edited by Patrick Joyce. New York: Routledge, 81–96.

Prasse-Freeman, Elliott. 2022. Resistance/refusal. Politics of manoeuvre under diffuse regimes of governmentality. *Anthropological Theory* 22 (1): 102–127.

Prasse-Freeman, Elliott and Ko Kabya. 2021. Revolutionary responses to the Myanmar coup. *Anthropology Today* 37 (3): 1–2.

Rankin, George. 1939. Custom and the Muslim law in British India. In *Transactions of the Grotius Society.* Vol. 25: Problems of peace and war, papers read before the society in the year 1939, 89–118.

Rao, Ursula. 2003. Kommunalismus in Indien. Eine Darstellung der wissenschaftlichen Diskussion über Hindu-Muslim Konflikte [Communalism in India. A description of the academic discussion on Hindu-Muslim conflicts]. *Südasienwissenschaftliche Arbeitsblätter* 4. University of Halle-Wittenberg. http://www.suedasien.uni-halle.de/SAWA/Rao.pdf (accessed 17 July 2022).

Rapport, Nigel and Joanna Overing (eds). 2000. *Social and cultural anthropology. Key concepts.* London and New York: Routledge.

Ray, Rajat Kanta. 2003. *The felt community. Commonality and mentality before the emergence of Indian nationalism.* Oxford: Oxford University Press.

Reynolds, Edward. 2017. Description of membership and enacting membership. Seeing-a-lift being a team. *Journal of Pragmatics* 118: 99–119.

Rhoads, Elizabeth. 2018. Forced evictions as urban planning? Traces of colonial land control practices in Yangon, Myanmar. *State Crime Journal* 7 (2): 278–305.

———. 2020. Property, citizenship, and invisible dispossession in Myanmar's urban frontier. *Geopolitics,* DOI: 10.1080/14650045.2020.1808887.

Rhoads, Elizabeth and Courtney Wittekind. 2018. Rethinking land and property in a 'transitioning' Myanmar. Representations of isolation, neglect, and natural decline. *Journal of Burma Studies* 22(2): 171–213.

Ribot, Jesse and Nancy Peluso. 2003. A theory of access. *Rural Sociology* 68 (2): 153–181.

Robinne, François and Mandy Sadan (eds). 2007. *Social dynamics in the highlands of Southeast Asia. Reconsidering political systems of highland Burma by E.R. Leach.* Leiden and Boston: Brill.

Robinne, François. 2019. Thinking though heterogeneity. An anthropological look at contemporary Myanmar. *Journal of Burma Studies* 23 (2): 285–322.

Rosa, Hartmut, Lars Gertenbach, Henning Laux und David Strecker. 2010.

Theorien der Gemeinschaft. Zur Einführung [Theories of community. An introduction]. Hamburg: Junius.

Rosnow, Ralph and Gary Alan Fine. 1976. *Rumor and gossip. The social psychology of hearsay.* New York: Elsevier.

Rosnow, Ralph. 1991. Inside rumor. A personal journey. *American Psychologist* 46: 484–496.

Röttger-Rössler, Birgitt and Hans Jürgen Markowitsch (eds). 2009. *Emotions as bio-cultural processes.* New York: Springer.

Saberwal, Satish. 1981. Elements of communalism. *Mainstream* 21–28 March.

Sacks, Harvey. 1992. On doing 'being ordinary'. In *Structures of social action. Studies in conversation analysis*, edited by J. Maxwell Atkinson and John Heritage. Cambridge: Cambridge University Press, 413–429.

———. 1995. *Lectures on conversation.* Vol. 1 and 2. Oxford: Blackwell.

Sadan, Mandy. 2008. *A guide to colonial sources on Burma. Ethnic and minority histories of Burma in the India Office Records, British Library.* Bangkok: Orchid Press.

Saha, Jonathan. 2013. *Law, disorder and the colonial state. Corruption in Burma c. 1900.* Houndmills: Palgrave.

———. 2022. *Colonizing animals. Interspecies empire in Myanmar.* Cambridge: Cambridge University Press.

Sahlins, Marshall. 1972. *Stone age economics.* Chicago and New York: Aldine.

———. 2013. *What kinship is … and is not.* Chicago: University of Chicago Press.

Salmond, Anne. 1986. Towards a local anthropology. *Sites* 13: 39–48.

Sartre, Jean-Paul. 2007 [1946]. *Existentialism is a humanism*, translated by Carol Macomber. New Haven and London: Yale University Press.

———. 1992 [1943]. *Being and nothingness. A phenomenological essay on ontology.* New York et al.: Washington Square Press.

———. 2004 [1960]. *Critique of dialectical reason.* Vol 1. Translated by Alan Sheridan-Smith. London and New York: Verso.

Sathyamala, Christina. 2018. Meat-eating in India. Whose food, whose politics, and whose rights? *Policy Futures in Education* 17 (7): https://doi.org/10.1177/14782103187805.

Satyanarayana, Adapa. 2001. 'Birds of passage'. Migration of South Indian labour communities to South-East Asia; 19–20th centuries, *A.D. ILAS/ IISG CLARA Working Paper* 11. Amsterdam.

Sax, William and Jan Weinhold. 2010. Rituals of possession. In *Ritual matters. Dynamic dimensions in practice*, edited by Christiane Brosius and Ute Hüsken. New Delhi: Routledge, 236–252.

Sax, William and Helene Basu (eds). 2015. *The law of possession. Ritual, heal-*

ing and the secular state. New York: Oxford University Press.

Scheff, Thomas. 1988. Shame and conformity. The deference-emotion system. *American Sociological Review* 53: 395–406.

Schegloff, Emanuel. 2007. *Sequence organization in interaction. A primer in conversation analysis*. Cambridge: Cambridge University Press.

Scheper-Hughes, Nancy. 1992. *Death without weeping. The violence of everyday life in Brazil*. Berkeley: University of California Press.

————. 2000. The global traffic in human organs. *Current Anthropology* 41 (2): 191–224.

Scheper-Hughes, Nancy and Margaret Lock. 1987. The mindful body. A prolegomenon to future work in medical anthropology. *Medical Anthropology Quarterly*, 1 (1): 6–41.

Schissler, Matt, Matt Walton and Phyu Phyu Thi. 2017. Reconciling contradictions. Buddhist-Muslim violence, narrative making and memory in Myanmar. *Journal of Contemporary Asia* 47 (3): 376–395.

Schlehe, Judith and Evamaria Sandkühler (eds). 2014. *Religion, tradition and the popular. Transcultural views from Asia and Europe*. Bielefeld: Transcript.

Schober, Juliane. 2011. *Modern Buddhist conjunctures in Myanmar. Cultural narratives, colonial legacies, and civil society*. Honolulu: University of Hawai'i Press.

Schonthal, Benjamin. 2016. Making the Muslim other in Myanmar and Sri Lanka. In *Islam and the state in Myanmar. Muslim-Buddhist relations and the politics of belonging*, edited by Melissa Crouch. New Delhi: Oxford University Press, 234–257.

Schütz, Alfred and Thomas Luckmann. 2003 [1975]. *Strukturen der Lebenswelt* [The structures of the life-world]. Konstanz: UVK.

Scott, James. 1990. *Domination and the arts of resistance. Hidden transcripts*. Ann Arbor: Edwards Brothers.

Seeley, J.R. 2010 [1883]. *The expansion of England. Two courses of lectures*. New York: Cambridge University Press.

Shibutani, Tamotsu. 1996. *Improvised news. A sociological study of rumor*. Indianapolis, IN: Bobbs-Merrill.

Sihlé, Nicolas. 2015. Towards a comparative anthropology of the Buddhist gift (and other transfers). *Religion Compass* 9 (11): 352–385.

Silva, Sónia. 2017 [2015]. Mobility and immobility in the life of an amputee. *In What is existential anthropology?* Edited by Michael Jackson and Albert Piette. Oxford: Berghahn Books, 125–154.

Siok-Hwa, Cheng. 1968. *The rice industry of Burma, 1852–1940*. Kuala Lumpur: University of Malaya Press.

Singh, Bhrigupati. 2011. Agonistic intimacy and moral aspiration in popular

Hinduism. A study in the political theology of the neighbour. *American Ethnologist* 38 (3): 430–450.

Sinha, Mrinalini. 2006. *Specters of mother India. The global restructuring of empire.* Durham and London: Duke University Press.

Skidmore, Monique. 2004. *Karaoke fascism. Burma and the politics of fear.* Philadelphia: University of Pennsylvania Press.

Smith, Donald. 1965. *Religion and politics in Burma.* Princeton: Princeton University Press.

Smith, Anthony. 1998. *Nationalism and modernism. A critical survey of recent theories of nations and nationalism.* London: Routledge.

Spivak, Gayatri. 1988. Can the subaltern speak? In *Marxism and the interpretation of culture,* edited by Cary Nelson and Lawrence Grossberg. Urbana and Chicago: University of Illinois Press, 271–313.

———. 1993. *Outside in the teaching machine.* New York: Routledge.

Stadtner, Donald. 2011. *Sacred sites of Burma. Myth and folklore in an evolving spiritual realm.* Bangkok: River Books.

Stasch, Rupert. 2009. *Society of others. Kinship and mourning in a West Papuan place.* Berkeley: University of California Press.

Staples, James. 2018. Appropriating the cow. Beef and identity politics in contemporary India. In *Farm to fingers. The culture and politics of food in contemporary India,* edited by Kiranmayi Bhushi. Cambridge: Cambridge University Press, 58–79.

Star, Susan Leigh. 2010. This is not a boundary object: reflections on the origin of a concept. *Science, Technology, and Human Values* 35(5): 601–617.

Star, Susan Leigh and James R. Griesemer. 1989. Institutional ecology, "translations" and boundary objects. Amateurs and professionals in Berkeley's museum of vertebrate zoology, 1907–1939. *Social Studies of Science* 19 (3): 387–420

Stein, Burton. 1998. *A history of India.* Oxford: Blackwell.

Stietencron, Heinrich von. 2005. *Hindu myth, Hindu history. Religion, art and politics.* New Delhi: Orient Longman.

Stoler, Ann and Frederick Cooper (eds). 2002. *Carnal knowledge and imperial power. Race and the intimate in colonial rule.* Berkeley: University of California Press.

Strathern, Andrew and Michael Lambek. 1998. Introduction. Embodying sociality. Africanist-Melanesianist comparisons. In *Bodies and persons. Comparative perspectives from Africa and Melanesia,* edited by Michael Lambek and Andrew Strathern. Cambridge: Cambridge University Press, 1–25.

Strathern, Marilyn. 2000. *The gender of the gift. Problems with women and problems with society in Melanesia.* Berkeley: University of California Press.

Sullivan, Daniel and Roman Palitsky. 2018. An existential psychological perspective on the human essence. In *The Oxford handbook of the human essence*, edited by John Dovidio and Martijn van Zomeren. Oxford: Oxford University Press, 21–34.

Symes, Michael. 1955. *Journal of his second embassy to the court of Ava in 1802*, edited by D.G.E. Hall. London: George Allen and Unwin.

Talbot, Cynthia. 1995. Inscribing the Other, inscribing the self. Hindu-Muslim identities in pre-colonial India. *Comparative Studies in Society and History* 37 (4): 692–722.

Tambiah, Stanley. 1990. *Magic, science and religion, and the scope of rationality*. Cambridge: University Press.

Tanaka, Shogo. 2015. Intercorporeality as a theory of social cognition. *Theory and Psychology* 25 (4): 455–472.

Taussig, Michael. 1992. *The nervous system*. New York and London: Routledge.

———. 2018 [1993]. *Mimesis and alterity. A particular history of the senses*. Abingdon and New York: Routledge.

Taylor, Charles. 1984. Foucault on freedom and truth. *Political Theory* 12: 152–183.

Taylor, Robert. 2009 [1987]. *The state in Myanmar*. Singapore: NUS Press.

Tedlock, Dennis and Bruce Mannheim (eds). 1995. *The dialogic emergence of culture*. Urbana and Chicago: University of Illinois Press.

Temple, Richard. 1887. *India during the jubilee reign*. Digital Library of India Item 2015.91981 (accessed 31 October 2019).

———. 1925. Buddermokan, *Journal of Burma Research Society* 15 (1): 1–33.

Ten Have, Paul. 2004. *Understanding qualitative research and ethnomethodology*. London: Sage.

Than, Tharaphi. 2014. *Women in modern Burma*. Milton Park and New York: Routledge.

Than Pale. 2018. Justice seeking strategies in everyday life. Case study among urban migrants in Yangon. *Independent Journal of Burmese Scholarship*. 1 (2): 151–179.

Thant Myint-U. 2001. *The making of modern Burma*. Cambridge: Cambridge University Press.

Thin Lei Win. 2015. Monogamy law takes aim at new target. *Myanmar Times* 11 December. https://www.mmtimes.com/national-news/yangon/18102-monogamy-law-takes-aim-at-new-target.html (accessed 18 July 2022).

Tilley, Charles. 1999. *Metaphor and material culture*. Blackwell Publishers.

———. 2011. Materialising identities. An introduction. *Journal of Material Culture* 16: 347–357.

Tinker, Hugh. 1979. A forgotten long march: The Indian exodus from Burma, 1942. *Journal of Southeast Asian Studies.* 6 (1): 1–15.

———. 1993 [1974]. *A new system of slavery. The export of Indian labour overseas 1830–1920.* London: Hansib.

Turkle, Sherry. 2011. *Evocative objects. Things we think with.* Cambridge, Mass.: MIT Press.

Turnell, Sean and Alison Vicary. 2008. Parching the land? The Chettiars in Burma. *Australian Economic History Review.* 48,1: 1–25.

Turner, Alicia. 2014. *Saving Buddhism. The impermanence of religion in colonial Burma.* Honolulu: University of Hawai'i Press.

———. 2019. Buddhist nationalism and the enduring myth of Burmese women's 'freedom'. Intersections of colonial secularism and gender. Unpublished paper presented at Duke University, 20 February.

Turner, Edith. 2012. *Communitas. The anthropology of collective joy.* New York: Palgrave MacMillan.

Turner, Terence. 1994. Bodies and anti-bodies. Flesh and fetish in contemporary social theory. In *Embodiment and experience. The existential ground of culture and self,* edited by Thomas Csordas. Cambridge and New York: Cambridge University Press, 27–47.

Veer, Peter van der. 1993. The foreign hand. Orientalist discourse in sociology and communalism. In *Orientalism and the postcolonial predicament. Perspectives on South Asia,* edited by Carol Breckenridge and Peter van der Veer. Philadelphia: University of Pennsylvania Press, 23–44.

———. 1994. *Religious nationalism. Hindus and Muslims in India.* California: University of California Press.

———. 2001a. *Imperial encounters: Religion and modernity in India and Britain.* Princeton: Princeton University Press.

———. 2001b. Communalism. In *International Encyclopedia of the Social and Behavioural Sciences:* 2286–2288.

———. 2014. *The modern spirit of Asia. The spiritual and the secular in China and India.* Princeton and Oxford: Princeton University Press.

Wade, Francis. 2017. *Myanmar's enemy within. Buddhist violence and the making of a Muslim 'Other'.* London: Zed.

Walther, Gerda. 1923. *Ein Beitrag zur Ontologie der sozialen Gemeinschaften. Mit einem Anhang zur Phänomenologie der sozialen Gemeinschaft* [A contribution to the ontology of social communities. With an appendix on the phenomenology of the social community]. Halle a.d.S.: Niemeyer.

Walton, Matthew, and Susan Hayward. 2014. Contesting Buddhist narratives. Democratization, nationalism, and communal violence in Myanmar. *Policy Studies (Southeast Asia)* 71. Honolulu: East-West Center. http://www.eastwestcenter.org/publications/contesting-buddhist-narratives-democratization-nationalism-and-communal-violence-in-mya (accessed 17 July 2022).

Walton, Matthew, Melyn McKay and Khin Mar Mar Gyi. 2015. Women and Myanmar's "Religious protection laws". *Review of Faith and International Affairs* 4: 36–49.

Walton, Matthew. 2017. *Buddhism, politics and political thought in Myanmar.* Cambridge: Cambridge University Press.

———. 2015. Burmese Buddhist politics. In *Oxford Handbook Online.* October 2015. https://www.oxfordhandbooks.com/view/10.1093/oxfordhb/9780199935420.001.0001/oxfordhb–9780199935420-e–21 (accessed 19 July 2022).

Watson, James. 1996. Fighting with operas. Processionals, politics and the spectre of violence in rural Hong Kong In *The politics of cultural performance. Essays in honor of Abner Cohen,* edited by David Parkin, Lionel Caplan and Humphrey Fisherx. London: Berghahn, 23–44.

Weick, Karl. 1993. The collapse of sensemaking in organizations. The Mann Gulch disaster. *Administrative Science Quarterly* 3: 628–652.

Wenger, Etienne. 1998. *Communities of practice. Learning, meaning, and identity.* New York: Cambridge University Press.

Wengrow, David. 2019. Rethinking cities, from the ground up. https://medium.com/whose-society-whose-cohesion/rethinking-cities-from-the-ground-up–73d92059b15f (accessed 17 July 2022).

Werbner, Pnina (ed.) 2008. *Anthropology and the new cosmopolitanism. Rooted, feminist and vernacular perspectives.* Oxford and New York: Berg.

Williams, Raymond. 1976. *Keywords.* New York: Oxford University Press.

Willford, Andrew and Kenneth George (eds). 2005. *Spirited politics. Religion and public life in contemporary Southeast Asia.* Ithaca, NY: Cornell Southeast Asia Program Publications.

Wingfield, Chris. 2012. Photographing 'the bridge.' Product and process in the analysis of a social situation in non-modern Zululand. In *Photography in Africa. Ethnographic perspectives,* edited by Richard Vokesx. Suffolk: James Currey, 23–44.

Wolputte, Steven van. 2004. Hang on to your self. Of bodies, embodiment, and selves. *Annual Review of Anthropology* 33: 251–269.

Ye Mon. 2016. Chinese minority to get 'Bamar' designation. *Myanmar Times,* 30 March 2016. https://www.mmtimes.com/national-news/19717-chinese-minority-to-get-bamar-designation.html (accessed 17 July 2022).

Yegar, Moshe. 1972. *The Muslims of Burma. A study of a minority* group. Wiesbaden: Otto Harrassowitz.

Yin May, 1962. Greater Rangoon. A study in urban geography. Unpublished

Master's Thesis. Department of Geography. University of Rangoon.

Yule, Henry and A.C. Burnell. 1903. *Hobson-Jobson*. London: John Murray.

Zillinger, Martin. 2017. Graduated publics. Mediating trance in the age of technical reproduction. *Current Anthropology* 58 (15): 41–55.

Zin New Myint. 1998. Geographical study of the urban growth of Yangon city. Unpublished Master's Thesis, Department of Geography, University of Yangon.

Laws

The Burma Laws Act. 1898.

The Lower Burma Town and Village Lands Act, Burma Act IV. 1898/1899.

The Citizenship Act. 1982.

The Trusts Act (India Act II). 1882.

The Condominium Law (Pyiaungsu Hluttaw Law). No 24. 2016.

The Constitution of the Republic of the Union of Myanmar. 2008.

The Constitution of the Socialist Republic of the Union of Burma. 1974.

The Constitution of the Union of Burma. 1947.

Muslim Personal Law (Shariat) Application Act. 1937.

The Farmland Law. No 11. 2012.

The Buddhist Women's Special Marriage and Succession Act. 1954

The Monogamy Law. No 54. 2015.

The Buddhist Women's Special Marriage Law. No 50. 2015.

The Population Control Act. No 28. 2015.

The Conversion Law. No 48. 2015.

The Code of Civil Procedure (India Act 1908). 1909.

The Code of Civil Procedure Amendment Act. [1956], 2014.

Land and Revenue Act (India Act II) 1876s. Substituted by Act II. 1945.

The Upper Burma Land and Revenue Regulation (Regulation III). 1889.

The Mussalman Wakf Validating Act. No 6. 1913.

The Mussalman Wakf Act. No 42. 1923.

The Dissolution of Muslim Marriages Act. 1939.

Cases

King-Emperor vs. E Maung and Six Others, 3 Lower Burma Rulings 131 (1906).

Muthusami Mudaliar vs. Masilamani (1909).

Chit Maung vs. Ma Yait and Ma Noo, 7 Lower Burma Rulings 362, No 26 (1913).

Ma Yait v. Maung Chit Maung and Maung Chit Maung V Ma Yait and Another, 11 Lower Burma Rulings 155 (1921).

Civil Regular Suit No 311. High Court Rangoon (1935).

Habiba vs. Swa Kyan, A.I.R, Ran 463 / R.L.R, 322 (1937).

Shiwadhari Shukla vs. Daw Daw Nu; Judgment of the High Court of Judicature at Rangoon (1953).

Official Documents

India Office Library and Records (IOR), Boards Collections, F/4/365, no. 9093 for 1812–1813.

India Office Library and Records (IOR), V/10/497. Report on the Administration of British Burma during 1881–1882. Rangoon: Government Press.

Final Report of the Riot Inquiry Committee 1939. Rangoon: Government Printing and Stationary.

Ministry of Religious Affairs (MORA). n.d. Objective. http://www.mora.gov.mm/mora_ministry1.aspx (accessed 2 November 2019; link no longer active).

Trust scheme of the Kalai unorthodox Hindu temple. In accordance with Civil Appeal, No 53 Rangoon High Court. 1953.

Government [of India] to Phayre, India Political Proceedings (IPP). 200/38. No 124. 1853.

Colour Section

Fig. 0.1: In front of the Mogul Shia Mosque. Fuller details on page 2.

Fig. 4.4: Entering the temple for Shivaratri. Fuller details on page 150.

Fig. 4.5: Receiving and passing baskets filled with flower petals. Fuller details on page 152.

Fig. 4.6: Genealogy chart installed inside the prayer hall. Fuller details on page 155.

Fig. 4.7: The late U Sanny (left) and the late U Thin Thain Moung (right) flanking the portrait of U Ohn Ghine in U Sanny's living room. **Fuller details on page 156.**

Fig. 5.8: Mukhtar Bhai's 'Shia shrine'. **Fuller details on page 203.**

Fig. 6.3: Embodying Rubab. Fuller details on page 211.

Fig. 6.4: Women decorating the cradle of Ali Asghar. Fuller details on page 215.

Index

Aba Boe Min Khaung 144
abil (white powder used as an offering) 95, 100, 104
access, theory of 190
adultery 199–200
Africa 53, 78*n*32
Afsheen, Karmel 181*n*8
Aga Khan 184
Agamas 95
Ahl-ul-bayt ('People of the House')
205, 209
Akyab 53
alam (battle standard) 205, 208–10,
215
Alaungpaya, King 50
Alayhi al-Salām (a.s., 'Peace be upon
him') 2*n*1
Alex, Gabriele 119
Alexander, Catherine 61
Alexander the Great 66*n*11
All Myanmar Hindu Central Council
153
amanat ('trust') 192
Amina Begum 222
Amit, Vered 14, 113–14
Amrith, Sunil 49, 53, 55, 78
amulets 97
ancestors 33, 65–6, 70*n*18, 137, 158,
160, 162, 235
Andaman Islanders 83–4, 89–90
Andaman Islands 84–5, 93
Andaman Sea 11, 84, 88
Andra Pradesh 53. *See also* Madras
Anglo-Burma War, First 30*n*1, 49, 52,
62; Second 50, 60, 63; Third 50

Anglo-Burmese 73, 81*n*37
Anglo-Indian administration 37, 72
Anglo-Indians 74*n*23
Animism 81*n*36
Animist 196*n*18
anjuman 206–7, 210*n*6, 216–17, 230,
234. *See also* worship: places of
Anjuman-e-Abbasia 210, 215–16
Anjuman-e-Hizbul-mehdi 219*n*11
anthropocentrism 116
anthropography 116
anthropologists 3, 14, 18–19, 21, 25,
108, 115–17, 229, 231, 239
anthropology 7, 21, 188; of Albert
Piette 23; approach to gossip 228;
approach to possession 108; of
belonging 213, 239; classic texts of
216; of community 18–19, 33; dialogical 23*n*14; of emotion 184; and
empire-building 37; of ethnic groups
8*n*5; existential 10, 20–1, 23*n*13, 25,
116, 242; fieldwork 137; legal 37,
158, 227–8; literature 60, 108, 207,
221; religious 150; sociocultural
106–7; of the state 227*n*17; of war
251
anthropos 24
Antweiler, Christoph 188
Appadurai, Arjun 22, 35*n*3, 37, 43,
46–8, 75, 147–8, 150–1, 165, 168,
201, 243. *See also* Tenkalai
Arab traders 77
Arabian Sea 66*n*13
Arakan 49, 83
Arba'een 2–3, 205–6, 208–9, 211,
217–20, 222, 230

291

Bodhi tree 142–3, 145–6, 154
bodies, dead 250; infants' 212–13
body 1, 3, 20–2, 24, 106, 108, 112,
115, 119–20, 130, 136, 197, 199,
205, 207, 210, 212–13, 220–2,
234–6, 245, 250–1; anthropological
studies of 207n3; boundaries of 221;
cognitive approaches to 22; collective 3; of community 234; of the deceased 68n16; divine 148; existence
as 221n13; existing one's 20, 236,
245; Foucault's concept of 235n20;
governance through 136, 235n20,
243; individual 110, 120, 185, 215,
221, 254; as instrument of resistance
251; Merleau-Ponty on 221n13; of
others 205; Sartre's theory of 207,
220, 222, 234, 236; of sovereign deity 148; theories of 221n12, 221n13.
See also embodiment
body and pain 236
body language 99
body of people 120
body politic 193, 235n20, 249
Bogyoke Aung San Market 94n1
Bogyoke Aung San Street 94
Boissevain, Jeremy 216
Bombay Burmah Company 67, 79
bombings 79, 160
Botataung Pagoda 140, 142n5
'boundary objects' 125
Bourdieu, Pierre 115, 245
'bovine politics' 144n9
Bowman, Glenn 136n22
Brac de la Perrière, Bénédicte 107
Brahman 96n8
Brahmanic origins 96
Brahmaputra River 49
Brahmin subcastes 176
Brahminical theory 39
Brahminism 42
Brahmins 46, 146, 176
bram ('energy') 129
Bramma 129
Breckenridge, Carol 17

Britain 26, 84, 248, 250; colonial 34–5,
37, 63, 67, 92, 94n1, 131–3, 136,
158, 198, 249; conquest of Burma
42, 51, 59, 67, 74n22; contemporary
politics of 248. *See also* England;
Great Britain
British & Burmese Steam Navigation
Co 179n6
British, civilizing mission of 157
British empire 5, 15, 26, 30, 33–4, 41,
45, 48, 50, 52, 54, 73, 162, 247
British Home Office 249
British immigration system 249
British India Steam Navigation
Company (BISN) 53
British Library 32
Brouwer, Jan 96n8
Brubaker, Rogers 17, 24
Bruun, Maya 61
Buddha 11, 69–70, 95n6, 99, 118,
128–36, 140–2, 145–6, 169, 206; as
a Hindu god 128–36; statues of 58,
100, 118, 127–8, 143, 145, 169
Buddha-bha-tha-lu-myo ('Buddhist eth-
nicity') 75n25
Buddhification 142
Buddhism 16, 70, 73, 78n33, 81,
131n18, 142, 169–70, 206, 223, 226;
Hinduism and 128, 169
Buddhist, community 70, 78, 206;
fasts 164; law 139, 199; monasteries
163; monks 126, 132, 169–70, 244;
monuments 140n3; temples 12, 31,
169; traditions 126n15; water-pouring ceremony 149. *See also* worship:
places of
Buddhist Bama majority 25, 28n19,
87, 226, 231, 247. *See also* Bama
Buddhist Special Marriage and
Succession Bill 199
Buddhist women 155, 165, 199–201;
and Muslim men 201; narratives of
200
Buddhist Women Special Marriage
and Succession Act 199
Buddhist Women's Special Marriage

Mauss, Marcel 151
mauvaise foi ('bad faith') 28
Mawlamyine 157, 176, 231*n18*. *See
also* Moulmein
maximal integration behaviour 124–7
Mazindarani family 182
McCrae, Alister 55
McNamara, Roger 74*n22*
Mecca 58*n3*, 208
media 233; foreign 132*n20*
mediatized performances 102
Medin, Douglas 24
Meikhtila 91
Memon Association 81
Memon community 57, 83
Memon Jamaat 68, 83, 86–8, 91, 93
Memons 17, 57*n2*, 66–8, 83, 87,
90–1, 93, 237, 253; ancestors of 93;
of Chicago 66*n12*; conversion to
Islam 66*n12*, 67; Kuch community
in South Africa 66*n12*; Kutchi 66;
mixed 87; pure 92. *See also* Halai
Memon
memory, storing 128
Merchant Street 215
Merleau-Ponty, Maurice 128, 207*n3*,
221*n13*
methodological individualism 19
mhanap dharam ('a good human being') 131
Michelangelo 116*n14*
microanalysis 24, 242
Middle East 175
migration. *See* India, migration from;
India, return migration to
military dictatorship 86*n40*, 203, 251,
253–4
Mill, John Stuart 42*n9*, 76*n29*
Miller, Daniel 188–9
Mingala Taungnyunt township 13
'minimal integration behaviour'
109–17, 126
'the minimum of human presence'
112–13
'the minimum of remains' 112–13

minorities, ethno-religious 9, 15–16,
25, 72–3, 76*n28*, 78, 126, 157, 194,
199, 242, 246
minority groups, literature on 29
Mitchell, Jon 128
mode mineur ('the minor mode') 116
Modonesi, Massimo 26, 247
Mogul Shia Mosque 2, 181–3, 190,
192, 205, 210, 215–16, 224, 232,
237
Mogul Street 63
Moguls 42, 180–1
Moharram 3*n2*, 44, 206, 214, 225–6,
239
mohinga (Burmese fish noodle soup)
57
'Mone Wun (Bama)' (ethnic Chinese)
75*n27*
Mongols 214*n9*
Monguadi 82
monks and nuns 170*n38*
Monogamy Law 199
Montgomery 63
Moomal, Ebrahim 66*n12*
Moore, Sally Falk 227*n17*
Morgan, Lewis Henry 38
Morgenstein Fuerst, Ilyse 39*n6*
Moroccan trance brotherhoods 125
Moses, statue of 116*n14*
mosques 13–15, 17, 31, 70, 81–2, 90,
99, 179, 181–3, 187, 190, 192, 213,
224–5, 229, 232, 246, 253; set on
fire 71. *See also* worship: places of
muezzin 50, 90
musicians 100, 104, 109, 118–19, 124
Muslim, communalism in India
131*n18*; conquerors 34; families
58, 79*n34*, 177*n2*; men, Buddhist
women and 199, 201; men, offspring
of 165; organizations 57, 65, 87;
personal law 177*n2*, 185*n13*; women
201
Muslim Marriages Act 185*n13*
Muslim Personal (Shariat) Application
Act 185*n13*